Rough Mason, Mason, Freemason, Accepted Mason

Oscar Patterson III

Hamilton Books

Lanham • Boulder • New York • Toronto • Plymouth, UK

Copyright © 2017 by Hamilton Books
4501 Forbes Boulevard, Suite 200, Lanham, Maryland 20706
Hamilton Books Acquisitions Department (301) 459-3366

Unit A, Whitacre Mews, 26-34 Stannary Street,
London SE11 4AB, United Kingdom

Library of Congress Control Number: 2017944075
ISBN: 978-0-7618-6960-3 (pbk : alk. paper)—ISBN: 978-0-7618-6961-0 (electronic)

Cover Art: *The Building of a Palace* by Piero di Cosimo (1462-1522) is an allegory of the art of building that was created between 1515 and 1520. It was commissioned by the Arte dei Maestri di Pietre e di Legname (Masters of Stone and Wood) in Florence and owned by the Medici family. It is considered by scholars to be an accurate representation of the construction of an idealized Renaissance palace. It is now on exhibit in the John and Mable Ringling Museum of Art in Sarasota, Florida.

∞™ The paper used in this publication meets the minimum requirements of American National Standard for Information Sciences Permanence of Paper for Printed Library Materials, ANSI/NISO Z39.48-1992.

In Memory of James S. Davis

Comrade in Arms, Americal Division, Vietnam

Worshipful Master, Ashlar Lodge No. 98 2013

Mentor

Friend

Brother

Contents

Acknowledgments

This manuscript began several years ago as I undertook to research the history of Freemasonry. There is in existence in the modern world such an organization, but where and when did began and how it came into its present form are open to question. Libraries are replete with books that attempt to explain the organization. But as I read, I became disenchanted with what I found. This fueled my quest. There had to be more to the story than the myths and fables that were and are so prevalent.

I wish to express my sincere appreciation to Robert P. Harry, Jr., Past Grand Master of Masons of Florida for reading the manuscript and providing critical editing and suggestions. Most Worshipful Harry has been my mentor and guide throughout my Masonic life and I am so very grateful to have him leading my steps and being my friend.

Edward R. Suart, Past District Deputy Grand Master and Historian at Ashlar Lodge No. 98 in St. Augustine provided me with many valuable manuscripts and articles. He reviewed the text in-depth and made essential comments and grammatical corrections.

David Pierucci has sat on my left as Secretary and, more importantly, has been a good friend and Masonic Mentor. His input is invaluable and sincerely appreciated. He is also a member of Hope Lodge 2813 in Savanna La Mar, Jamaica and graciously introduced me to his Jamaican Brothers and the English Constitution Freemasonry. He read the manuscript while sitting at his mountain-top retreat in that tropical nation.

To my Brothers throughout Masonry, especially those at Ashlar Lodge No. 98, I offer my deepest appreciation. You took me in; made me part of your Great Fraternity; and encouraged me to achieve far beyond what I thought possible when I began my Masonic journey. You also encouraged my Masonic research and writing by obtaining copies of my book *Interpret-*

ing Masonic Ritual and reading my articles published in various Masonic journals. To you I offer my deepest gratitude. You encouraged me to seek further knowledge and to share what I had learned.

Above all, to my wife, Julie, my soul-mate and best friend—and too often a "Masonic Widow" —I offer my sincerest appreciation for your support and encouragement. If not for a visit you made in, I may never have sought the privileges of Freemasonry. Your tour of the Grand Lodge of Pennsylvania's magnificent building led you to return with me "in tow". You then encouraged me to seek membership and have supported me whole-heartedly as I moved through the chairs, served as a District Committeeman and State Chairman, and sat in the East. You attended one installation on our twenty-fifth wedding anniversary and graciously allowed me to miss your birthday another year to accept an Honorary Membership. You have ridden with me at the county fair and been at my side for installations and banquets. To you goes my eternal love and affection. Forever and always.

Introduction

Every person, organization, government, and nation had a beginning. Free-masonry is no different. Yet no organization comes to be as it is in a vacuum. History is a massive web of interrelated events and an understanding of the fact requires some level of mastery of research methodology and specialized knowledge.

Historians are part of a guild as surely as were ancient masons. Both groups focused their attention on creating strong foundations and preparing others to follow in their lead. There is in history no isolated, single, true tradition. History is collaboration as surely as is that of the construction of any magnificent edifice and involves discourse as well as the exchange of ideas. History also requires constant reassessment and it is anti-historical to be overly obsessed with a single point of view of the past.

The study of history is about getting the story *relatively* straight. Theories abound, but they must be tested and retested as new evidence is discovered and old evidence disproved. Essential to an understanding of history is context. It is inescapable that history happens within the context of a given time, set of attitudes, perspectives, and laws. To overlook this is to subvert the outcome of any historical analysis.

To understand the history of a group or organization requires thinking about the time and placed of origination as well as the people involved. Just as we have cultural awareness, we so too should have historical awareness. A principal venue for the historical record is the law. And while culture, those phenomena that seem to hold us together, may give us clues to understand history, it is through the political expression of the law that the official record survives. The law is the essence which provides continuity and predictability.

Throughout man's time on earth, fabulists and myth-makers provided their accounts of history in a quest to provide points of origin for then existing practices and privileges. What they did was, for them, historical, cultural, and political. Their work was often heavily influenced and highly constrained by sovereign powers which included church and state as well as available resources.

The study of history is also the study of literature. It is a matter of fixing the texts in their historical context and coming to grasp with the diversity as well as the polarity of meanings and readings. History does not yet provide a unified or general theory of the past. It is too full of complexity and permutations. To come to an understanding of the past, it is necessary for the historian to become familiar with his predecessors as well as his contemporaries, and to take into consideration those who live through and wrote about each age: what motivated them and what their audience took both to and from these histories as well what those audiences expected of the histories being produced.

Finally, a historian should endeavor to come to grasps with the nature of human variation which produces in its wake widely divergent interpretations of any given set of facts. This is essential to understanding the legitimate intent and designated meaning of the author.

Chapter One

Making a Mason

Medieval Masons.

Freemasonry is a Moral Order, instituted by virtuous men, with the praise-worthy design of recalling to our remembrance the most social pleasures founded on Liberality, Brotherly Love and Charity. It is a system of morality, veiled in allegory and illustrated by symbols. Truth is its center—the point

1

whence its radii diverge—pointing out to its disciples a correct knowledge of the Great Architect of the Universe and the moral laws which He has ordained for their government.
—National Masonic Convention, Baltimore, Maryland, 1843

Freemasonry is the oldest still-functioning Fraternity in the western world. Its principle tenets are brotherly love, relief, and truth, and all Freemasons are governed by fortitude, prudence, temperance, and justice. Freemasons place their trust in Deity and endeavor to do unto their neighbors as their neighbors should do unto them. They are quiet and peaceful citizens, true to their country and just to their government. They do not engage in political disputes as an organization and are accepting of all religions that profess a belief in a Supreme Being. While it is possible to trace Freemasonry's existence in some form since the sixteenth century, more solid documentation is available for the period after the early eighteenth century and the founding of The Grand Lodge of England.

In the United States, regular Freemasonry is organized by jurisdiction with each state hosting a Grand Lodge. There is no central authority for Freemasonry in the United States. Outside the United States, in England, for example, Freemasonry is organized under a national Grand Lodge which issues warrants or charters for the formation of Lodges within its jurisdiction. Freemasonry in the United States is considered to be a direct descendant of the Grand Lodge of England and still follows many of the practices of that institution.

MEDIEVAL MASON

That some form of organized masonry began with the *masoun* or rough mason of medieval Europe who progressed through "the ranks" of layers, pavers, and masons to become freemasons is well documented in the records of the operative guilds. Guilds were, essentially, trade unions that protected the rights of labored as they ensured the quality of the finished product. They also served to provide essential education for future generations and to protect the trade secrets of the craft. One of the most important of these secrets was methods of recognition. In this pre-literate age, those methods included manual signs, grips, and the exchange of specific passwords or *shibboleths*. The nature of the masonic trade—the erection of large stone structures—necessarily required a certain degree of movement among highly skilled workers. The signs, grips, and words were tests of a mason's qualifications as well as his introduction to others of the same trade. Prior to being accepted into a lodge where he was unknown and being allowed to function as a full mason or freemason, and to ensure that he was "worthy and well qualified" (that he could create a sustainable arch, for example) it was necessary that he be "tested." This was generally done by the use of the "secrets" as noted—

signs, grips, and words—that were received "mouth to ear" upon the successful completion of a period of apprentice and an examination or presentation of a finished piece of work to an examining committee. The original testing and qualification was time-consuming and expensive.

In the operative trade or guild, it was often the custom for the master or foreman to remove the central post supporting the frame for the arch. If it collapsed, it collapsed on him. This rather drastic approach to quality control ensured that the master or foreman properly instructed apprentices and fellows of the craft, and that they properly supervised the labor of their workers. To qualify as a fellow of the craft it was essential that an apprentice mason prove that he possessed the skills and knowledge essential to successful building construction. This required a young man to enter the trade at age eleven or twelve as an apprentice and work under the direct supervision of a master for seven or more years. At the conclusion of the well-supervised and arduous seven years of labor, the apprentice presented a final piece of work to be evaluated by the master. The movie "The Red Violin" suggests the outcome of this form of evaluation of workmanship. If found worthy the apprentice was advanced to the rank of fellow of the craft where he generally remained for the rest of his working life.

This system of training, evaluation, and advancement is not that unusual today. For example, United Scenic Artists, a modern labor union which is an autonomous local of the International Alliance of Theatrical Stage Employees, utilizes a similar system. After being trained and engaged in the profession for some period (training may come through a university degree), the candidate applies for recognition. He or she is assigned a take-home project followed by a written examination, personal interview, and portfolio review of previous work. The candidate is then required to execute an on-site practical project for evaluation by a panel of judges. For those with significant prior experience—three years or more of satisfactory practice in the trade often under the supervision a guild member—a take-home project, portfolio review, interview, and examination of samples of previous work without the practical examination suffice to demonstrate proficiency.

Nor is a form of apprenticeship and evaluation restricted just to unions. Parachute riggers in the United States military work under the direct supervision of senior Noncommissioned Officers. During training, riggers are required to jump with a parachute they packed and continue to do so on a regular basis upon successful completion of the school and assignment as a rigger with an airborne unit. In a similar fashion, aircraft mechanics often participate in a check ride before certifying the craft airworthy. And in very public demonstration of an engineer's faith in her and her husband's work, Emily Warren Roebling, wife of Washington Roebling and his successor as field engineer on the Brooklyn Bridge, hitched a team of horses to a wagon and with a rooster as a passenger became the first person to traverse the full length of that famous bridge.

The men who erected the great cathedrals of Europe and other impressive structures were skilled craftsmen much valued for their knowledge and dedication to their craft. They were *masons.* But some were freer than others. The use of the term "free" in freemason has often been interpreted to mean free of obligation to church or secular authority and thus free to "roam at will", to be true "traveling men." While this did become the case in the mid-seventeenth century and continued into the nineteenth century [1] , all masons of the eleventh through fifteenth centuries were as subject to government (crown) and church authority as any other *freeman.* The original use of the term *free* associated with "mason" resulting in *freemason* was used to identify those skilled artisans who could work in free stone creating the beautiful carvings and other ornaments found in medieval architecture, especially gothic. [2] The term *freemason* thus differentiated those highly skilled, highly paid craftsmen who most often worked at a *piece rate* from rough masons such as layers, pavers and hewers who received a daily wage (see Chapter III for a more complete outline). Freemasons also tended to be independent masters or contractors with their own apprentices who demanded and received a high level of respect while enjoying a significant amount of authority and the right to independently negotiate for their services.

All masons, however, found it necessary to band together because of the very nature of their craft. A cursory survey of any great cathedral reflects the conditions necessary for their erection and supports the contention that, unlike other craftsmen such as metal smiths, saddlers, or goldsmiths, masons could not easily acquire positions, perform work, or complete a finished work in his chosen materials alone. A large-scale, coordinated, well-funded effort was necessary to quarry, cut, finish, deliver, and erect the thousands of stones used in any given project. Early masons were very similar to modern construction workers: a wage-earner paid according to a time or piece rate. And he did not work in isolation any more than do members of a twenty-first century construction crew; but rather as part of a larger force directed by a master, overseer, clerk, or foreman and often under the watchful eye of a master of the work or architect appointed by crown or ecclesiastical authorities. Within this system fathers taught their sons and uncles their nephews without formal indentures, but this produced insufficient numbers of skilled workmen. A system of formal apprenticeship was thus necessary and became common among all craft guilds in order to train and certify the work of skilled craftsmen.

Life-spans during those centuries coupled with difficulties in traveling great distances and the length of time required to complete massive construction projects such as a cathedral or castle meant that most medieval masons ended their careers in the very lodges built in the quarries or at the construction sites where they first began work at age eleven or twelve. In addition, medieval building records—and there are a number extant—indicate that the clear majority of masons never exceeded the journeyman status or fellow of the craft. They were neither masters nor contractors which further restricted their "traveling." The existing records further indicate that those designated as master masons were most often supervisors or contractors who performed as much as administrators as they did as operative workmen. During this ancient period, men who were not operative masons—real masons—were an integral part of the craft structure and served as haulers, clerks, stewards, and, even, contractors.

The antiquity of the masons' organizations in England has generated much speculation and mythology. It is obvious from the remnants of Roman structures still dotting the English countryside that there was some form of masonic trade prior to the sixth century. There is no evidence, though, among the existing Roman archives of an organized masons' guild in England at that time. Roman building projects, Hadrian's Wall, for example, were under the auspices of the Roman military not civilian contractors. In the historical record, the first reference to anything masonic is found in Bede's *The Ecclesiastical History of the English Nation and Lives of Saints and Bishops*. Bede writes that in the year 675 Bishop Benedict crossed into Gaul and carried back with him some masons to build a church in the Roman style and that he also brought from Gaul makers of glass which was at that time an unknown skill in Britain. "This was done, and they came, and not only finished the work required, but taught the English nation their handicraft."[3] Yet earlier in the same text, for the year 619, Bede writes that a great fire consumed the city of London and that "The church of the Four Crowned Martyrs was in the place where the fire raged."[4] The four crowned Martyrs were the patron saints of Roman masons[5] which suggested to some scholars that while mason/soldiers may have remained in Britain after the Roman withdrawal, none were left by the year 675.

The Four Crowned Martyrs or *Sancti Quatuor Coronati* refers to nine men identified by the Catholic Church as martyrs. They are divided into two groups: Severus (or Secundius), Severian(us), Carpophorus (or Carpoforus), and Victorinus (or Victorius, Vittorinus): and Claudius, Castorius, Symphorian (Simpronian), Nicostratus, and Simplicius. *The Golden Legend* recounts that they were not actually known at the time of their death but "were learned thorough the Lord's revelation after many years had passed."[6] The four in group one, all of whom were soldiers or military clerks, were executed at the order of the Emperor Diocletian for refusing to sacrifice to Aesculapius, the Roman god of medicine. According to the legend, they were buried in the cemetery of Santi Marcellinoe Pietro e Laterano by Pope Miltiades and St. Sebastian. Of greater interest to ancient operative masons (and to Freemasons) is group two.

Tradition teaches that these five were sculptors or freemasons who refused to make a statue of Emperor Diocletian and to offer sacrifice to other Roman Gods. The Emperor ordered them sealed in lead coffins and tossed into the sea from a cliff in Pannonia. *The Catholic Encyclopedia* reports that "they were condemned to death as Christians . . . towards the end of 305."[7] They were venerated as saints early in English Christian history when Augustine of Canterbury coming to the island from a monastery near the basilica of Santi Quattro Coronati in Rome arriving in Kent in 597 and their relics came to England in 601. This reference in *The Catholic Encyclopedia* may be construed to support Bede's reference to a church dedicated to the masonic martyrs prior to the reintroduction of masons into Britain in 675. The connection with sculpture or stone work linked the martyrs to the guild in England, Germany, and Italy. A sculpture created by Nanni di Banco located in Orsanmichele near Florence depicts the martyrs and was commissioned by the guild of stone and woodworkers of which he was a member.

Outside Bede, there is no reference to masons or to any guild in the other great chronicles to include *The Anglo-Saxon Chronicles*, *The Croyland Chronicle*, or *The Doomsday Book*. The existing evidence suggests stone buildings were rarely built prior to the twelfth century and that organized masonry arose in England only after the Norman Conquest when kings, nobles, and churchmen from William I onward, erected buildings such as Westminster Abbey, the Tower of London, and other royal edifices. The account books for the reign of Henry III (1216-1307) as well as those of Edward I (1272-1307) and Edward III (1327-1377) indicate a strong royal passion for building and the development of an organization of masons to perform the labor.

Given the nature of the masonic lodges necessary for the erection of these magnificent edifices, it was inevitable that customs would be established to govern the relationship between the employer and the employee. Similarly, these organizations facilitated the administrative functions necessary to house, feed, pay, and supervise the workmen as well as to make available to them a ready supply of useable materials and suitable working tools.

The Regis Manuscript, a long poem in Old English, dated to about 1390, and the *Cooke Manuscript*, a prose or ledger-type document also in Old English dated to about 1410, list the articles and points developed within the medieval craft to regulate its practices. Both documents in their entirety as well as *The Graham Manuscript* and *Schaw Statutes* are in Chapter IV. The articles in these documents are directed chiefly to the masters—the person or craftsman in charge—noting that they should be loyal to their lord—the person paying the bills; not waste his goods by giving more pay to any man than he deserved; taking and training apprentices only as needed (and keeping them in training for at least seven years); dismissing insufficiently skilled workers; and not supplanting another because "no man can so well finish a piece of work as he that began it."[8]

The points are directed to the laborers or fellows. They were to love God and regard their fellows as brethren; to keep their secrets; to "tell it to no man wheresoever you go, the counsel of the hall, and even of bower, keep it well to great honor, lest it would turn thyself to shame, and bring the craft into great shame;"[9] to take his pay meekly and to avoid quarreling; to keep the seventh commandment "thou shalt not steal;" and, if a warden, to be a true and fair mediator between his master and his fellows. The mason also pledged himself to keep the mysteries of the craft which included such arcane knowledge as how to create a true square within a square; how to build an arch that would support substantial weight; how to create a design using nothing more than a string and several stakes or points; and how to orient a building correctly. In the modern world, many masonic mysteries are now taught in high school plane and solid geometry, algebra, and drafting.

By the middle of the fifteenth century, the London Company or guild had established its ordinances which were revised in 1481, 1521, and subsequent years, remaining in force until the early nineteenth century when the government had so fully taken over the duties and responsibilities of the guild that they were, effectively, put out of business. This same pattern of shift from guild control to government control may be noted throughout England and Scotland as well as in Europe and was not restricted to masons (see Chapter III).

OPERATIVE TO SPECULATIVE

By the end of the sixteenth century, political and religious events, began to erode the influence of the guilds and the very reason for their existence, but they did not disappear. Instead, they reinvented themselves—some suggest that they returned to their roots—and became [again?] social organizations that brought together like-minded men in pursuit of fellowship, enlightenment, and social standing. While it is most difficult to locate the exact beginnings of speculative masonry—modern Freemasonry—this much can be documented. Elias Ashmole wrote in his diary in October 1646 that "I was made a free-mason at Warrington in Lancashire."[10] The earliest record of the initiation of a non-operative mason is found in the minutes of the Lodge of Edinburgh at Mary's Chapel dated July 1634 when Lord Alexander and his brother, Anthony, were admitted. This Lodge is still in existence today. The oldest existing records of any Masonic Lodge date to January 1599 and are from Lodge Aitchison's Haven in East Lothian, Scotland. That Lodge closed in 1852. Minutes dating to July 1599 from the Lodge of Mary's Chapel, noted above, still exist, as well. There are no equally ancient records from English Lodges. But from the early medieval period, there had been throughout England and Scotland associations of stonemasons, and by the late 1500s there were at least thirteen of what appear to be speculative Lodges in Scotland from Edinburgh to Perth. It will not be until the early eighteenth century, however, that any type of institutional structure appears. This move toward national unity through the grand lodge system originated in England between 1717 and 1723. It was copied in Ireland (1725) and Scotland (1736).

In 1686, Dr. Robert Plot would write that it was the custom to admit men into the Society of Freemasons throughout the nation, "especially in Staffordshire." He also informs us that this Lodge consisted of at least five members of The Ancients of the Order and that a Fellow of the Society was called an "accepted mason."[11] Other early freemasons included Rundle Holme, made a Freemason in Chester in 1666 along with twenty-six other "Brethren", and the Lodge roll of the Old Lodge at York for the years 1712-1730 still exists.

HOW TO MAKE A MASON

Elias Ashmole was born in 1617. He studied and worked at Oxford University, probably in the library. He was admitted to the Middle Temple (the bar) in London in 1657, but having married a rich widow, he does not seem to have practiced law at any length. On 16 October 1646, he wrote in his diary: "4:30 p.m., I was made a free-mason at Warrington in Lancashire with Col. Henry Mainwaring of Karincham in Cheshire."[12] He then gives the names of those in attendance.

Prior to the second decade of the 18th century, there is not a single reference to three separate degrees in Freemasonry in any minutes of any lodge in existence. "Making a brother" or "Making a Free Mason," as Ashmole notes, were the only designations provided. All candidates were simply "entered." The ritual for making a Mason consisted, based upon available records, of what we would think of today as parts of the first and second degrees accompanied with a charge and some type of lecture.

THE PROCESS

A man asked a Masonic friend to join the lodge. His qualifications were debated in open lodge at length and his name put to a vote. If he was approved, he was sent a summons, usually written, to appear with his proposer at a specified place on a given date. There was no waiting for investigation. It was assumed that if a Brother of a lodge recommended a man for membership he knew the candidate well and personally, and was positive that his record would survive the test of open debate in the lodge. Brethren at that time would never have considered proposing someone whom they did not know and know well.

At the initiation, the candidate first took an obligation on the Volume of Sacred Law to preserve the *mysteries* not the *secrets* of the craft. The words and signs were communicated to him by his proposer who then asked him to demonstrate his proficiency for all present. A charge was given informing the new Mason of his duty to God, his master, and his fellow men. A history of the craft was generally read. This history could be found in one of several ancient documents such as the *Regius Manuscript* or poem, the *Cooke Manuscript*, or *Grande Lodge Manuscript No. 1.* It may even have been taken from an early form of the *Graham Manuscript*. Each of these ancient charges varied markedly in its account of the craft's history with the Legend of Hiram absent. Instead, we find the Legend of Noah as used by Antediluvian or Noachida Masons (see Albert Mackey's *The History of Freemasonry*). While Noah is mentioned in passing in the *Regius* poem (abt. 1390), a longer version of the story is found in the Cooke Manuscript of 1410 and the Graham manuscript of the early 1700s.

THE LEGEND OF NOAH

Lamech, the great, great, great, grandson (sixth generation) of Adam had two wives and four children: sons Jabal, founder of geometry and builder of the first stone house; Jubal, a musician and founder of music; Tubal, the first blacksmith and worker in brass; and a daughter, Naamah, the founder of weaving. Knowing that God would destroy the world, these four erected a pillar of marble and a pillar of brick on which they inscribed on each side the mysteries of their crafts and sciences. After the flood, Noah's great grandson, Nimrod, finds the marble pillars and the knowledge thereon contained is imparted to mankind.

The *Graham Manuscript*, dated to 1726, adds more to the legend. After Noah's death, Shem, Ham and Japheth, the sons of Noah, go to their father's grave in search of a valuable secret. They find nothing but a "dead body all most consumed." Shem, taking the body by a finger and the finger coming off, says "here is yet marrow in this bone." Ham, taking the body by the hand, which also comes off, says "but a dry bone." Japheth then says "it stinketh." They then proceed to raise the body by the elbow supporting it foot-to-foot, knee-to-knee, breast-to-breast, cheek-to-cheek, and hand-to-back, and cry out "Help O Father." "And so," states the manuscript, "they agreed for to give it a name that is known to freemasonry to this day."

These Masonic versions of the Legend of Noah probably originated in the Noah mystery play produced by the various craft guilds in England from the thirteenth through the sixteenth centuries which were suppressed during the Reformation (mid 1500s to early 1600s) and virtually eradicated during the Commonwealth under Cromwell (1649-1660). There are eight extant but different versions of the Noah mystery play each of which may have contributed some part to the Masonic ritual of the early eighteenth century.

THE RITUAL

The process of making a mason was simple. The lodge was opened and the Master asked if anyone was in waiting to be "made a Mason." The wardens and proposer (there were no deacons) retired to prepare the candidate—divested of minerals and metals, and so forth—and he was asked some basic questions similar to the modern Senior Deacon's anteroom lecture. The wardens returned to the lodge while the candidate and his proposer waited in complete silence in the totally dark anteroom for at least thirty minutes.

A set of figures were drawn on the floor with charcoal or chalk within an oblong square. Symbols were added and a tracing board put in place. When all was in order, the proposer brought the candidate into the lodge "upon the point of a sword or spear" and in later generations, led by a deacon with a sword. Prayer may or may not have been offered based on the tradition of that lodge. Moderns tended to omit the prayer upon admission while Ancients (Antients) included it. The candidate was presented to the lodge through the circumambulation. He was then led to the altar and given the obligation which, since it was only one degree, included most of the penalties in the full modern ritual. The candidate then kissed the Volume of Sacred Law and said "*fune merum genio*" which is Latin for "pour out the good wine for our pleasure." The brothers drank a toast given by the Master to the "heart that conceals and to the tongue that never reveals." After which each drew his glass, now empty, across his throat.

With the trestle board (not to be confused with the tracing board) already in place, the pattern on the floor and the emblems on the tracing board were explained. The new brother was then instructed to "wash away" the figures on the floor, retire to the preparation room, recover his valuables, and return to the lodge.

Upon his return, he was presented with a white leather apron and its meaning explained. The craft then assembled in a circle, hands joined crossways to form a chain, and the ceremony was ended. After the ceremony of "making a Mason" was concluded, the members sat around the trestle board feasting, toasting, and reciting the Apprentice lecture which was given in the form of a catechism with the Master asking the questions. Each brother could propose a toast as he desired upon answering a question. If a brother did not know the answer to the Master's question, he would stand, clap his hands, place his right hand on his left breast, give a very low bow, take a drink, and pass the question to the next brother in line. The lodge was finally closed with the Senior Warden simply saying, "Our Master's will and pleasure is that this lodge stands closed till" after which he would give the date and time of the next meeting. This concluded the initiation or "making a Mason," but for the new member, the journey had barely begun. There followed many, many extensive communications which included comprehensive and considered lessons in and discussions of morality, architecture, mathematics, natural science, art, literature, philosophy, and the myriad other topics covered in the seven liberal arts and sciences. Yes, there was congeniality, brotherly love, and conviviality (and a few glasses were undoubtedly emptied), but above all and paramount to the Craft was education, philosophical discussion, and moral and ethical development.

The Master Mason Degree in the symbolic lodges appears to have been an innovation of the Grand Lodge system sometime after 1725. Most Freemasons remained Fellow Crafts all of their days. Bro. George Bell, for example, was a Fellow Craft when he served as Deputy Grand Master in 1751. It is not until 1777 that the first and second degrees are noted as having been given on different evenings and, if the third degree was worked with any regularity between 1725 and 1760, few brothers knew about it and even fewer participated. It is possible that the third or Master Mason degree was worked in a separate or Master's Lodge and by invitation only with the first record of a separate Master Mason degree dated 1756.

Considering all available information and research, the precise origin of the three-degree system remains a true Masonic Mystery. Was there any formally authorized work prior to 1717 or did individual Lodges establish and promulgate their particular work? Who authorized and wrote the degrees after 1717? Did the Grand Lodge of England derive its ritual from operative lodges then in existence in London or elsewhere? Were the original rituals derived from or, even, part of the mystery play tradition of the operative crafts which had been suppressed? How much did the French have to do with English lodge practices, and the English with the French? Who wrote the story of Hiram and why? Does the Hiramic Legend relate to the Jacobean Rebellion or to the restoration of the English Monarchy after the Commonwealth? Is the Hiram Legend a retelling of the Noah mystery or does it symbolize something else—politically, morally, philosophically, or historically?

The ancient and honorable Fraternity of Freemasons never ceases to challenge us, but that is the way of our time-honored institution.

THE LEGEND OF NOAH ACCORDING TO GRAHAM 1725

(Spelling taken from the original)
Shem ham and jepheth ffor to go their father
noahs grave for to try if they could find anything about him ffor to lead
    them

to the valuable secret which this famieous preacher had for I hop all will
allow that all things needful for the new world was in the ark with noah
Now these 3 men had already agreed that if they did not find the very
    thing
If self that the first thing what they found was to be to them as a secret
    they not
doubting but did most ffirmly believe than God was able and would also
    prove
willing through their faith prayer and obedience for to cause what they
    did
find for to prove as vertuable to them as if they had received the secret at
ffirst from God himself at its head spring so came to the Grave finding
nothing save the dead body all most consumed away takeing a
greip at a ffinger
it came away so from Joynt to Joynt so to the wrest so to the Elbow so
    they
Reared up the dead body and supported it setting ffoot to ffoot knee to
    knee
Breast to breast Cheeck to cheeck and hand to back and cryed out
help o ffather as if they had said o ffather of heaven helpo us no Earthly
    ffather
cannot so Laid down the dead body again and now knowing what
to do – so one said is et marrow in this bone and the second said but a
dry bone and the third said it stinketh so they agreed for to give it a name
as is known to free masonry to this day so went to their undertakings
the virtue did not proceed from what they ffound or how it was called but
ffrom ffaith and prayer o thu it continued the will pass for the deed.

MODERN FREEMASONRY: WHAT IT HAS ACCOMPLISHED

Modern Freemasonry dates itself from the formation of the Grand Lodge of
England in or about the year 1717. According to at least one source, four
London lodges of Freemasons, gathered to form the Grand Lodge, but the
minutes of the Grand Lodge do not commence until the year 1723 and no
minutes from individual lodges in London seem to have survived. In 1723
the first edition of the Constitutions appeared and the Duke of Montagu was
elected Grand Master. Tradition holds that the great architect Christopher
Wren was the starting point for the organization. Wren, officially "Master of
the Work" under Charles II (1630-1685) after the great fire of 1666, and
other notable architects and masons are reported to have been part of the
fraternity. But when Wren died in 1723, only two contemporary sources
referred to him as a Freemason. Inigo Jones (1573-1652) and a contemporary

of Wren is also reported to have been a Freemason but there no existing records supporting this claim. References to Jones's association with the fraternity date from 1725 and 1848.

When English, Scottish, and Irish Freemasons migrated to the American colonies, they brought with them their Masonic fraternity and, obsessed with the new ideal of freedom and enlightenment, the Fraternity, which was open to men of every social rank, of every faith, and every political persuasion, was the perfect organization for the emerging nation. The colonists valued friendship second only to protecting one's reputation. Your good name was everything. Government existed for the purpose of enlisting private individuals to carry out public ends. Important offices were to be held by only the most trustworthy—those who had already proven themselves of worth. These good men were expected to provide political and public leadership. They developed such leadership skills in their Masonic Lodge. The Lodges also provided sound education in the arts and sciences in those days before state universities and public schools.

"It would be difficult," writes Gordon Wood in *The Radicalization of the American Revolution,* "to exaggerate the importance of Masonry for the American Revolution. It not only created national icons that are still with us; it brought people together in new ways and helped fulfill the republican dream of reorganizing social relationships. . .Masonry was looking for the lowest common denominator of unity and harmony in a society increasingly diverse and fragmented. It became 'The Center of the Union'. . . it embodied the enlightened cosmopolitan dream."[13]

Freemasonry introduced us to and encouraged the development of individualism. Throughout the seventeenth and eighteenth centuries, the fraternity actively pressed for and taught its members the idea that each man and woman was entitled to respect as an individual. The Masonic Lodge served as the first model of democracy. Lodge members made their own by-laws and elected their own leaders. The very idea of election was unheard of except in the Lodge. When Freemasonry came to North America, much of this great nation's future was determined by Freemasons such as George Washington, Ben Franklin, Paul Revere, and Joseph Warren. In later years, men such as Andrew Jackson, James Polk, James Buchanan, James Garfield, William McKinley, Theodore Roosevelt, Howard Taft, Warren Harding, Franklin Roosevelt, Harry Truman, and Gerald Ford were Freemasons, and Masonic Lodges were among the first to break down the barriers of social class. Members of the British royal family sat with their own servants and presidents of the United States sat with carpenters, plumbers, and brick layers. Masonic principles and ritual teach that all men are equal and have inalienable rights to include life, liberty, and the pursuit of happiness.

The influence of Freemasonry on art, architecture, and science is virtually limitless. Christopher Wren, already noted as responsible for the rebuilding of London after the great fire of 1666 was reportedly a Freemason. The works of Mozart, Haydn, Susa, and Gilbert and Sullivan—all Freemasons— reflect Masonic themes. The authors of *War and Peace*, *The Man Who Would Be King*, and *Kim* were Freemasons. Some of the first hospitals and programs for deceased or disabled workers were created by the Fraternity. It is estimated that Freemasons contribute three million dollars daily to such charities as the Shrine Hospital System and other worthy causes. Freemasonry partners with public education by providing scholarships, treating children with dyslexia, and aiding our local schools monetarily and through the donation of time.

Freemasonry offers not only the traditional path of self-discovery and self-development, it offers training in leadership, organization, problem-solving, interpersonal skills, and values.

Freemasonry is more than a fraternity; it is a way of life and a commitment to the future.

NOTES

1. R.A. Leeson. *Traveling Brothers: The Six Centuries Road from Craft Fellowship to Trade Unionism.* (London: George Allen & Unwin., Ltd., 1979), pp. 23-40.

2. Douglas Knoop & G. P. Jones. *A Short History of Freemasonry to 1730.* (Manchester, UK: Manchester University Press, 1940), p.10.

3. Paul S. Boer, Sr. (ed.). *The Ecclesiastical History of the English Nation and Lives of Saints and Bishops.* (London: Veritatis Splendor Publications, 2014), pp. 503-504.

4. Boer, pp. 146-147.

5. http://www.catholic.org/saints/saint.php?saint_id=3430, retrieved, July 6, 2015.

6. William Jacobus. *The Golden Legend: Readings on the Saints.* (Princeton, NJ: Princeton University Press 1993), pp. 291-292.

7. "Four Crown Martyrs", *The Catholic Encyclopedia, Vol. 6,* (New York: Robert Appleton Company, 1909) p. 163.

8. Michael R. Poll (ed.) *Ancient Manuscripts of the Freemasons: The Transformation from Operative to Speculative Freemasonry,* (New Orleans: Cornerstone Books, 20130, p. 88.

9. Poll, p. 36.

10. Elias Ashmole. *Memoirs of the Life of that Learned Antiquary, Elias Ashmole, Esq; Drawn up By Himself by way of Diary. With an Appendix of Original Letters. Publish'd by Charles Burman,Esq.* (Farmington Hills, Michigan: Gale Ecco Publishing, 2010 reprint), p. 36.

11. Robert Plott. *The Natural History of Staffordshire by Robert Plot.* (Farmington Hills, Michigan: Gale Ecco Publishing, [1686] 2010 reprint), p. 316.

12. Ashmole, p. 36.

13. Gordon Wood. *The Radicalism of the American Revolution.* (New York; Vintage Books, 1993), p. 223.

Chapter Two

The Nature of History

The history of any organization, people, or civilization inevitably begins with questions about origins. "Where did I come from?" "Where did this begin?" "What does this mean?" These questions are often answered through legends, myths, history, and, at the personal level, genealogy. The study of history, however, requires mastery of methodology and specialized knowledge. History is a great art accomplished by members of a guild of historians that often looks not just to the facts as presented in the various narratives but searches for deeper meanings and truths. Advances in scholarship over the past 150 years have significantly improved our understanding of the past. One thing is certain, the historical context of an event is inescapable. This requires historians to read and analyze not just historical documents but also pamphlets, diaries, letters, and newspapers as well as the important philosophical, political, and religious works of the period they are studying to find clues about the "character of the age." They reach beyond the canonical seeking a larger world inhabited by men and women of all classes.

History has no grand design. Its progress cannot be neatly categorized. There are no rules or laws which govern what is and what is not important. There is no one right way to grasp history nor is there any guarantee that any given project or any given history is singularly more valid than other well-researched approaches to the subject. History is change, and change is a surprise because it does not always happen in a linear fashion. History is also about linkages, but these linkages often come about by accident rather than design.

In thinking about the past, historians seek to improve cultural awareness as they investigate the persistence of certain institutions, traditions, and conventions. They seek for those tangible things which led to the creation of a group or society and which hold or held it together. A significant factor in most cases is the law of the land or organization. But unlike the law, which is rather straightforward, history is filled with compromise. Law is intended to provide predictability; history is not predictable. The past, noted William Harvey, the discoverer of the circulatory system, was filled "with the common subterfuge of ignorance."[1] But as the seventeenth century emerged— and with it the beginnings of Freemasonry—there appeared in many nations men of genius in a quantity never before seen in history who sought not only to understand the past but to judge and utilize its impact on the present and the future. In a much-truncated alphabetical order they included Bacon, Bernini, Bernoulli, Boyle, Brahe, Caravaggio, Cervantes, Corneille, Dekker, Descartes, Donne, Dryden, El Greco, Galileo Galilei, Halley, Hals, Locke, Malpighi, Milton, Moliere, Monteverdi, Scarlatti, Shakespeare, Spinoza, van Leeuwenhoek, Velázquez, Vermeer, and Wren. Some of these were Freemasons, and others had Masonic ties.

Their approach to the understanding of history would evolve into what is currently referred to as *critical history*. This approach to the study of the past involves strict analysis of the nature of the evidence cited to support historic contentions. Just because something appears in an official document does not necessarily make it correct. Nor is something that contradicts established, official sources correct, either. Critical analysis requires the historian to approach sources without bias or preconceptions. It also requires the historian to consider *all* sources in a form of comparative content analysis. Some authors, past and present, attempt to create what the past was like without employing any or only a few carefully selected sources. Others place a strong emphasis on surviving sources without a critical analysis of the survivors. Our access to the past is through those sources, but they often are in conflict and, as with all history, represent the world-view of the author to include his biases and limitations.

History is not an empirical science. It cannot be tested or evaluated in a manner similar to astronomy even though some empirical guidelines may be utilized. For example, if one wished to prove that the sun rose in the east, they would arise each morning for years and record the point on the horizon where they witnessed the rising sun. They would do this year after year, decade after decade. And they would not be alone; thousands and thousands of other people at thousands of locations on the earth over thousands of years would make similar observations and reach the same conclusion. The sun rises in the east. And if you go outside tomorrow morning, you can make the same observation and reach the same conclusion. This is empirical, verifiable, repeatable science.

Or you may wish to prove that your lead fishing sinker will go down in water while your cork float or bobber will not. You gather one thousand tubs of water into which you drop your lead sinker and your cork float. The sinker always goes down; the float always floats. Your conclusion, based upon repeated testing and observation, is that lead objects sink and cork objects float. In this case, you may even be able to apply your conclusion to other bodies with similar properties. Based upon your observations of the sinkers and floats, you theorize that a steel ball (metal, heavy, round) will sink when dropped into water while a wooden ball (lighter, of similar construction as the cork) will float. You then experiment to prove your theory. This, too, is empirical science.

History, unlike science, can neither be repeated nor observed a second time. It is *done and over with* immediately after the first observation. There are no *instant replays* in history. History, therefore, must depend upon different levels of proof to verify what was reported. Were Germany and Japan defeated in World War II? The first-hand observations of millions of individuals from various locations and at various times verify this conclusion as do the surviving documents of surrender signed by officials from many nations as well the political and geographical structure of the real world after those surrenders in April and August 1945. Similarly, did William the Conqueror invade and capture what became England? Again, the records of survivors as well as the very shape of all history and politics after 1066 in England support that conclusion.

But all history is not as unequivocal in its interpretation nor does it always enjoy the unified conclusions of millions of observers. History is often more the art of probability than hard evidence or scientific analysis. The issue in history becomes not what makes events certain but rather what makes them more or less probable. The old maxim "winners write the history" is not always valid and has often been disproven. Critical analysis of history requires historians to carefully analyze, appraise, and balance every source. As will be noted later in this chapter, an inordinate amount of the historical record appears to have been destroyed purposely. An even greater part has simply been lost. For example, we have no extant first-hand accounts of the lives of Jesus or any of his immediate followers. Some of what may have existed may have been destroyed or not recopied because the accounts conflicted or were deemed improbable. Others did not survive because they were not considered important enough to be copied and recopied. Consider in relatively recent U.S. history how few letters exist that were written during the Civil War. There is no available estimate of the number of surviving Civil War letters, but considering that an estimated 2.75 million men and women served in the Union and Confederate military over four years and there were just as many if not more civilians writing to soldiers, it is obvious that the clear majority of personal, first-hand correspondence from that period has disappeared. And it must be kept in mind that most of what is extant comes not from the common soldiers who experienced the horrors of battle first-hand, but rather from their leaders, both military and political.

Prior to 1456, all documents were handwritten and, if they were to be maintained for posterity, they had to be carefully archived and recopied again and again. If a book or document was deemed questionable, it simply was not recopied or was archived in an inaccessible part of the library. There does exist in the surviving record, though, evidence of lost or yet to be found books. Some, like the *Dead Sea Scrolls* or the *Nag Hammadi Library* have been found in most serendipitous ways. The existence of other lost writings such as the *Q* document or the *Sayings of Jesus* may be inferred from existing documents or through direct reference by later writers. For example, most of what is known about Marcion and Marcionite Christianity comes from Tertullian who wrote five volumes attaching Marcion as well as from Epiphanius, Bishop of Salamis, not from Marcion or his immediate followers.

The question of forgeries of ancient documents must also be considered when making judgments about the past and how it was recorded. In the modern world, the exploits of Konrad Kujau and *The Hitler Diaries* are well known as are those of Mark Hofmann and *The Salamander Letter* or Mark Cusack with his *J.F.K. Letters*. But forgery is an ancient trade practiced by some noted artists and writers. Michelangelo created a sculpture of a sleeping Cupid which he artificially aged and sold to Cardinal Riario of Giorgo who, when he discovered it was a fraud, demanded his money back. What is interesting to art historians in this case is it was the forgery that served to promote Michelangelo's career.

At a more arcane and esoteric level is the reported discovery of a first-person reference to a *Secret Gospel of Mark*. It was found by a Biblical scholar in a book with no cover or title page and appeared be an eighteenth-century copy of an older document—a letter written by Clement of Alexandria who died about 215. But how does one authenticate any letter or document from antiquity? It is a complex and time-consuming task. It usually begins with an analysis of the handwriting by paleographers. Does the handwriting match the purported age and origin of the document? But anyone with patience, skill, and an artistic flair can learn how to imitate handwriting from any age or any person. Another way to determine the age of a document is chemical analysis of the ink and paper or parchment. Yet a third is to authenticate the text by making a point-by-point analysis of vocabulary, style, and modes of expression. Consider how a comedian or any other individual imitates a person. They focus on special words that the person uses. For example, Theodore Roosevelt is often parodied by using the word *bully*. How do we know if a speech is an authentic Roosevelt? Let us assume that he used that word at a frequency of about one time for every 1000 words spoken. To imitate Roosevelt, the imitator might use that special word one time for every 100 words spoken. This is too much Teddy to be Teddy. The same process or frequency count may be used to discovery a forgery.

But why would anyone forge a historic document? There are numerous reasons; money being a prime consideration—the *Hitler Diaries* brought more than $4 million and art forgeries for money are common (see the 1966 movie *How to Steal a Million*). It is even conceivable that a scholar might forge a document. Dionysius the Renegade forged Sophocles and then ridiculed Heraclides for not recognizing the forgery. When a scholar possesses a super-sized ego accompanied by disdain for other scholars, he might just perpetrate a ruse to "pull the wool over the eyes" of acknowledged experts simply to demonstrate, if only for himself, his superiority.

Most historical documents were not created to deceive but many early histories of various organizations, and Masonry is an organization, utilized what in their time passed for history to create traditional connections. Others were simply misinterpretations or misunderstandings of the evidence found or the documents discovered while still others were attempts to provide legitimacy to existing political, cultural, religious, or societal institutions.

Any analysis of historical documents is fraught with problems; even the most skilled researcher can be fooled. When discovering history, multitude possibilities should be considered and, through various research techniques, a sound theory established regarding the reliability of any document.

THE SEARCH

History does not proceed in a straight line from point to point, from event to event. History is best described as a vast web with multiple points interconnected through a swarm of paths. No event in history may be explained based upon a single event. An example of the result of such a multitude of forces is World War II. Fascism arose in Italy under Mussolini in the early 1920s; militarism became dominant in Japan in the same period; and the Nazi movement came to power in Germany almost simultaneously. Russia underwent the extreme turmoil of civil war and became the Soviet Union while experiencing severe economic deprivation and, under Stalin, genocide; and civil war accompanied the rise of Mao in China. Various nations, such as India, began their move toward independence. Add to the mix the abject failure of The League of Nations to prevent any aggression; the United States' failure to join that organization which had been championed by Woodrow Wilson; the world-wide economic collapse of the early 1930s; German perception that the Treaty of Versailles unfairly punished the German people; simmering anti-Semitism; German and Soviet political engagements; expanding nationalism (especially that of Japan) with the accompanying need for resources; American political isolationism; rapid advancements in technology; and, after the horrors of World War I, the tendency of the intelligentsia to ignore the impending markers of future destruction suggests that the cataclysm that began in 1932 inevitable. World War II, therefore, was not simply the result of Germany's invasion of Poland in 1939 nor of Japan's attack on Pearl Harbor in 1941. It was the result of a massive web of interrelated people, events, political movements, history, perceptions, and, even religion.

Yet reading history is not the single path to fully understanding man's past nor, as Edmund Burke wrote, a prevention against repeating past errors. The discovery of history can be both instructive and destructive. History operates from the safety of the distance of time and may appear to provide information that leads us all too easily to underestimate actions or connections or to incorrectly interpret events, documents, and artifacts. It may also, though, enable us to properly interpret past happenings and use the lessons learned to govern the present and plan for the future. We have made impulsive use of historical research too often to strengthen rather than liberate our preconceptions. For example, when historians and anthropologists began studying the Mayan culture of Central America they concluded that Mayan interest in astronomy and building as well as chronology indicated that they were a peaceful people focused on non-violent pursuits. And even though there was ample evidence in the carvings that covered most significant buildings that warfare was endemic; many early Mayan researchers chose to ignore the evidence because it did not support their preconceived notion of or desire to document a peaceful people. This choice to ignore what is now obvious may have been the result of a continuation of the agenda of the international peace movement which was prominent among academic and political thinkers and writers before and after World War I. Ultimately this approach did not serve to properly report and interpret Mayan history. Critical historical analysis does, however, enable us to express our faith in mankind's ability to correct misinformation and to properly establish his foundations and his beginnings.

The history of an organization is not that of spontaneous generation--the concept that each new organism was produced independently from some primordial substance or from nothing at all. History, like medicine, enables us to analyze the offspring as well as the parent. History and nature provide continuity with entities and, like blood, circulates, replicates, replenishes, changes, and sanitizes. As with any human organ, the study of history may carry out multiple functions. Ultimately, though, as noted by the English poet Alexander Pope, the proper study of mankind is man.

To study man and his organizations is the work not just of historians, but also of anthropologists, ethnologists, linguists, archeologists, psychologists, and a host of other scholars. Cultures and civilizations were active participants in our past, and functioned in conjunction with each other, not independently. Too much of popular history, however, is in the form of anecdotes which, though possibly accurate representations of a single time or set of words, are often taken out of context thus resulting in misrepresentations of the totality of events. These popular histories lead to unsupported myths and fantasies of origin and descent. Historical research, when properly done, often gives lie to popular misconceptions and accepted wisdom. That is its nature and its purpose.

Eusebius in his *Church History* recounts the story of Simon Magus taken from Acts 8: 9-24. Simon is described as a great magician who tried to convince the Samarians that his magic was miracles and he *the great power of God.* Eusebius is expanding, somewhat, on Justin Martyr who had written about Simon more than one hundred years earlier noting that the Romans became so convinced of Simon's divinity that they erected a statue to him on the Tiber Island with the inscription *Simoni Deo Sancto* or *To Simon, the Holy God.* When the base of the statue was excavated in 1574, however, it was found to read *Semoni Sanco Sancto Deo* informing us that the statue was erected to *Semo Sancus*, a deity worshiped by the Sabines in Rome not to Simon from the Book of Acts. But this misinterpretation became part of accepted church history for almost fourteen hundred years.

So, it is with the history of Freemasonry. Much of what purports to be Masonic history appears to be either misinterpretations of facts or outright fabrications. There is little definitive, straight line documentation linking the modern institution and its practices to any single ancient organization, or political or religious movement. Modern Freemasonry is the outgrowth of myriad organizations, practices, motivations, historical periods, as well as political and cultural systems. Much of what purports to be Freemasonic history is highly romanticized, mythological, and mystical *history* written by non-masons for non-masons and involves no authentic approach to historical analysis. Too much is self-published and tends to be created more to support a myth or a preconception than to clarify the murky history of the Fraternity. These histories also tend to over-use the word *secret* for its sensational nature and its ability to attract an audience.

Freemasonry is not a secret society nor is it a political conspiracy with tendrils extending into industry, commerce, the church, and the educational system. Freemasonry is a living organization with at least four hundred years of documented history. And throughout those four hundred years and across the globe, it has transformed, innovated, and adapted itself to meet the needs of changing generations, philosophies, perceptions, and interpretations of the past.

There are multiple keys to historical research among them being the use of primary sources. "History tries to describe past events as they really happen. It aims at faithful representation. Its concept of truth is correspondence with what was once reality."[2] It is, notes von Mises "the search after facts and events that really happen."[3] And while a given historian's account of the past is often influenced by his specific understanding of the problem and his world perspective, the work should be objective. Fiction, on the other hand, often depicts events that never happened and objectivity is not required, but this issue will be expanded on later as will other criteria used to determine what is to be considered historical. One problem, though, even with primary sources, is that of interpretation and value judgment. Historians are no more able to provide the ultimate truth or *definitive* history than anyone else. Another issue with historical analysis is the axiom that "winners write the history." When a victory is secured, efforts are made to obscure if not destroy evidence of past conflicts or differences of opinion. But such efforts are generally not successful, and there tend to be traces left that can be scrutinized and analyzed to discover the truth.

When Henry VII of England ascended the throne in 1485, he intended to marry Elizabeth of York, the daughter of Edward IV and make her Queen of England. He was confronted with the problem of *Titulus Regius* which had been promulgated by Richard III, Henry's predecessor whom he had defeated in battle at Bosworth Field. *Titulus Regius* had declared Elizabeth and her siblings to be bastards and thus not eligible to sit on the throne, even as consort. To address this issue, the order was suppressed by Henry and the Parliament roll on which it was recorded was burned by the public hangman. An additional order was issued that all copies were to be presented to the Chancellor before Easter 1486 for destruction on pain of imprisonment and fine. In the early sixteenth century, however, the original draft was found in the Tower of London and printed in 1611.

Another example of extraordinary survival may be found in the history of Hatshepsut of Egypt or the Foremost of Noble Ladies (1507–1458 B.C.E.). She was the fifth pharaoh of the Eighteenth Dynasty of Egypt coming to the throne in 1478 B.C.E. Considered by Egyptologists to be one of the most successful pharaohs, she was the daughter and only child of Thutmose I and his primary wife Ahmose. Near the end of the reign of Thutmose III attempts were made to eradicate Hatshepsut from the historical records. Images of her were carved off stone walls and at the Deir el-Bahari temple; her statues were shattered or disfigured and then buried in pits. An attempt was even made to wall up her obelisks at Karnak, but typical of the period and probably to save money, the new administration simply repurposed Hatshepsut's structures thus leaving traces of her reign for future Egyptologists to analyze.

What, then, determines what is included in any given history and what is accepted as authoritative? First, as Dan Brown notes in his discussion of the establishment of the Biblical canon, there is the tendency to accept most readily ancient documents, but this alone is no guarantee of final acceptance. *Codex Sinaiticus*, for example, which is dated between 330 and 360, includes "The Shepherd of Hermas," a book not found in the accepted canon. The *Muratorian Canon*, a fragment, consisting of 85 lines dated to the seventh century but containing features which suggest that it is a Latin translation of a Greek original written, possibly, as early as 170, maintains that "Hermas wrote [it] recently, in our times, in the city of Rome, while bishop Pius, his brother, was occupying the [episcopal] chair of the church of the city of Rome" [4] and thus, because it was too near to "our times" and the product of the brother of a recent bishop not an apostle was not worthy of inclusion in the canon even if it was permissible to read it in church but not as Scripture.

Other considerations for inclusion include authorship, acceptance, and point of view. As the *Muratorian Canon* notes about "The Shepard," the author was known, but he was only a bishop's brother, not an apostle. The pedigree of a document is critical to judging its content and establishing its place in the canon of history. Further, the general acceptance of a source among a knowledgeable population is also relevant. Some authors have proven themselves to be more reliable than others. Their contentions or reports are supported by other reliable sources, and there is a scholarly consensus about the documents relevancy and content.

British novelists L.P. Hartley in *The Go-Between* opened with the words "The past is a foreign country, they do things differently there." This implies, as all historians know, that when reporting on the past one must take into consideration the setting to include emotional, intellectual, cultural, religious, political, and social aspects of the society or group being studied. History is littered with letters, records, diaries, legal documents, and other bits and pieces of information. A history of an organization is not to be read as a phone book but within context to support inferences that lead to understanding. To do this, it is necessary to establish the significance and legitimacy of the source. Was there a Holocaust? Some writers content that there was not. The historically literate writer must access the source and use that assessment to validate or invalidate the claim.

Not everything that happened in the past is historically significant, and since significance tends to depend on perspective and purpose, not everything that is in a history book is important. Often it is there simply because the author was interested in it. Historical persons and events become significant when they can be linked to larger trends or events. What, then, is historically significant? It is best described as the collective evaluation or judgment of many historians that the event or person was probable as reported. And finally, and possibly most critically, what is the point of view of the document. Is it consistent with other documents of the period and does it report similar events in a comparable manner? Is it propaganda or particularly biased? What is the underlying theme of the document?

Fiction, on the other hand, while it does tend to give the reader a sense of presence, is not intended to accurately recount events but rather to enable the reader to view the world through the perspective of the characters. Fiction is a "web of imagination" constructed by the author. Fiction writers are more like advertising people or public relations specialists than tour guides. Historical fiction may be a stepping stone to history, but it should never be confused with the real thing. It may lead readers to study the history behind the novel and, as in the case of Dan Brown's *The Da Vinci Code* even compel scholars like Bart Ehrman to refute numerous historical and religious errors as he did in his 2004 book *Truth and Fiction in The Da Vinci Code. The Da Vince Code* has also served as a repository of errors about Freemasonry, its practices, and its history. The *Priory of Sinon* is a well-debunked piece of fiction created to enrich a single person. There is no documented link between the Templars and Freemasonry. In addition, neither Walt Disney nor Richard Wagner was a Mason; the association between Rosslyn Chapel and the Templars is spurious; and Brown's understanding of modern Freemasonry and church history are riddled with errors. In addition, and contrary to Brown's fiction, Da Vinci himself received only one Vatican commission and, as Ehrman clearly demonstrates, Constantine had nothing to do with the Biblical canon. "I have to keep emphasizing that Dan Brown was writing *fiction.* Even though he claims that his 'descriptions of . . . documents . . . are accurate,' in fact they are not . . . for some of us the historical record really does matter. . . All the more reason to know whether their [fiction writers] historical claims are true or flights of literary fancy." [5]

MASONIC HISTORY

The purpose of early Masonic histories, suggests Knoop and Jones, was to give the emerging fraternity something like the well-documented and still existing charters and records of privileges enjoyed by the operative guilds. It appears also that many well-meaning clergymen (many early Freemasons were clergymen) and others well-learned in *The Bible*, classical literature, what at that time purported to be history, and out of a desire to show the ancient nature of the Craft by demonstrating its Biblical as well as traditional connections, complied their histories much as Ussher compiled his chronology. Whatever their motives, these early compilers were honorable men who used the historical standards of their day which tended to be based on scripture and those authorities then known to them directly or indirectly to write their histories. These histories should not be taken seriously when compared to historical research conducted over the past two hundred years, but they do provide a solid foundation for Masonic allegory and ritual.

History today is much like a human being. When you look at the family tree of any person you note the web-like structure; the many individuals involved; the passage of time; the different countries and cultures; and the wide variety of events that contributed to the experiences of all who came before. What a person is today is the product of a long, involved past coupled with each person's unique set of experiences, education, expectations, views, politics, faith, and genetics. Consider the family tree that includes individuals who fought on both sides during the American Civil War with the grandfathers of those nineteenth century individuals including members of the Continental Army of the Revolution as well as Hessian soldiers paid by King George III. Further back that tree may include Normans and Saxons who fought on opposite sides at the Battle of Hastings with the Saxons being the descendants of Viking raiders who invaded England and settled near York and Normans who descended from Roman senators or centurions. The further back you go, the more intricate the connections become and may genetic tracers from a multitude of regions on several continents. Freemasonry is no different.

The human imperative to discover "where we came from" has fueled the practice of genealogy for generations; so too it has led to the desire to establish and understand the history of the Masonic fraternity. As with the genealogical quest, now so greatly facilitated by genetic analysis, new tools coupled with old analytical techniques and documents newly discovered or rediscovered provide many potential links. To understand fully the human organism, you must analyze the various genes which compose the final product. Each gene has its original but each may also have its mutation. Combined, the human is the product of that progression. Freemasonry is a similar combination or progression. To understand the modern structure one should consider all contributing factors and institutions, and determine which links are valid and which are not. Is there a link between ancient craft guilds and their practices and Freemasonry? Did the mystery religion traditions factor into early Masonic practices? How much of craft guild practice was a function of its involvement in the mystery play cycles? To what extent did the human focus on ritual practices through the ages contribute to Freemasonry? To what extend did the various cultural revolutions such as the Enlightenment and the Renaissance contribute to the founding of the Fraternity? The questions are endless, but they provide a beginning point.

The history of any group appears to issue from the primal search to determine "why it became what it did." In the seventeenth and eighteenth centuries, this question was commonly answered, as it had so often been done in the past, by fabulists and myth-makers with the ensuing rival accounts of the same phenomena. Did these fabulists and myth-makers realize that their search for origins tended to render them more defenders and persuaders than seekers for historical information? The answer is an emphatic "No." These antiquaries, as Knoop and Jones note, wrote out of an ancient and honorable interest in the Craft and its history. "The results, whatever the motives, cannot be taken seriously today; but the compilers probably did their best according to the standards of their time, basing their accounts upon scriptural and such other received authorities as were directly or indirectly known to them."[6]

These *historians* originated, studied, and wrote in a period before there was a fundamental grasp of historicity. They understood the need for chronology and thus presented their stories in such a manner, but there was little attempt to verify or document people or events, or account fully for motivations and variations in the narratives. They were, in a modern sense, naïve, but they were doing their best to illuminate man's condition and explain his past in light of current events and political realities. The problem with all history, however, is that of intent, especially original intent. The historical record does not always present a unanimous, single voiced account of the past nor does it come to us through perfect and complete records. In fact, for much of history, there is a significant lack of evidence of most events and as significant a misinterpretation of what evidence is or was available.

A major motivation that leads humans to study history appears to be the security which such study implies. There is security in reviewing the artifacts and writings of past eras. The past does not appear to change. Much like Monday-morning quarterbacking, it is safe. But it really is not. With each succeeding generation of scholars, there are new realities to be pondered or brought into the open made possible by some recent discovery or some old discovery reevaluated and reinterpreted. When we read ancient texts in the light of new findings about language, meaning, and history, we discover that we can now know things of which our ancestors had no knowledge or even suspicion. All historians feel some degree of self-satisfaction in this process. Consider medicine as example. Reading Morgagni's (1682-1771) clinical notes, we discover that he described hardening of the arteries and myriad other conditions, and even demonstrated that strokes were not the result of a lesion on the brain long before such medical diagnosis became standard or any treatment devised. Morgagni made the observations, but it depended upon future generations to interpret them correctly and to use them clinically.

Yesterday may be a comfortable place to be, but it is not conducive to full understanding or to the utilization of that understanding to address current concerns. The Greeks and Romans, notes J.G.A. Pocock, were not fully aware, as we are aware, of civilizations that existed in their immediate past. For them, there was no past world of which they felt the need to possess evidence, to explore, or to explain. They were centered on *the here and now* comparing their civilization with others then in existence and assuming that the past had been no different. As historiography moved into the medieval period and then the Renaissance, coupled with an emphasis on classical learning and antiquity, it began to focus on the past. The men of these periods sought to *model themselves upon antiquity* by accepting newly rediscovered teachings as authoritative. But, the imaginative mind of the Middle Ages, especially, led to a composite reading of ancient texts that mixed the past with the present. Medieval and Renaissance art is replete with images of Hector and Alexander, both ancient Greek characters, depicted as European knights in full armor; of Christ's trial taking place in a feudal castle according to feudal law and tradition; and numerous images of various Middle

Eastern Biblical characters and events depicted in European settings with European faces dressed as Europeans of the period in which the art was produced. In addition, prior to the modern age, history traditionally focused primarily on what the writer perceived as important people doing important things with men being the central character in most histories and narratives.

Common men and just about all women tended to be omitted from the historical record or only described in a cursory manner. For example, as R.V. Turner and Helen Castor note, while we have a detailed description of Henry II of England to include his hair color, complexion, freckles, eye color, and even his chosen hair style (closely shorn), there is no similar record of Eleanor of Aquitaine, his wife. She was a woman and thus unworthy of such note. And when there are records of the appearance of an individual, either in the chronicles or other sources, they do not always reflect the historical record. Henry V of England had been shot full in the face with a cross bow bolt at age sixteen. Such an injury would suggest that his outward appearance was not especially pleasing and though often described as muscular, manly, and kingly, the one accepted portrait, a profile with a tonsure hair style, does not suggest a handsome man by modern standards. Yet the dramatic depictions of the man by actors such as Kenneth Branagh and Laurence Olivier never suggest this youthful facial wound or the appearance seen in the only accepted portrait.

One aspect of modern perception must not be overlooked in this discussion. So much of what modern man—especially twentieth and twenty-first century man—thinks he knows about history comes not from the historical record but from media, especially films and television. Even in the sixteenth through the nineteenth centuries, dramas and fictionalized history created vivid images of the past. Shakespeare depicts Richard III as a crooked, limping hunchback. History suggests otherwise. He was a warrior king who fought and won battles in full body armor and rode considerable distances on horseback. Similarly, cinematic representations of Catherine, first wife of Henry VIII of England, are most often of a dark-haired, dark-eyed female with a pale complexion. Both the historical record and period paintings indicate that she had chestnut hair, blue eyes, and the ruddy cheeks of her French, English, and Norman ancestors who included John of Gaunt and Edward III. Finally, though at six feet and two inches, General George Patton was an inch taller than George C. Scott, Patton's voice was far from the sonorous tone of Scott's. Why, then, do some historians, dramatists, and others write their histories as they do and did? Why not report accurately and without bias so that future generations would be fully cognizant of the nature of their past?

Pocock suggests that early attempts to establish the history and antiquity of so many political, social, and governmental institutions was based on the concept of *the immemorial* and encouraged the creation of legends about remote times when true heroes and people of great stature were the creators of so many things. Legally, in England, for example, this *immemorial* custom was often considered binding in the present based on the past. The practical utility of any history is that it provides moral and practical guides of what to do and what to avoid in the present. These accounts of ancient heroes, customs, and mores by historians and others thus took an active part in shaping the present.

LEGEND, MYTH, AND HISTORY

The words *legend* and *myth* are often used interchangeably to refer to past events, especially those of which there is little or no documentation. There are significant differences, however. A legend appears to have some basis in fact with the inclusion of historical names and events. History becomes legend when it is exaggerated or romanticized. The founding of any great nation contains such legends. Did George Washington throw a silver dollar across the Delaware or the Potomac or Rappahannock River? Probably not. While silver dollars were first minted in 1793 six years before Washington died, the width of the rivers tends to refute the legend, but it persists. The truth of Washington's existence has been adapted to meet allegorical needs. Myths, on the other hand, are archetypical storytelling which seek to explain difficult concepts using personifications and allegories. Myths tend not to be chronological and are often cyclical in form. The basic content of a myth tends to be timeless with the events being symbolic rather than expressions of actual events.

Some significant differences between legends and myths are summed up in the table below.

History tends to focus less on abstractions and conceptual indispositions, and more on factuality. In history, the study of the text becomes a matter of anchoring the words in context with the understanding that not all texts are verbal. There does not appear to be a great general theory of history but rather plurality and diversity. History is complex and filled with permutations. It is a puzzle with most of the parts missing or defaced.

Legend	Myth
Events occurred, people existed but the evidence has been exaggerated or is insubstantial.	No documentation of people or events
Tends to focus on recent past.	Focus is on ancient past.
Facts are execrated, even fictional.	No evidence to support story.
Notable, documented historical figures.	Gods and the supernatural.
Heroic deeds.	Explanation of natural phenomena through symbolism, no objective proof.

A historian must diligently strive to work through the legend as in the case of Heinrich Schliemann and the discovery of Troy. The legend, propounded by Schliemann, is that he became fascinated with Troy when his father read him the *Iliad*. This long poem led him to search for proof of Troy, the Tiryns, and Mycenae by first going into business to make his fortune and then utilizing those funds to search Hissarlik in Turkey for the fabled city. The historical record tells a different story. Schliemann was a brilliant, talented con man who, nevertheless, changed the course of archeology. He traveled the world visiting Russia, England, Mexico, Greece, India, Egypt, and Turkey. He went to ancient monuments, sat in on university classes, attended lectures in comparative literature and languages, wrote reams of pages in his diary, and made friends and enemies wherever he went.

There is no doubt that by 1868 at age 46 Schliemann was focused on archaeology, particularly the history of the Trojan War. In June of that year he was in Pompeii and in July at Mount Autos, said to have been the site of the palace of Odysseus. Schliemann returned to Paris in the fall of 1868 and became an expert on Troy and Mycenae. In 1871, shortly after marrying seventeen-year-old Sophia Engastromenos and based upon a long exchange of letters with British archeologist Frank Calvert, Schliemann focused his work in Hissarlik, one of three candidates for the site of Troy. He assumed that Homeric Troy was the oldest (an invalid assumption), he quickly moved through the upper levels of the mound until he reached fortifications which he identified as ancient Troy. In May 1873, Schliemann reported finding a cache of gold objects which he designated *Priam's Treasure.* Subsequent excavations indicate that the site originally designed by Schliemann as the Troy of the *Iliad* was of early Bronze Age origins long before the Mycenaean Age and that the treasure reportedly found there did not appear to belong to the Trojan Wars.

Did Schliemann discover the Troy of the *Iliad*? Obviously not; Troy is still being discovered with recent archeology showing that the city was far larger than originally envisioned, extending well into the surrounding plain and that the site had been used by the Greeks as well as the Romans. The site of Troy is now believed to have housed nine cities and indicates at least 46 levels of habitation. But with Schliemann, the myth of Troy took on new life; but further research supported only part of his original contention. Myth became reality. History presents many of the same problems: a dearth of evidence; misunderstanding of what is found; and the tendency of some historians to fail the test of serendipity and creativity by creating false links between disconnected things to force relationships.

One great myth that even in the modern era is often still believed though repeatedly disproved is that the earth was accepted by everyone as flat until Columbus and Magellan demonstrated otherwise in the late fifteenth and early sixteenth centuries. Pythagoras had theorized the spherical shape of the earth in the sixth century B.C. Eratosthenes, a Hellenistic mathematician and astronomer based in Alexandria, calculated the circumference of the world in the third century B.C. based upon observations made in a deep well in Syene in what is now Egypt using accepted mathematical formulas (geometry) and established its circumference as 39,690 kilometers, an error of only 389 lilometers. There is even evidence that Columbus had access to and probably consulted Henricus Martellus' map of the world created about 1491. This map, with its accompanying notes and annotations, shows a spherical earth with Asia, Africa, and Europe clearly delineated. It does not, however, show the New World, an error that would have resulted in Columbus thinking that he had landed close to Japan not the Bahamas. This map, as had other maps of antiquity, represented the earth as spherical, not flat.

FINDING HISTORY

The dissolution of the Monasteries in England under the reign of Henry VIII between 1536 and 1541 resulted in the destruction of virtually all records of churches, monasteries, convents, and other religious institutions in England, Ireland, and Wales. These records included not only ecclesiastical writings but also birth, death, and marriage records; records of land transactions; family genealogies; and diaries and chronicles. It is estimated that this loss represented about fifty percent of the written record of English history. During the English Civil War (1642-1651) and the following Commonwealth (1649-1653), a significant part of what remained disappeared. This was followed in 1660 by the Great Fire of London and, in the twentieth century, by the destruction that resulted from the Blitz. Other great losses of historical records include the burning of the library at Alexandria, the sack of Rome, the destruction of the House of Wisdom in Baghdad, and the fall of Constantinople in 1453.

The library at Alexandria, founded in 235 B.C., underwent successive attacks beginning in 48 B.C. and ending with the final and complete destruction of the institution in 391 A.D. The numerous sackings of Rome began with the attack by the Gaul's in 390 B.C and was followed by subsequent attacks in 410 through 546, 1084, and 1527. These attacks and sacks removed from existence an untold wealth of information. The Mongols' destruction of the House of Wisdom in Baghdad in 1258 resulted in the loss to the western world of Greek documents salvaged at Rome's fall thus removing from the Western tradition what had been salvaged from previous sacks of the Eternal City. In the New World, the written record of the Mayan culture was virtually destroyed by Catholic missionaries and only three codices remain. The Nazi regime and other fascist groups throughout Europe burned books on a scale unmatched in previous history. Anyone doing genealogical research in the United States becomes quickly aware of the destruction of primary documents over the relatively short 408-year history of this nation, especially during the Civil War of 1861-1865.

In the recent history of the United States, the 1921 fire in the basement of the Department of Commerce Building in Washington, DC, destroyed ninety percent of 1890 US Census records leaving a 20-year gap in the genealogical record. The July 1973 fire at the St. Louis National Personnel Records Center destroyed an estimated eighty percent of all U.S. Army personnel records from late 1912 to January 1960 (World War I and World War II) and seventy-five percent of U.S. Air Force records from late 1947 to January 1964 with the total estimated loss of between sixteen and eighteen million files. In the twenty-first century, reports indicate that six percent of all PCs fail annually or 4.6 million loss episodes each year. It is also estimated that more than forty percent of all companies experience some degree of data loss annually. All of which suggest the flawed logic that there are sound records of our past. Add to this fact that prior to 1436 and the invention of the printing press, the concept of readily available records in multiple copies was unthinkable. And until the development of electronic computing and digital storage in the second half of the twentieth century, information archiving was a cumbersome affair requiring large spaces and complete with a variety of dangers from fire to water, moths, and beetles.

A summary of the history of that great charter of liberties commonly known as the *Magna Carta* (generally considered the most significant early influence on the rule of constitutional law in the English-speaking world) is a prime example of problems with how historical documents have been maintained and interpreted. *Magna Carta* was not the first written law, even in England. Sumerian tablets from Mesopotamia contain laws written prior to 2,100 B.C.E. The Code of Hammurabi was incised into a stone stele in 1754 B. C. E. The Ten Commandments were placed into written form in the sixth century B.C.E and the Roman Code of Justinian and Salic law of the fifth century both laid down rules for human society. It is the legend more than fact that has given *Magna Carta* its place in Western history.

King John of England was well versed in law. He was trained by his father, Henry II, to know how government worked—inside and out—and how to manipulate it to his wishes. Eventually, John ran afoul of his barons, but more importantly, the Catholic Church. He was excommunicated by Innocent III in 1207 and England was placed under interdict—no church services: no weddings, funerals, or masses. A typical comment made about John was that written by Matthew Paris: "Foul as it is, hell itself is defined by the fouler presence of John."[7] There is no original of the document in existence. What survive today are four different copies in written form which are engrossments or written records of an oral agreement hammered out months before in June 1215. Two of the surviving copies are located in the British Museum in London; one is at Lincoln Cathedral; and a fourth is housed at

Salisbury Cathedral. Even though the language is virtually identical in the four copies, a form of heavily abridged Latin, one is square; two are what in modern typography would be considered *portrait* and one *landscape.* John signed none of them. One of the copies in the British Library does display the melted remains of the king's seal rather than his signature. The British Library copy was exposed to fire in 1731 (which melted the seal) and a poorly done restoration attempt served to wash off much of the ink and half-dissolve significant parts of the parchment thus requiring the utilization of imaging technology to read the text. They are magnificent documents, none the less, and provide a foundation for an understanding of English and American law. They do not, however, provide the researcher all answers to all questions about the evolution of English or American legal systems.

A significant part of the historical record has been lost and this includes documents relating to the founding of Freemasonry. The entire history of Masonry, operative and speculative, is spotty. For the craft guilds, trade secrets were paramount which discouraged putting them in any tangible form. Likewise, the very nature of speculative Freemasonry with its focus on mystery (see Chapter VII) and secrecy resulted in a dearth of historical records. In Chapter III may be found four primary documents associated with the Fraternity including the most ancient, the *Regius* manuscript or poem. Appendix I provides a list of more than 140 other such documents. Appendix II provides a list of English Liberate, Charter, and Chancery rolls or ledgers which relate directly to the operative guild from which the modern Fraternity appears to have evolved. It is possible, therefore, using such documents and other available information, to construct a plausible history of Freemasonry and to draw conclusions based on that construct. Searching outside traditional sources and considering contributing factors is essential to understanding and to the development of the history of any organization.

NOTES

1. Robert Willis, M.D. *The Works of William Harvey.* (London: Sydenham Society, 1847), p. 116.

2. Ludwig von Mises. *Theory and History: An Interpretation of Social and Economic Evolution.* (Auburn, AL: Ludwig von Mises Institute, 1957), p. 274.

3. Von Mises, p. 274.

4. *The Muratorian Fragment.* Located at http://www.bible-researcher.com/muratorian.html, line 73.

5. Ehrman, *Truth and Fiction*, p. 190.

6. Douglas Knoop & G.P. Jones. *The Genesis of Freemasonry: An Account of the Rise and Development of Freemasonry in Its Operative, Accepted, and early Speculative Phase.* (Manchester, UK: Manchester University Press, 1949), p. 1.

7. Dan Jones, "The Mad King and Magna Carta," *Smithsonian, Vol. 46, No.4,* p. 54.

Chapter Three

The Legend Begins

There are still in existence about 140 Masonic manuscripts known collective-
ly as the *Old Charges* or *Constitutions* and include rituals as well as catechisms. They include:

OLD CHARGES
Halliwell Manuscript or *Regius Poem*
The Matthew Cooke Manuscript
The Dowland Manuscript
Grand Lodge No. 1
LATER MANUSCRIPTS
Lansdowne
York No. 4
Melrose No. 2
RITUALS
Edinburgh Register House
Airlie
Trinity College, Dublin
The Haughfoot fragment
Graham Manuscript
MINUTES
Mary's Chapel
York Minutes
London Grand Lodges
OTHER DOCUMENTS
Fabric Rolls of York Minster
Statutes of Ratisbon
Schaw Statutes

Kirkwell Scroll
London Masons' Ordances 1481 and *1521.*
CATECHISMS
Three Distinct Knocks at the Door
Edinburgh Register House
The Grand Mystery of Free-Mason's Discover'd
Prichard's Masonry Dissected
(A more complete list may be found in Appendix I.)

These manuscripts outline the history of the Craft as well as its organization and regulation. They are considered the primary documents from the
operative and early speculative periods when each Lodge maintained a handwritten copy of its charges inscribed either on a vellum or parchment scroll
or entered in the first pages of the minute books. This was their authority to
meet as a lodge and to exercise certain privileges and duties. Of the old
charges, the *Regius Poem* is unique in that it is set in verse. Excluding the
Schaw Manuscript, these charges open with a prayer, an invocation for God's
assistance, or a general declaration of purpose. What follows includes a
history of the craft which varies from document to document; a capitulation
of the seven liberal arts and sciences, especially geometry; and a set of rules
and regulations for masters and fellows. These early documents demonstrate
the evolution of the craft's legend and often begin with Noah and the flood
and concluding with the establishment of the masonic guild at York by
Athelstan.

REGIUS POEM OR HALLIWELL MANUSCRIPT

The *Regius Poem* or *Halliwell Manuscript* is accepted as the most ancient of
these documents with modern analysis dating it to about 1390. The manuscript appeared in several estate or personal inventories as it changed hands
and was finally deposited in the Royal Library before being donated to the
British Museum in 1757 by King George II. It was first referred to as a
Freemasonic document in 1838 by James Halliwell. It is listed in an inventory of 1734 as simply *A Poem of Moral Duties.* Halliwell, though not a
Freemason, published a short paper about the manuscript in 1840 giving it
the 1390 date. It is assumed, based on the numerous Biblical allusions, writing style, Latin grammar, fineness of the script, and other exegesis, that the
poem was written by a Catholic priest or monk. It was for a time mistakenly
assumed that the document was written about 1440 to counter the 1425 edicts
banning guild meetings.

Albert Mackey suggests that the extant rhymed verse manuscript is a
copy of two earlier documents with what he refers to as "a carless admix-

ture."[1] The poem consists of 5,260 words in 794 lines written in a fine hand on sixty-four pages of small quarto vellum. It appears to come from the German stone mason tradition which suggests that the author was familiar with the thoughts and principles of the Germanic guild in the medieval period. The original legend was modified by masons from France or Gaul. The *Regius Poem* makes no mention of King Solomon's Temple which constitutes such an important part of modern Freemasonic ritual and legend. It does, however, note the Four Crowned Martyrs-*Sancti Quatuor Coronati*--of Roman origin also referenced by Bede but absent from later manuscripts (see Chapter I). What is interesting about the document is that while the poem attributes masonry in England to Athelstan, it makes no reference to Edwin of the later York Legend nor is there any reference to St. Alban or Bishop Benedict noted by Bede. This poem does, however, provide the beginnings of craft history in England which will become known as *The Legend of the Craft*. This legend, first recorded in this late fourteenth century document, it will soon expand to include accounts of Lamech's sons and the pillars (The Legend of Noah); Hermes; the Tower of Babel; Nimrod; Euclid; the Temple of Solomon; St. Alban; and the more complete York legend.

MATTHEW COOKE MANUSCRIPT

The Matthew Cooke Manuscript or *Gothic Constitution* is the oldest Freemasonic document written in prose. The document includes the legend of the children of Lamech with Jabal's discovery of geometry; Jubal's development of music; Tubal's creation of metallurgy;and Naamah's invention of weaving as well as their inscription of these mysteries on pillars that would be discovered after the great flood. Nimrod, the Tower of Babel, Euclid and, even, Egyptians are found in Cooke's rendition of Masonic history. This manuscript is written on sheets of vellum 112 millimeters by 86 millimeters (4 3/8 inches by 3 3/8 inches) and bound into a book between oak covers. The Middle English of the documents supports a date of around 1450. The *Regius Poem* and *The Cooke Manuscript* demonstrate early masons' attempts to establish their *immemorial* history (see Pocock on immemorial histories) and, for *Cooke,* possibly, determine their privileges considering the 1425 ban on assemblies. These documents endeavor to prove that the Craft had ancient royal approval and that even the King's (Athelstan) son was associated directly with masonry.

GRAHAM MANUSCRIPT

The Graham Manuscript, which dates from about 1725 and comes after the foundation of the Grand Lodge of England, is the first to offer the Legend of

Hiram Abiff though in greatly abbreviated form with the older Legend of Noah (see Chapter I) being retained. The first reference to the death of Hiram Abiff is found in Pritchard's *Masonry Dissected* even though there are references to Hiram in the 1723 and 1738 Anderson's *Constitution.* The existing version of Graham was discovered in Yorkshire in 1930 but the location of its origin is unknown. It is filled with editorial errors which indicate that it is a copy of an earlier document. Unlike the older documents, this manuscript is written in a catechism format with set questions and answers.

SCHAW STATUTES

The Schaw Statutes were written by William Schaw, Master of the Works under James VI (1566-1625) of Scotland [who was King of England as James I successor to Elizabeth I] and later general warden of all Scottish stonemasons' lodges. He was responsible not only for the general oversight of royal building projects but also the operations of a fraternity *already* in existence. Schaw's task was to codify and create uniformity in the rules governing both the fraternity and the trade. His rules or statutes cover the proper qualifications of a person admitted into the craft; provisions for the sick and widows; and the formalization of an already existing oath. The statutes also provided rules for the election of wardens; set in writing the seven-year apprenticeship; and established examinations for promotion to *fellow of the craft.* The document did meet opposition which focused, primarily, on which existing Lodge would be declared Lodge No. 1. The issue was settled in 1599 with Edinburgh being declared first or principle Lodge and Kilwinning in West Scotland the second and head Lodge.

The four *Old Charges* noted above are given in their entirety below. A more detailed discussion of the various theories of Freemasonic origin and legend may be found in Mackey's *The History of Freemasonry* to include the Andersonian, Prestonian, Hutchinsonian, and Oliverian theories.

Regius Poem.

Thonkyd be god
our glorious
ffadir and foū
der and former of heuen
and of erthe. and of alf
thyngis that in hym is
that he wolde fochelaue of
his glorious god hed for to
make fomony thyngis of di
ners vertu for mankynd.
ffor he made all thyngis for
to be abedient ⁊ loget to man
ffor all thyngis that ben cones
tible of holfome nature he

Cooke Manuscript.

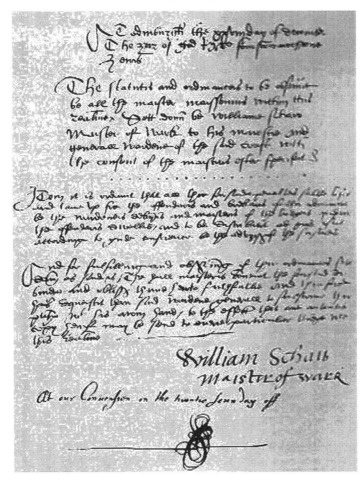

Schaw Statutes.

REGIUS MANUSCRIPT 1390

Here begin the constitutions of the art of
Geometry according to Euclid.
Whoever will both well read and look
He may find written in old book
Of great lords and also ladies,
That had many children together, y-wisse;
And had no income to keep them with,
Neither in town nor field nor frith;
A council together they could them take,
To ordain for these children's sake,

How they might best lead their life
Without great dis-ease, care, and strife;
And most for the multitude that was coming
Of their children after their ending
They send them after great clerks,
To teach them then good works;
And pray we them, for our Lord's sake.
To our children some work to make,
That they might get their living thereby,
Both well and honestly full securely.
In that time, through good geometry,
This honest craft of good masonry
Was ordained and made in this manner,
Counterfeited of these clerks together;
At these lord's prayers they counterfeited geometry,
And gave it the name of masonry,
For the most honest craft of all.
These lords' children thereto did fall,
To learn of him the craft of geometry,
The which he made full curiously;
Through fathers' prayers and mothers' also,
This honest craft he put them to.
He learned best, and was of honesty,
And passed his fellows in curiosity,
If in that craft he did him pass,
He should have more worship than the lasse,
This great clerk's name was Euclid,
His name it spread full wonder wide.
Yet this great clerk ordained he
To him that was higher in this degree,
That he should teach the simplest of wit
In that honest craft to be parfytte;
And so each one shall teach the other,
And love together as sister and brother.
Furthermore yet that ordained he,
Master called so should he be;
So that he were most worshipped,
Then should he be so called;
But masons should never one another call,
Within the craft amongst them all,
Neither subject nor servant, my dear brother,
Though he be not so perfect as is another;

Each shall call other fellows by cuthe,
Because they come of ladies' birth.
On this manner, through good wit of
geometry,
Began first the craft of masonry;
The clerk Euclid on this wise it found,
This craft of geometry in Egypt land.
In Egypt he taught it full wide,
In divers lands on every side;
Many years afterwards, I understand,
Ere that the craft came into this land.
This craft came into England, as I you say,
In time of good King Athelstane's day;
He made then both hall and even bower,
And high temples of great honour,
To disport him in both day and night,
And to worship his God with all his might.
This good lord loved this craft full well,
And purposed to strengthen it every del,
For divers faults that in the craft he found;
He sent about into the land
After all the masons of the craft,
To come to him full even straghfte,
For to amend these defaults all
By good counsel, if it might fall.
An assembly then he could let make
Of divers lords in their state,
Dukes, earls, and barons also,
Knights, squires and many mo,
And the great burgesses of that city,
They were there all in their degree;
There were there each one algate,
To ordain for these masons' estate,
There they sought by their wit,
How they might govern it;
Fifteen articles they there sought,
And fifteen points there they wrought,
Here begins the first article.
The first article of this geometry;-
The master mason must be full securely
Both steadfast, trusty and true,
It shall him never then rue;
And pay thy fellows after the cost,

As victuals goeth then, well thou woste;
And pay them truly, upon thy fay, (faith)
What they deserven may;
And to their hire take no more,
But what that they may serve for;
And spare neither for love nor drede,
Of neither parties to take no mede;
Of lord nor fellow, whoever he be,
Of them thou take no manner of fee;
And as a judge stand upright,
And then thou dost to both good right;
And truly do this wheresoever thou gost,
Thy worship, thy profit, it shall be most.
Second article.
The second article of good masonry,
As you must it here hear specially,
That every master, that is a mason,
Must be at the general congregation,
So that he it reasonably be told
Where that the assembly shall be holde;
And to that assembly he must needs gon,
Unless he have a reasonable skwasacyon,
Or unless he be disobedient to that craft
Or with falsehood is over-raft,
Or else sickness hath him so strong,
That he may not come them among;
That is an excuse good and able,
To that assembly without fable.
Third article.
The third article forsooth it is,
That the master takes to no 'prentice,
Unless he have good assurance to dwell
Seven years with him, as I you tell,
His craft to learn, that is profitable;
Within less he may not be able
To lords' profit, nor to his own
As you may know by good reason.
Fourth article.
The fourth article this must be,
That the master him well besee,
That he no bondman 'prentice make,
Nor for no covetousness do him take;
For the lord that he is bound to,

May fetch the 'prentice wheresoever he go.
If in the lodge he were ty-take,
Much dis-ease it might there make,
And such case it might befal,
That it might grieve some or all.
For all the masons that be there
Will stand together all y-fere.
If such one in that craft should dwell,
Of divers dis-eases you might tell;
For more ease then, and of honesty,
Take a 'prentice of higher degree.
By old time written I find
That the 'prentice should be of gentle kind;
And so sometime, great lords' blood
Took this geometry that is full good.
Fifth article.
The fifth article is very good,
So that the 'prentice be of lawful blood;
The master shall not, for no advantage,
Make no 'prentice that is outrage;
It is to mean, as you may hear
That he have all his limbs whole all y-fere;
To the craft it were great shame,
To make a halt man and a lame,
For an imperfect man of such blood
Should do the craft but little good.
Thus you may know every one,
The craft would have a mighty man;
A maimed man he hath no might,
You must it know long ere night.
Sixth article.
The sixth article you must not miss
That the master do the lord no prejudice,
To take the lord for his 'prentice,
As much as his fellows do, in all wise.
For in that craft they be full perfect,
So is not he, you must see it.
Also it were against good reason,
To take his hire as his fellows don.
This same article in this case,
Judgeth his prentice to take less
Than his fellows, that be full perfect.
In divers matters, know requite it,

The master may his 'prentice so inform,
That his hire may increase full soon,
And ere his term come to an end,
His hire may full well amend.
Seventh article.
The seventh article that is now here,
Full well will tell you all y-fere
That no master for favour nor dread,
Shall no thief neither clothe nor feed.
Thieves he shall harbour never one,
Nor him that hath killed a man,
Nor the same that hath a feeble name,
Lest it would turn the craft to shame.
Eighth article.
The eighth article sheweth you so,
That the master may it well do.
If that he have any man of craft,
And he be not so perfect as he ought,
He may him change soon anon,
And take for him a more perfect man.
Such a man through rechalaschepe,
Might do the craft scant worship.
Ninth article.
The ninth article sheweth full well,
That the master be both wise and felle;
That he no work undertake,
Unless he can both it end and make;
And that it be to the lords' profit also,
And to his craft, wheresoever he go;
And that the ground be well y-take,
That it neither flaw nor grake.
Tenth article.
The tenth article is for to know,
Among the craft, to high and low,
There shall no master supplant another,
But be together as sister and brother,
In this curious craft, all and some,
That belongeth to a master mason.
Nor shall he supplant no other man,
That hath taken a work him upon,
In pain thereof that is so strong,
That weigheth no less than ten ponge,
but if that he be guilty found,

That took first the work on hand;
For no man in masonry
Shall not supplant other securely,
But if that it be so wrought,
That in turn the work to nought;
Then may a mason that work crave,
To the lords' profit for it to save
In such a case if it do fall,
There shall no mason meddle withal.
Forsooth he that beginneth the ground,
If he be a mason good and sound,
He hath it securely in his mind
To bring the work to full good end.
Eleventh article.
The eleventh article I tell thee,
That he is both fair and free;
For he teacheth, by his might,
That no mason should work by night,
But if be in practising of wit,
If that I could amend it.
Twelfth article.
The twelfth article is of high honesty
To every mason wheresoever he be,
He shall not his fellows' work deprave,
If that he will his honesty save;
With honest words he it commend,
By the wit God did thee send;
But it amend by all that thou may,
Between you both without nay.
Thirteenth article.
The thirteenth article, so God me save,
Is if that the master a 'prentice have,
Entirely then that he him teach,
And measurable points that he him reche,
That he the craft ably may conne,
Wheresoever he go under the sun.
Fourteenth article.
The fourteenth article by good reason,
Sheweth the master how he shall don;
He shall no 'prentice to him take,
Unless diver cares he have to make,
That he may within his term,
Of him divers points may learn.

Fifteenth article.
The fifteenth article maketh an end,
For to the master he is a friend;
To teach him so, that for no man,
No false maintenance he take him upon,
Nor maintain his fellows in their sin,
For no good that he might win;
Nor no false oath suffer him to make,
For dread of their souls' sake,
Lest it would turn the craft to shame,
And himself to very much blame.
Plural constitutions.

At this assembly were points ordained mo, Of great lords and masters also. That who will know this craft and come to estate, He must love well God and holy church algate, And his master also that he is with, Wheresoever he go in field or frythe, And thy fellows thou love also, For that thy craft will that thou do.

Second Point.
The second point as I you say,
That the mason work upon the work day,
As truly as he can or may,
To deserve his hire for the holy-day,
And truly to labour on his deed,
Well deserve to have his mede.
Third point.
The third point must be severele,
With the 'prentice know it well,
His master's counsel he keep and close,
And his fellows by his good purpose;
The privities of the chamber tell he no man,
Nor in the lodge whatsoever they don;
Whatsoever thou hearest or seest them do,
Tell it no man wheresoever you go;
The counsel of hall, and even of bower,
Keep it well to great honour,
Lest it would turn thyself to blame,
And bring the craft into great shame.
Fourth point.
The fourth point teacheth us also,
That no man to his craft be false;
Error he shall maintain none

Against the craft, but let it gone;
Nor no prejudice he shall not do
To his master, nor his fellow also;
And though the 'prentice be under awe,
Yet he would have the same law.
Fifth point.
The fifth point is without nay,
That when the mason taketh his pay
Of the master, ordained to him,
Full meekly taken so must it byn;
Yet must the master by good reason,
Warn him lawfully before noon,
If he will not occupy him no more,
As he hath done there before;
Against this order he may not strive,
If he think well for to thrive.
Sixth point.
The sixth point is full given to know,
Both to high and even to low,
For such case it might befall;
Among the masons some or all,
Through envy or deadly hate,
Oft ariseth full great debate.
Then ought the mason if that he may,
Put them both under a day;
But loveday yet shall they make none,
Till that the work-day be clean gone
Upon the holy-day you must well take
Leisure enough loveday to make,
Lest that it would the work-day
Hinder their work for such a fray;
To such end then that you them draw.
That they stand well in God's law.
Seventh point.
The seventh point he may well mean,
Of well long life that God us lene,
As it descrieth well openly,
Thou shalt not by thy master's wife lie,
Nor by thy fellows', in no manner wise,
Lest the craft would thee despise;
Nor by thy fellows' concubine,
No more thou wouldst he did by thine.
The pain thereof let it be sure,

That he be 'prentice full seven year,
If he forfeit in any of them
So chastised then must he ben;
Full much care might there begin,
For such a foul deadly sin.
Eighth point.
The eighth point, he may be sure,
If thou hast taken any cure,
Under thy master thou be true,
For that point thou shalt never rue;
A true mediator thou must needs be
To thy master, and thy fellows free;
Do truly all that thou might,
To both parties, and that is good right.
Ninth point.
The ninth point we shall him call,
That he be steward of our hall,
If that you be in chamber y-fere,
Each one serve other with mild cheer;
Gentle fellows, you must it know,
For to be stewards all o-rowe,
Week after week without doubt,
Stewards to be so all in turn about,
Amiably to serve each one other,
As though they were sister and brother;
There shall never one another costage
Free himself to no advantage,
But every man shall be equally free
In that cost, so must it be;
Look that thou pay well every man algate,
That thou hast bought any victuals ate,
That no craving be made to thee,
Nor to thy fellows in no degree,
To man or to woman, whoever he be,
Pay them well and truly, for that will we;
Thereof on thy fellow true record thou take,
For that good pay as thou dost make,
Lest it would thy fellow shame,
And bring thyself into great blame.
Yet good accounts he must make
Of such goods as he hath y-take
Of thy fellows' goods that thou hast spende,
Where and how and to what end;

Such accounts thou must come to,
When thy fellows wish that thou do.
Tenth point.
The tenth point presenteth well good life,
To live without care and strife;
For if the mason live amiss,
And in his work be false y-wisse,
And through such a false skewsasyon
May slander his fellows without reason,
Through false slander of such fame.
May make the craft acquire blame.
If he do the craft such villainy,
Do him no favour then securely,
Nor maintain not him in wicked life,
Lest it would turn to care and strife;
But yet him you shall not delayme,
Unless that you shall him constrain,
For to appear wheresoever you will,
Where that you will, loud, or still;
To the next assembly you shall him call,
To appear before his fellows all,
And unless he will before them appear,
The craft he must need forswear;
He shall then be punished after the law
That was founded by old dawe.
Eleventh point.
The eleventh point is of good discretion,
As you must know by good reason;
A mason, if he this craft well con, (know,
That seeth his fellow hew on a stone,
And is in point to spoil that stone,
Amend it soon if that thou can,
And teach him then it to amend,
That the lords' work be not y-schende,
And teach him easily it to amend,
With fair words, that God thee hath lende;
For his sake that sit above,
With sweet words nourish his love.
Twelfth point.
The twelfth point is of great royalty,
There as the assembly held shall be,
There shall be masters and fellows also,
And other great lords many mo;

There shall be the sheriff of that country,
And also the mayor of that city,
Knights and squires there shall be,
And also aldermen, as you shall see;
Such ordinance as they make there,
They shall maintain it all y-fere
Against that man, whatsoever he be,
That belongeth to the craft both fair and free.
If he any strife against them make,
Into their custody he shall be take.
Thirteenth point.
The thirteenth point is to us full lief,
He shall swear never to be no thief,
Nor succour him in his false craft,
For no good that he hath byraft;
And thou must it know or sin,
Neither for his good, nor for his kin.
Fourteenth point.
The fourteenth point is full good law
To him that would be under awe;
A good true oath he must there swear
To his master and his fellows that be there;
He must be steadfast and also true
To all this ordinance, wheresoever he go,
And to his liege lord the king,
To be true to him over all thing.
And all these points here before
To them thou must need be y-swore,
And all shall swear the same oath
Of the masons, be they lief be they loath.
To all these points here before,
That hath been ordained by full good lore.
And they shall enquire every man
Of his party, as well as he can,
If any man may be found guilty
In any of these points specially;
And who he be, let him be sought,
And to the assembly let him be brought.
Fifteen point.
The fifteenth point is of full good lore,
For them that shall be there y-swore, (sworn)
Such ordinance at the assembly was laid
Of great lords and masters before said;

For the same that be disobedient, y-wisse,
Against the ordinance that there is,
Of these articles that were moved there,
Of great lords and masons all y-fere,
And if they be proved openly
Before that assembly, by and by,
And for their guilt's no amends will make,
Then must they need the craft forsake;
And no masons craft they shall refuse,
And swear it never more to use.
But if that they will amends make,
Again to the craft they shall never take;
And if that they will not do so,
The sheriff shall come them soon to,
And put their bodies in deep prison,
For the trespass that they have done,
And take their goods and their cattle
Into the king's hand, every delle,
And let them dwell there full still,
Till it be our liege king's will.
Another ordinance of the art of geometry.
They ordained there an assembly to be
-holde,
very year, wheresoever they would,
To amend the defaults, if any were found
Among the craft within the land;
Each year or third year it should be holde,
In every place weresoever they would;
Time and place must be ordained also,
In what place they should assemble to,
All the men of craft there they must be,
And other great lords, as you must see,
To mend the faults that he there spoken,
If that any of them be then broken.
There they shall be all y-swore,
That belongeth to this craft's lore,
To keep their statutes every one
That were ordained by King Athelstane;
These statutes that I have here found
I ordain they be held through my land,
For the worship of my royalty,
That I have by my dignity.
Also at every assembly that you hold,

That you come to your liege king bold,
Beseeching him of his high grace,
To stand with you in every place,
To confirm the statutes of King Athelstane,
That he ordained to this craft by good reason.
The art of the four crowned ones.
Pray we now to God almight,
And to his mother Mary bright,
That we may keep these articles here,
And these points well all y-fere,
As did these holy martyrs four,
That in this craft were of great honour;
They were as good masons as on earth shall
go,
Gravers and image-makers they were also.
For they were workmen of the best,
The emperor had to them great luste;
He willed of them an image to make
That might be worshipped for his sake;
Such monuments he had in his dawe,
To turn the people from Christ's law.
But they were steadfast in Christ's lay,
And to their craft without nay;
They loved well God and all his lore,
And were in his service ever more.
True men they were in that dawe,
And lived well in God's law;
They thought no monuments for to make,
For no good that they might take,
To believe on that monument for their God,
They would not do so, though he were wod;
For they would not forsake their true fay,
And believe on his false lay, (law)
The emperor let take them soon anon,
And put them in a deep prison;
The more sorely he punished them in that
place,
The more joy was to them of Christ's grace,
Then when he saw no other one,
To death he let them then gon;
Whose will of their life yet more know
By the book he might it show
In the legend of sanctorum

The names of the quatuor coronatorum.
Their feast will be without nay, (doubt)
After Hallow-e'en the eighth day.
You may hear as I do read,
That many years after, for great dread
That Noah's flood was all run,
The tower of Babylon was begun,
As plain work of lime and stone,
As any man should look upon;
So long and broad it was begun,
Seven miles the height shadoweth the sun.
King Nebuchadnezzar let it make
To great strength for man's sake,
Though such a flood again should come,
Over the work it should not nome;
For they had so high pride, with strong boast
All that work therefore was lost;
An angel smote them so with divers speech,
That never one knew what the other should
tell.
Many years after, the good clerk Euclid
Taught the craft of geometry full wonder
wide,
So he did that other time also,
Of divers crafts many mo.
Through high grace of Christ in heaven,
He commenced in the sciences seven;
Grammar is the first science I know,
Dialect the second, so I have I bliss,
Rhetoric the third without nay, (doubt)
Music is the fourth, as I you say,
Astronomy is the fifth, by my snout,
Arithmetic the sixth, without doubt,
Geometry the seventh maketh an end,
For he is both meek and hende,
Grammar forsooth is the root,
Whoever will learn on the book;
But art passeth in his degree,
As the fruit doth the root of the tree;
Rhetoric measureth with ornate speech
among,
And music it is a sweet song;
Astronomy numbereth, my dear brother,

Arithmetic sheweth one thing that is another,
Geometry the seventh science it is,
That can separate falsehood from truth, I
know.
These be the sciences seven,
Who useth them well he may have heaven.
Now dear children by your wit
Pride and covetousness that you leave it,
And taketh heed to good discretion,
And to good nurture, wheresoever you come.
Now I pray you take good heed,
For this you must know nede,
But much more you must wyten,
Than you find here written.
If thee fail thereto wit,
Pray to God to send thee it:
For Christ himself, he teacheth ous
That holy church is God's house,
That is made for nothing ellus
But for to pray in, as the book tellus;
There the people shall gather in,
To pray and weep for their sin.
Look thou come not to church late,
For to speak harlotry by the gate;
Then to church when thou dost fare,
Have in thy mind ever mare
To worship thy lord God both day and night,
With all thy wits and even thy might.
To the church door when thou dost come
Of that holy water there some thou nome,
For every drop thou feelest there
Quencheth a venial sin, be thou ser.
But first thou must do down thy hood,
For his love that died on the rood.
Into the church when thou dost gon,
Pull up thy heart to Christ, anon;
Upon the rood thou look up then,
And kneel down fair upon thy knen,
Then pray to him so here to worche
After the law of holy church,
For to keep the commandments ten,
That God gave to all men;
And pray to him with mild steven

To keep thee from the sins seven,
That thou here may, in this life,
Keep thee well from care and strife;
Furthermore he grant thee grace,
In heaven's bliss to have a place.
In holy church leave trifling words
Of lewd speech and foul bordes,
And put away all vanity,
And say thy pater noster and thine ave;
Look also that thou make no bere,
But always to be in thy prayer;
If thou wilt not thyself pray,
Hinder no other man by no way.
In that place neither sit nor stand,
But kneel fair down on the ground,
And when the Gospel me read shall,
Fairly thou stand up from the wall,
And bless the fare if that thou can,
When gloria tibi is begun;
And when the gospel is done,
Again thou might kneel down,
On both knees down thou fall,
For his love that bought us all;
And when thou hearest the bell ring
To that holy sakerynge,
Kneel you must both young and old,
And both your hands fair uphold,
And say then in this manner,
Fair and soft without noise;
"Jesu Lord welcome thou be,
In form of bread as I thee see,
Now Jesu for thine holy name,
Shield me from sin and shame;
Shrift and Eucharist thou grant me bo,
Ere that I shall hence go,
And very contrition for my sin,
That I never, Lord, die therein;
And as thou were of maid y-bore
Suffer me never to be y-lore;
But when I shall hence wend,
Grant me the bliss without end;
Amen! Amen! so mote it be!
Now sweet lady pray for me."

Thus thou might say, or some other thing,
When thou kneelest at the sakerynge.
For covetousness after good, spare thou not
To worship him that all hath wrought;
For glad may a man that day be,
That once in the day may him see;
It is so much worth, without nay, (doubt)
The virtue thereof no man tell may;
But so much good doth that sight,
That Saint Austin telleth full right,
That day thou seest God's body,
Thou shalt have these full securely:-
Meet and drink at thy need,
None that day shalt thou gnede; (lack)
Idle oaths and words bo, (both)
God forgiveth thee also;
Sudden death that same day
Thee dare not dread by no way;
Also that day, I thee plight,
Thou shalt not lose thy eye sight;
And each foot that thou goest then,
That holy sight for to sen,
They shall be told to stand instead,
When thou hast thereto great need;
That messenger the angel Gabriel,
Will keep them to thee full well.
From this matter now I may pass,
To tell more benefits of the mass:
To church come yet, if thou may,
And hear the mass each day;
If thou may not come to church,
Where that ever thou dost worche,
When thou hearest the mass knylle,
Pray to God with heart still,
To give they part of that service,
That in church there done is.
Furthermore yet, I will you preach
To your fellows, it for to teach,
When thou comest before a lord,
In hall, in bower, or at the board,
Hood or cap that thou off do,
Ere thou come him entirely to;
Twice or thrice, without doubt,

To that lord thou must lowte;
With thy right knee let it be do,
Thine own worship thou save so.
Hold off thy cap and hood also,
Till thou have leave it on to do.
All the time thou speakest with him,
Fair and amiably hold up thy chin;
So after the nurture of the book,
In his face kindly thou look.
Foot and hand thou keep full still,
For clawing and tripping, is skill;
From spitting and sniffling keep thee also,
By private expulsion let it go,
And if that thou be wise and felle,
Thou has great need to govern thee well.
Into the hall when thou dost wend,
Amongst the gentles, good and hende,
Presume not too high for nothing,
For thine high blood, nor thy cunning,
Neither to sit nor to lean,
That is nurture good and clean.
Let not thy countenance therefore abate,
Forsooth good nurture will save thy state.
Father and mother, whatsoever they be,
Well is the child that well may thee,
In hall, in chamber, where thou dost gon;
Good manners make a man.
To the next degree look wisely,
To do them reverence by and by;
Do them yet no reverence all o-rowe,
Unless that thou do them know.
To the meat when thou art set,
Fair and honestly thou eat it;
First look that thine hands be clean,
And that thy knife be sharp and keen,
And cut thy bread all at thy meat,
Right as it may be there y-ete.
If thou sit by a worthier man,
Then thy self thou art one,
Suffer him first to touch the meat,
Ere thyself to it reach.
To the fairest morsel thou might not strike,
Though that thou do it well like;

Keep thine hands fair and well,
From foul smudging of thy towel;
Thereon thou shalt not thy nose smite.
Nor at the meat thy tooth thou pike;
Too deep in cup thou might not sink,
Though thou have good will to drink,
Lest thine eyes would water thereby-
Then were it no courtesy.
Look in thy mouth there be no meat,
When thou beginnest to drink or speak.
When thou seest any man drinking,
That taketh heed to thy carpynge,
Soon anon thou cease thy tale,
Whether he drink wine or ale,
Look also thou scorn no man,
In what degree thou seest him gone;
Nor thou shalt no man deprave,
If thou wilt thy worship save;
For such word might there outburst.
That might make thee sit in evil rest.
Close thy hand in thy fist,
And keep thee well from "had I known".
In chamber, among the ladies bright,
Hold thy tongue and spend thy sight;
Laugh thou not with no great cry,
Nor make no lewd sport and ribaldry.
Play thou not but with thy peers,
Nor tell thou not all that thou hears;
Discover thou not thine own deed,
For no mirth, nor for no mede:
With fair speech thou might have thy will,
With it thou might thy self spylle.
When thou meetest a worthy man,
Cap and hood thou hold not on;
In church, in market, or in the gate,
Do him reverence after his state.
If thou goest with a worthier man
Then thyself thou art one,
Let thy foremost shoulder follow his back,
For that is nurture without lack;
When he doth speak, hold thee still,
When he hath done, say for thy will,
In thy speech that thou be felle,

And what thou sayest consider thee well;
But deprive thou not him his tale,
Neither at the wine nor at the ale.
Christ then of his high grace,
Save you both wit and space,
Well this book to know and read,
Heaven to have for your mede.
Amen! Amen! so mote it be!
So say we all for charity.*

COOKE MANUSCRIPT 1450

Thanked be God,
our glorius
father and found-
er and former of Heaven
and of earth and of all
things that in him is,
that he would vouchsafe, of
his glorious God-head, for to
make so many things of di
vers virtue for mankind;
for He made all things for
to be obedient and subject to man,
for all things that are comes
tible of wholsome nature he
ordained it for mans suste-
nance. And also he hath given
to man wits and cunning
of divers things, and crafts,
by the which we may
travel in this world to
get with our living to make
divers things to God's pleasure, and also for our ease and
profit. The which things
if I should rehearse them it
were too long to tell, and to
write. Wherefore I will leave (them),
but I shall shew you some,
that is to say how, and in what
wise, the science of Geometry

first began, and who were
the founders thereof, and of
other crafts more, as it is noted
in the Bible and in other
stories.
How and in what man-
ner that this worthy
science of geometry began, I
will tell you, as I said before. Ye shall understand
that there be 7 liberal sciences,
by the which 7 all sciences
and crafts, in the world, were
first found, and in espwciall
for he is causer of all, that is to
say the science of geometry of all
other that be, the which 7 sciences are called thus. As for the
first, that is called [the] fundament
of science, his name is grammar,
he teacheth a man rightfully to
speak and to write truly. The
second is rhetoric, and he teacheth a man to speak formab-
ly and fair. The third is
dialecticus, and that science teacheth
a man to discern the truth
from the false, and commonly it is
called art or sophistry. The fourth
is called arithmetic, the which
teacheth a man the craft of
numbers, for to reckon and
to make account of all things.
The fifth [is] geometry, the which
teacheth a man all the metcon,
and measures, and ponderacion,
of weights of all mans craft.
The 6th is music, that teacheth
a man the craft of song, in
notes of voice and organ,
and trumpet, and harp, and of all
others pertaining to them. The
7th is astronomy, that teacheth

man the course of the sun,
and of the moon, and of other
stars and planets of heaven.
Our intent is principally to
treat of [the] first
foundation of the worthy science
of geometry, and we were
the foundes thereof, as I said
before. There are 7 liberal
sciences, that is to say, 7 sciences, or
crafts, that are free in themselves, the which 7 live
only by geometry. And geometry is as much to say
as the measure of the earth,
"Et sic dicitur a geo ge quin R ter
a latin et metron quod est
mensura. Una Geometria in
mensura terra vel terrarum,"
that is to say in English, that
gemetria is, I said, of geo that is
in gru, earth, and metron, that is
to say measure, and thus is this
name of Gemetria comounded
and is said [to be] the measure of the earth.
Marvel ye not that I
said, that all sciences live
all only, by the science of geometry, for there is none [of them] artifici-
al. No handicraft that is wrought
by mans hand but it is
wrought by geometry, and a
notable cause, for if a man
work with his hands he worketh with some manner [of] tool, and
there is none instrument, of material things, in this world
but it come[s] of the kind of
earth, and to earth it will
turn again, and there is none
instrument, that is to say a tool
to work with, but it hath
some proportion, more or less.

And proportion is measure,
the tool, or the instrument,
is earth. And geometry is
said [to be] the measure of [the] earth, Wherefore, I may say that men live
all by geometry, for all
men here in this world live
by the labour of their hands.
Many more probations I
will tell you, why that
geometry is the science that all reasonable men live by, but I
leave it, at this time, for the long
process of writing. And now
I will proceed further on my matter.
Ye shall understand that
among all the crafts of the
world, of man's craft,
Masonry hath the most notabil-
ity and most part of this
science, geometry, as it is
noted and said in history,
as in the Bible, and in the
master of history. And in [the] Policronicon
a chronicle printed, and in the
histories that is named Bede.
"De Imagine Mundi;" et Isodorus
"Ethomolegiarum." Methodius,
Episcopus et Martiris, and others,
many more, said that masonry is
principal of geometry, as
me thinketh it may well
be said, for it was the first
that was founded, as it is
noted in the Bible, in the first
book of Genesis in the 4th
chapter; and also all the doctors aforesaid accordeth thereto,
and some of them saith it
more openly, and plainly,
right as it saith in the Bi
ble, Genesis.
Adam's line lineal

son, descending down
the 7th age of Adam before
Noah's flood, there was a man that
was named Lamech the
which had 2 wives, the
one hight Adah, and another
Zillah; by the first wife, that
hight Adah, he begat 2 sons
that one hight Jabal, and the other
hight Jubal. The elder son,
Jabal, he was the first man
that ever found geometry and
Masonry, and he made houses,
and [is] named in the Bible
"Pater habitancium in tento-
ris atque pastorum," that is to
say, father of men dwelling
in tents, that is, dwelling
houses. And he was Cain's
master mason, and governor
of all his works, when
he made the city of Enock,
that was the first city;
That was the first city that
ever was made, and that made
Cain, Adam's son, and
gave to his own son Enock,
and gave the city the name
of his son, and called it
Enock. And now it is
called Ephraim, and there was
[the] science of Geometry, and masonry, first occupied, and
contrenid, for a science and
for a craft, and so we may
say that it was [the] cause and foundation of all crafts, and
sciences, and also this man,
Jaball, was called "pater
pastorum."
The master of stories
saith, and Bede, De Im-
agine Mundi, {the] Policronicon, and

other more say that he was
the first that made depercession
of land, that every man might
know his own ground,
and labour thereon, as for
his own. And also he de-
parted flocks of sheep, that
every man might know his
own sheep, and so we may
say that he was the first
founder of that science. And his
brother Jubal, or Tubal,
was [the] founder of music and
song, as Pythagoras saith
in [the] Policronicon and the
same saith Isodore in his
Ethemologies, in the 6th book,
there he saith that he was
the first founder of music,
and song, and of organ and
trumpet, and he found that
science by the sound of pon-/deration
of his brother's hammers, that
was Tubal Cain.
Soothly as the Bible
saith in the chapter,
that is to say, the 4th of Genesis,
that he saith Lamech begot upon
his other wife, that hight Zillah,
a son and a daughter, the names of
them were called Tubal Cain,
that was the son, and his daughter [was]
called Naamah, and as the Policronicon saith, that some men
say that she was Noah's wife:
whether it be so, or no, we affirm/ it not.
Ye shall understand
that this son Tubal Cain
was [the] founder of smiths'
craft, and of other crafts of
metal, that is to say, of iron,
of brass, of gold, and of silver,
as some doctors say, and his

sister Naamah was finder of
weavers-craft, for before that time
was no cloth woven, but
they did spin yarn and
knit it, and made them such
clothing as they could,
but as the woman Naamah
found the craft of weaving,
and therefore it was called women's craft, and these 3
brethren, aforesaid, had knowledge that God would take vengeance for sin, either by fire,
or water, and they had greater
care how they might do to
save the sciences that they [had] found,
and they took their counsel
together and, by all their witts,
they said that [there] were 2 manner of
stone[s] of such virtue that the one
would never burn, and that stone
is called marble, and that the other stone
that will not sink in water and
that stone is named latres, and
so they devised to write all
the sciences that they had found in
these 2 stones, [so that] if that God would
take vengeance, by fire, that the
marble should not burn.
And if God sent vengeance,
by water, that the other should not
drown, and so they prayed their
elder brother Jabal that [he] would
make 2 pillars of these 2
stones, that is to say of marble
and of latres, and that he would
write in the 2 pillars all
the science[s], and crafts, that all they
had found, and so he did
and, therefore, we may say that
he was most cunning in
science, for he first began
and performed the before

Noah's flood.
Kindly knowing of
that vengeance, that God
would send, whether it
should be by fire, or by water,
the brethren had it not
by a manner of a prophecy, they
wist that God would send one thereof, and therefore they wrote
their science[s] in the 2 pillars
of stone, and some men say
that they wrote in the stones
all the 7 science[s], but as
they [had] in their mind[s] that a vengeance should come. And
so it was that God sent vengeance so that there came such
a flood that all the world was
drowned, and all men were
dead therein, save 8 persons,
And that was Noah, and his
wife, and his three sons, and
their wives, of which 3
sons all the world came of,
and their names were na-
med in this manner, Shem, Ham,
and Japhet. And this flood was
called Noah's flood, for he, and
his children, were saved therein. And after this flood many
years, as the chronicle telleth,
these 2 pillars were found,
and as the Pilicronicon saith, that
a great clerk that [was] called Pythagoras
found that one, and Hermes, the
philosopher, found that other, and
they taught forth the sciences that
they found therein written.
Every chronicle, and his-
tory, and many other
clerks, and the Bible in principal, witnesses of the making
of the tower of Babel, and it

is written in the Bible, Genesis
Chapter x., how that Ham, Noah's
son begot Nimrod, and he
waxed a mighty man upon the
earth, and he waxed a strong
man, like a giant, and he was
a great king. And the beginning of his kingdom was [that of the]
true kingdom of Babylon, and
Arach, and Archad, and Calan, and
the land of Sennare. And this
same Nimrod began the tower
of Babylon . . . and
he taught to his workmen the
craft of measures, and he had
with him many masons, more than
40 thousand. And he loved and
cherished them well. And it
is written in [the] Policronicon, and
in the master of stories, and in
other stories more, and this in part
witnesseth [the] Bible, in the same
x. chapter [of Genesis,] where he saith that A-
sur, that was nigh [of] kin to
Nimrod, [and] went out of the land of
Senare and he built the city [of]
Nineveh, and Plateas, and other
more, this he saith "de tra illa
et de Sennare egressus est Asur,
et edificavit Nineven et Plateas
civitatum et Cale et Jesu quoque,
inter Nineven et hoec est Civitas
magna."
Reason would that we should
tell openly how, and in
what manner, that the charges
of mason-craft was first founded and who gave first the name
of it of masonry. And ye
shall know well that it [is] told
and written in [the] Policronicon and
in Methodius episcopus and Martyrus
that Asure, that was a worthy lord

of Sennare, sent to Nimrod
the king, to send him masons
and workmen of craft that might
help him to make his city
that he was in will to make.
And Nimrod sent him 30 [380]
hunred of masons. And when they
should go and [he should] send them forth he
called them before him and said
to them--"Ye must go to my cousin Asur, to help him to build
a city; but look [to it] that ye be well
governed, and I shall give
you a charge profitable for
you and me.
When ye come to that lord
look that ye be true to
him like as ye would be to
me, and truly do your labour
and craft, and take reasonable your meed therefore as ye
may deserve, and also that ye
love together as ye were
brethren, and hold together
truly; and he that hath most cunning
teach it to his fellow; and
look ye govern you against
your lord and among
yourselves, that I may have
worship and thanks for
my sending, and teaching,
you the craft." and they re-/ceived
the charge of him that was their
master and their lord, and
went forth to Asur, and
built the city of Ninevah, in
the country of Plateas, and other
cities more that men call Cale
and Jesen, that is a great city
between Cale and Nineveh.
And in this manner the craft
of masonry was first preferred and charged it for a science.

Elders that were before us,
of masons, had these
charges written to them as
we have now in our char-
ges of the story of Euclid,
as we have seen them written
in Latin and in French both;
but how that Euclid came to [the knowledge of]
geometry reason would we
should tell you as it is
noted in the Bible and in other
stories. In the twelfth chapter of Genesis
he telleth how that Abraham came to
the Land of Canaan, and our
Lord appeared to him and said, I
shall give this land to thy
seed; but there fell a great hunger
in that land, and Abraham took
Sarah, his wife, with him and
went into Egypt in pilgrim-
age, [and] while the hunger [en]dur-
ed he would bide there. And A-
braham, as the chronicle saith,
he was a wise man and a
great clerk, and couthe all
the 7 science[s] and taught
the Egyptians the science of
geometry. And thid worthy
clerk, Euclid, was his
clerk and learned of him.
And he gave the first name
of geometry, all be that it
was occupied before it had
no name of geometry. But
it is said of Isodour, Ethe-
mologiarum, in the 5th booke Ethe-
molegiarum, capitolo primo, saith
that Euclid was one of the first
founders of geometry, and
he gave it [that] name, for in
his time that was a wa- [there]
ter in that land of Egypt that
is called [the] Nile, and it flowed

so far into the land that men
might not dwell therein.
Then this worthy
clerk, Euclid, taught
them to make great walls
and ditches to holde out the
water; and he, by geometry,
measured the land, and depar-
ted it in divers parts, and
made every man close his
own part with walls and
ditches, and then it became
a plenteous country of all
manner of fruit and of young
people, of men and women,
that there was so much people
of young fruit that they could
not well live. And the lords
of the country drew them [selves] together and made a council
how they might help their
children that had no livelihood,
competent and able, for to find
themselves and their children
for thy had so many. And
among them all in council
was this worthy clerk Euclid,
and when he saw that
all they could not bring
about this matter he said
to them-"Will ye take your sons
in governance, and I shall teach
them such science that they
shall live thereby gentle-
manly, under condition that
ye will be sworn to me to
perform the governance that
I shall set you to and
them both." And the king
of the land and all the lords,
by one assent, granted thereto.
Reason would that every man
would grant to that

thing that were profitable to himself, and they took their sons
to Euclid to govern
them at his own will, and
he taught to them the craft,
Masonry, and gave it the
name of geometry, because
of the parting of the ground that
he had taught to the people,
in the time of the making
of the walls and ditches a-
foresaid, to close out the
water, and Isodore saith, in his
Ethemologies, that Euclid
calleth the craft geometry;
and there was this worthy clerk
gave it name, and taught
it the lords' sons of the
land that he had in his teaching.
And he gave them a charge that
they should call here each
other fellow, and no otherwise, because that they were
all of one craft, and of one
gentle birth born, and lords'
sons. And also he that were
most of cunning should be
governor of the work, and
should be called master, and
other charges more that are
written in the book of charges. And so they wrought
with lords of the land, and made
cities and towns, castles
and temples, and lords' palaces.
What time that the chil-
drewn of Israel dwelt
in Egypt they learned the
craft of masonry. And
afterward, [when] they were
driven out of Egypt, they
came into the land of behest,
and is now called Jerusalem,

and it was occupied and charges there hel. And the making
of Solomon's temple that
king David began. (King
David loved well masons,
and he gave them right nigh
as they be now.) And at the
making of the temple in
Solomon's time as it
is said in te Bible, in the
3rd book of Regum in tercio
Regum capitolo quinto, that
Solomon had 4 score
thousand masons at
his work. And the king's
son, of Tyre, was his master
Mason. And [in] other chronicles it is said, and in old
books of masonry, that
Solomon confirmed the charges that David, his father, had
given to masons. And Solomon himself taught them
there manners [with] but little [their ?]
difference from the manners
that now are used. And from
thence this worthy science
was brought into France
and into many other regions
Sometime there was
a worthy king in
France that was called Ca-
rolus secundus, that is to say,
Charles the Second, and this
Charles was elected king
of France, by the grace of
God and by lineage also. And
some men say that he was
elected by fortune, the which
is false, as by [the] chronicle he
was of the king's blood
royal. And this same King,
Charles, was a mason

before that he was king, and
after that he was king he loved
Masons and cherished them,
and gave them charges and
manners at his device, [of] the which
some are yet used in France;
and he ordained that they
should have [an] assembly once
in the year, and come and
speak together, and for to be
ruled by masters and fellows
of all things amiss.
And soon after that came
Saint Adhabell into England,
and converted Saint Alban
to Christianity. And Saint
Alban loved well masons,
and he gave them first their
charges and manners first
in England. And he or-
dained convenient [times] to pay
for the travail. And after
that was a worthy king
in England that was called
Athelstan, and his young-
est son loved well the
science of geometry, and
he wist well that hand-craft
had the practice of the sci
ence of geometry so well
as masons, wherefore he
drew him to council and learned [the] practice of that science
to his speculative, for of speculative he was a master,
and he loved well mason-
ry and masons. And
he became a mason him-
self, and he gave them charges
and names as it is now
used in England, and in
other countries. And he
ordained that they shouuld have

reasonable pay and purchas-
ed a free patent of the king
that they should make [an] assembly when they saw a reasonable time and come together to
their councillors of which
charges, manners, and assembly,
as it is written and taught in the
book of our charges, wherefore
I leave it at this time.
Good men for this
cause and this manner
Masonry took [its] first beginning. It befel sometime[s]
that great lords had not so
great possessions that they
might not advance their
free begotten children, for
thet had so many, therefore
they took counsel how they
might their children advance
and ordain them honestly to
live. And [they] sent after wise
masters of the worthy science of geometry that they, through
their wisdom, should ordain
them some honest living.
Then one of them, that had the
name which was called
Englet, that was most subtle
and wise founder, ordained
an art and called it Ma-
sonry, and so with his art, honestly, he taught the children
of great lords, by the prayer of the fathers and the free-
will of their children, the
which when they [were] taught with
high care, by a certain time,
they were not all alike able
for to take of the [a]foresaid art
wherefore the [a]foresaid master,
Englet, ordained [that] they [who] were

passing of cunning should
be passing honured, and
ded to call the cunninger master
for to inform the less of cunning masters, of the which
were called masters, of nobility of wit and cunning
of that art. Nevertheless they commanded that they that were less
of wit should not be called
servant, nor subject, but fellow,
for nobility of their gentle
blood. In this manner was the
[a]foresaid art begun in the
land of Egypt, by the [a]foresaid
master Englet, and so it went
from land to land, and from kingdom to kingdom. After that, many years, in the time of King-
Athelstan, which was some
time king of England, by
his councillors, and other greater
lords of the land, by common
assent, for great default
found among masons, they
ordained a certain rule
amongst them: one time of
the year, or in 3 years as need
were to the king and great
lords of the land, and all the
comonalty, from province to province,
and from country to country,
congregations should be made,
by masters, of all masters,
Masons, and fellows in the
[a]foresaid art, and so, at such
congregations, they that be made
masters should be examined,
of the articles after written, and
be ransacked whether they be
able and cunning to the pro-
fit of the lords [having] them to serve
and to the honour of the [a]foresaid

art. And, moreover, they should
receive their charge that they
should well and truly dis-
pend the goods of their lords,
as well the lowest as the
highest, for they be their lords,
for the time, of whom they take
their pay for their service
and for their travail. The
first Article is this,--That every
master of this art should be
wise and true to the lord that he
serveth, dispending his goods
truly as he would his own
were dispensed, and not give
more pay to no mason than
he wot he may deserve, after the
dearth of corn and victual in the
country, no favour withstanding,
for every man to be rewarded
after his travail. The second
Article is this,--That every master
of this art should be warned,
before, to come to his congregation,
that they come duly, but if they
may [be] excused by some manner [of]
cause. But, nevertheless, if they
be found rebel[lious] at such congregations, or faulty in any
manner [of] harm of their lords,
and reproof of this art, they
should not be excused in no
manner [with]out taking peril of death,
and though they be in peril
of death, they shall warn the
master that is principal of the
gathering of his decease. The
[third] Article is this,--That no master
take no [ap]prentice for [a] less term
than 7 year[s] at the least, because such as be within [a]
less term may not, profitably,
come to his art nor able

to serve, truly, his lord [and] to
take as a mason should
take. The 4th Article is this,--
That no master, for no profit, take
no [ap]prentice, for to be learned,
that is born of bond blood,
for, because of his lord, to
whom he is bond, will take
him as he well may, from
his art and lead him, with him, out
of his lodge, or out of his
place, that he worketh in, for
his fellows, peradventure, would help
him and debate for him, and
thereof manslaughter might
[a]rise, it is forbid[den.] And also
for another cause of his art,
it took beginning of great
lords' children, freely begotten,
as it is said before. The
5th Article is this,--That no master
give more to his [ap]prentice in
time of his [ap]prenticehood, for
no profit to be take[n], than he
note[s] well he may deserve
of the lord that he serveth, nor not
so much that the lord, of the place
that he is taught in, may
have some profit of his teaching. The 6th Article is
this,--That no master for no coveteous-
ness, nor profit, take no [ap]pren-
tice to teach that is imperfect, that
is to say, having any maim
for the which he may not
truly work as he
ought for to do. The 7th
Article is this,--That no master be
found wittingly, or help
or procure. to be [a] maintainer and
sustainer [of] any common night wal-
ker to rob, by the which
manner of night-walking

they may not fulfil their day's
work and travail, [and] through
the condition their fellows might
be made wroth. The 8th
Article is this,--That if it befal
that any mason that be perfect, and
cunning, come for to seek
work and find an imperfect
and uncunning working,
the master of the place shall receive the perfect, and do away the
imperfect, to the profit of his lord.
The 9th Article is this,--That
no master shall supplant
another for it is said, in the
art of masonry, that no man
should make end so well
of work begun by ano-
ther, to the profit of his lord,
as he [that] began it, for to end
it by his matters, or to whom
he sheweth his matters.
This council is made by divers lords and masters of
divers provinces and divers
congregations of masonry
and it is, to wit, that who that
coveteth for to come to the
state of the [a]foresaid art it be-
hoveth them first, principally,
to God and holy church, and
all-halows, and his master
and his fellows as his own
brethren. The second Point,--
He must fulfil his day's
work truly that he taketh for
his pay. The 3rd [Point].--That he can
hele the counsel of his fellows
in lodge, and in chamber,
and in every place there as Masons
be. The 4th Point,--That he be
no deceiver of the [a]foresaid art,
nor do no prejudice, nor sustain

no articles, against the art,
nor against none of the art,
but he shall sustain it
in all honour, inasmuch
as he may. The 5th Point,--
When he shall take his
pay, that he take it meekly,
as the time is ordained by
the master to be done, and that
he fulfil the acceptations
of travail, and of rest,
ordained and set by the
master. The 6th Point,--If
any discord shall be be-
tween him and his fellows he
shall obey him meekly, and
be still at the bidding of
his master, or of the warden
of his master, in his master's
absence, to the holy-day following, and that he accord
then at the disposition of his
fellows, anot upon the work-
day for letting of their
work and profit of his lord.
The 7th Point,--That he covet
not the wife, not the daughter,
of his masters, neither of his
fellows, but if it be in marriage, nor hold concubines,
for discord that might fall a-
mongst them. The 8th
Point,--If it befal him
for to be warden under
his master, that he be true mean
between his master and his
fellows, and that he be busy in
the absence of his master to
the honour of his master and profit of the lord that he serveth.
The 9th Point,--If he be wiser,
and subtler than his fellow
working with him in his

lodge, or any other place,
and he perceive it that he should
leave the stone that he worketh upon, for default of cunning,
and can teach him and a-
mend the stone, he shall in-/form
him and help him, that the more
love may increase among them,
and that the work of the lord be not
lost. When the master and the fellows be forewarned [and] are
come to such congregations,
if need be, the Sheriff of the
Country, or the Mayor of the
City, or Alderman of the Town,
in which the congregations is
holden, shall be fellow, and [as] soci-
ate, to the master of the congregation, in help of him, against re-
bels and [for the] up-bearing the right
of the realm. At the first beginning new men, that never were
charged before, be charged
in this manner,--That [they] should
never be thieves, nor thieves'
maintainers, and that [they] should
truly fulfil their day's
work, and travail, for their
pay that they shall take of
their lord, and [a] true account
give to their fellows, in things
that be to be accounted of
them, and to hear, and them
love as themselves. And they
shall be true to the King
of England, and to the realm,
and that they keep, with all their
might, and all the Articles
aforesaid. After that it shall
be enquired if any master, or
fellow, that is warned, have
broke[n] any Article beforesaid,
the which, if they have done,

it shall be determined there.
Therefore, it is to wit, if
any master, or fellow, that is
warned before to come to
such congregations and be
rebell[ious], and will not come, or
else have trespassed against
any Article beforesaid, if it
may be proved, he shall forswear his Masonry and shall
no more use his craft; the
which, if he presume for to do,
the Sheriff of the Country, in which
he may be found working,
he shall [im]prison him and take all
his goods into the king's hand
till his grace be granted him and shew-
ed. For this cause, principally, where
these congregations ordained
that as well the lowest, as
the highest, should be well
and truly served in
his art, beforesaid, throughout all the kingdom of
England. Amen: So
Mote it be.

GRAHAM MANUSCRIPT 1725

The whole Institutions of Free-Masonry opened and proved by the best of Tradition and still some referance to Scripture.

Ffirst observe that all our signes is taken from the square according to every subject in handleing this is proved by the 9 vers of the 6 chapter of ffirst book of kings.

The Sallutation is as follows:

Ffrom whence came you?

I came ffrom a right worshipfull Lodge of Masters and ffellows (1) belonging to God and holy saint John who doth greet all perfect brothers of our holy secrets so do I you if I find you be one.

I greet you well Brother craveing your name?

J and the other is to say his is B.

The examination as ffollows:

How shall I know you are a ffree Mason?

By true words signes and tokens from my entering.

How were you made a ffree Mason?

By a true and perfect Lodge.

What is a perfect Lodge?

The senter of a true heart.

But how many masons is so called?

Any od number from three to 13.

Why so much ado and still having od numbers?

Still in refferance ffrom the blesed trinity to the comeing of christ with his 12 apostles.

What was the first step towards your entering?

A willing disire for to know the secrets of free masonry.

Why is it called free masonry (2)?

First because a ffree gift of God to the children of men secondly free from the intruption of infernall spirits thirdly a ffree union amonge the brothers of that holy secret to remain for ever.

How came you into the Lodge?

Poor and penyless blind and Ignorant of our secrets.

Some reason for that?

In regard our saviour became poor ffor our redemption so I became poor at that time for the knowledge of God contracted in the square.

What did you see in the Lodge when you did see?

I saw truth the wolrd and Justice and brotherly Love.

Where?

Before Me.

What was behind you?

Perjury and hatred of Brotherhood ffor ever if I discover our Secrets without the consent of a Lodge Except that have obtained a trible Voice (3) by being entered passed and raised and Conformed by three severall Lodges and not so Except I take the party sworn to be true to our articles.

How stood your Lodge at your entering?

East west and south.

Why not north also?

In regard we dwell at the north part of the world we burie no dead at the north side of our churches so we cary a Vacancey at the north side of our Lodges.

Why east and west?

Because churches stands eats and west and porches to the south.

Why doth churches stand east and west?

In ffour references.

What are they?

First our first parance was placed Eastward in edin - secondly the East winde dryed up the sea before the children of Israell so was the temple of the Lord to be builded - thirdly these who dwell near the Equenoxall the sun riseth and seteth west on them - fourthly the stare appeared in the East that advertised both the sheep heards and wise men that our saviour was come in the flesh.

Who Conducted you into the Lodge?

The warden and the oldest fellow craft.

Why not the youngest fellow craft?

In regard our Saviour exorted the chiefe to Serve at the table that being an exortation to Hummility to be observed by us for ever.

What poster did you pass your oath in?

I was nether siting standing goeing running rideing hinging nor flying naked nor cloathed shode nor bairfoot.

A reason fffor such poster?

In regard one God one man makes a very christ so one naked object being half naked half cloathed half shode half bairfoot half kneeling half standing being half on all was one on the whole this sheweth a humble and obedient heart for to be o ffaithfull ffollower of that Just Jesus.

What were you sworn to?

For to hale and conceal our secrets.

What other tenours did your oath Cary?

My second was to obey God and all true Squares made or sent from a brother my third was never to steall Least I should offend God and shame the square my fourth was never to commite adultery with a brothers wife nor tell him a willfull lie my fift was to disire no unjust revange of a brother but Love and relieve him when its in my power it not horting my self too far.

I pass you have been in a Lodge yet I demand how many Lights belongs to a Lodge?

I answer 12.

What are they?

The first three jewells is ffather son holy ghost sun moon Master Mason square Rule plum Lyne Mell and cheisall.

Prove all thses proper?

As ffor the blesed trinity they affurd reason as ffor the sun he renders Light day and night as ffor the moon she is a dark body off water and doth receive her Light ffrom the sun ans is also queen of waters which is the best of Leavells as ffor the Master Mason he teaches the trade and ought to have a trible voice in teaching of our secrets if he be a bright man because we do be Leive into a Supper oratory power for alltho the 70 had great power Yet the 11 had mor for they chused matthias in place of Judas as ffor square Rule plum lyne mell and cheisall they are six toolls that no mason can performe true work without the major part of them.

What refferance can be prest on the 12 Lights?

We draw refferance from the 12 patriarches and also from the 12 oxen we reid of at the 7 chapter of first king that caryed up the molten sea of brass which was tipes of the 12 disciples was to be tought by christ.

I pass you entered yet I demand if you were raised?

Yes I was.

Into what were you raised?

I was raised into knowled of our primitive both by tradition and scripture.

What is your foundation words at the Laying of a builiding where you exspect that some inffernall squandering spirit hath haunted and posable may shake your handy work?

O come Let us and you shall have.

To whom do you speak?

To the blesed trinity in prayer.

How do you administer these words?

Kneeling bairhead fface towards the east.

What mean you by the exspreshion thereof?

We mean that we forsake self righteiouness and differs ffrom these babal-lonians who presumed to build to heaven but we pray the blesed trinity to Let us build trueLy and square and they shall have the praise to whom it is due.

When was these words made or what need was for them?

I answere into the primitive before the ghospell spraid the world being incumbered with infernall squandering spirits except that men did build by ffaith and prayer their works were oft asulted.

But how came that the works of the Baballonians [Babylonians] stood before all this or yet the brightness off the gospell?

I yet by your own question answere you because the presumption of the Baballonians aforesaid had vexed the God head in so much the Langvage was Confounded ffor their sake so that no mankind ffor ever was to do the Like again without a devine Lisiance which could not be had wtout faith and prayer.

Tradition that ?

We have it by tradition and still some refferance to scripture cause shem ham and Japheth ffor to go to their father noahs grave for to try if they could find anything about him ffor to Lead them to the vertuable secret which this famieous preacher had fot I hop all will allow that all things needful for the new world was in the ark with noah.

Now these three men had allready agreed that if they did not ffind the very thing it self that the first thing that they found was to be to them as a secret they not Douting but did most ffirmly be Leive that God was able and would also prove willing through their fatih prayer and obedience for to cause what they did find for to prove as vertuable to them as if they had received the secret at ffirst from God himself at its head spring so came to the Grave finding nothing save the dead body all most consumed away takeing a greip at a ffinger it came away so from Joynt to Joynt so to the wrest so to the Elbow.

So they Reared up the dead body and suported it setting ffoot to ffoot knee to knee Breats to beast Cheeck to check and hand to back and cryed out help o ffather as if they had said o father of heaven help us now for our Earthly ffather cannot so Laid down the dead body again and not knowing what to do.

So one said here is yet marrow in this bone and the second said but a dry bone and the third said it stinketh so they agreed for to give it a name as is known to free masonry to this day so went to their undertakings and afterwards works stood: yet it is to be beleived and also understood thet the vertue did not proceed from what they ffound or how it was called but ffrom ffaith and prayer so thus it Contenued the will pass for the deed.

While the reigne of king alboyne then was born Bazalliell [Bezalel] (4) who was so Called of God before conceived in the [womb] and this holy man knew by inspiration that the secret titles and primitive pallies of the God head was preservitiv and he builded on them in so much that no infernall squandering spirit durst presume to shake his handy work so his works became so ffameious while the two younger brothers of the fforesaid king alboyin disired for to be instructed by him his noble asiance by which he wrought to which he agreed conditionally they were not to discover it without a another to themselves to make a trible voice so they entered oath and he tought them the heorick and the practick part of masonry and they did work.

Then was masons wages called up in that realme then was masons numbered with kings and princes yet near to the death of Bazalliell he disired to be buried in the valey of Jehosephate and have cutte over him according to his diserveing which was performed by these two princes and this was cutte as follows.

Here Lys the flowr of masonry superiour of many other companion to a king and to two princes a brother Here Lys the heart all secrets could conceall Here lys the tongue that never did reveal.

Now after his death the inhabitance there about did think that the secrets of masonry had been totally Lost because they were no more heard of for none knew the secrets therof Save these two princes and they were so sworn at their entering not to discover it without another to make a trible voice.

Yet it is to be beleiued and allso under stood that such a holy secret could never be Lost while any good servant of God remained alive on the earth for every good servant of God had hath and allways will have a great part of that holy secret alltho they know it not themselves nor by what means to make use therof for it hapened with the world at that time as it did with the Sammaritan church about christ they were Seeking ffor what they did not want.

But their deep Ignorance could not disarne it so all this contenued dark and obscure while the ffour hundred and ffour Score off year after the children of Israell came out of the Land off Egypt in the ffourth year of Sollomons reigne over Israell that sollomon begun to Build the house of the Lord which his father david should have builded but was not admited to performe it because his hands was gultie of blood wars being on every side.

So all reffered while the days off Sollomon his son that he be gun to build the house of the Lord now I hope all men will give ffor granted that all things needffull ffor carying on off that holy errection was not holden ffrom that wise king.

To this we must all allow Els we must charge God with unJustice which no ffraill mortall dare presume to charge God with nether can his devine goodness be Guilty off now we read at the 13 vers off the 7 chapter of ffirst book of kings that Sollomon sent and ffet hiram out off tyre he being a widdows son of the tribe of naphtale and his father was a man of tyre a worker in brass ffilled with wisdom and Cunning to work all works in brass and he came to king sollomon and wrought all his work ffor him.

The Exsplanation of these verses is as ffollows:

The word Cunning renders ingenuity as ffor wisdom and understanding when they are both found in one person he can want nothing: so by this present scripture must be allowed that the widows Son whose name was hiram had a holy inspiration as well as the wise king sollomon or yet the holy Bazalliell. Now it is holden fforth by tradition that there was a tumult at this Errection which should hapened betwext the Labrours and masons about wages and ffor to call me all and to make all things easie the wise king should have had said be all of you contented ffor- you shall be payed all alike yet give a signe to the Masons not known to the Laborours and who could make that signe at the paying place was to be payed as masons the Laborours not knowing thereof was payed as fforesaid.

This might have been yet if it was so we are to Judge very Mercyfull on the words of the wise king sollomon ffor it is to be understood and allso beleived that the wise king meant according to every mans disarveing yet the 7 vers of the 6 chapter off ffirst book off kings reads me still Better where it is said the House when it was in Building was build of ston made ready beffore it was brought theither so that there was nether hammer nor ax nor any tooll off Iron heard in the house when it was in Building.

Ffrom whence may be gathered that all things was flitted affore hand yet not posable to be caryed on without a motion and when all things were sought ffrom the horasin off the heavens to the plate fform off the earth there could be nothing ffound more be Comeing more becomeing then then the square ffor to be their signe ffor to signifie what they would have each other to do.

So the work went on and prospered which could not well go amiss being they wrought ffor so good a Master and had the wisest man on earth for to be their overseer therefore in so parts by Merite yet Much mor by ffree grace Masonry obtained a name and a new command.

Their name doth signifie strength and their answere beauty and theire command Love ffor proofe hereoff read the 7 and 6 of ffirst book off kings where you will finde the wonderfull works off hiram at the building off the house of the Lord.

So all Being ffinised then was the secrets off ffree Masonry ordered aright as is now and will be to the End of the world for such as do rightly understand it.

In three parts in refferance to the blesed trinity who made all things yet in 13 brenches in refferances to Christ and his 12 apostles which is as follows a word ffor a devine Six ffor the clargey and 6 ffor the ffellow craft and at the ffull and totall agreement therof to ffollow with five points off ffree Masons fellowshipe which is ffoot to ffoot knee to knee breast to breast cheeck to cheeck and hand to Back which ffive points hath refferance to the ffive cheife signes which is head ffoot body hand and heart and allso to the ffive points off artitectur and allso to the ffive orders of Masonry yet takes thire strength ffrom five primitive one devine and ffour temporall which is as ffollows ffirst christ the chiefe and Cornnerston secondly Peter called Cephas thirdly moses who cutte the commands ffourthly Bazalliell the best of Masons ffifftly hiram who was ffilled with wisdom and understanding.

You[r] ffirst is...
Your Second is...
Your third is...
You[r] ffourth is...
Your ffift is...
Your sixt is...
Your seven is...
Your eight is...
Your nineth is...
Your tent is...
you[r] Elewent is...
your twelt is...
You[r] thirteen is

Tho[mas] Graham Chanceing Master of Lodges
outher Enquam Ebo
October ye 24 1726
To all or any off our ffretarnity
that intends to Learn by this.

SCHAW STATUTES 1598 AND 1599

Edinburgh, the 28th day of December AD1598.

The Statutes and Ordinances to be observed by all the Master Masons within this realm. Set down by William Schaw, Master of Work to His Majesty and Warden General of the said Craft, with consent of the Masters specified hereafter.

(1) First, they shall observe and keep all the good ordinances established before, concerning the privileges of their craft, by their predecessors of good memory; and especially. They shall be true to one another and live charitably together as becometh sworn brethren and companions of the Craft.

(2) They shall be obedient to their wardens, deacons, and masters in all things concerning their craft.

(3) They shall be honest, faithful, and diligent in their calling, and deal uprightly with their masters, or the employers, on the work which they shall take in hand, whether it be piece-work with meals and pay [task, melt, & fie], or for wages by the week.

(4) None shall undertake any work great or small, which he is not capable to perform adequately, under penalty of forty pounds lawful money or else the fourth part of the worth and value of the work, besides making satisfactory amends to the employers, according as the Warden General may direct or, in the absence of the latter, as may be ordered by the wardens, deacons, and masters of the sheriffdom in which the work is undertaken and carried on.

(5) No master shall take away another master's work after the latter has entered into an agreement with the employer by contract or otherwise, under penalty of forty pounds.

(6) No master shall take over any work at which other masters have been engaged previously, until the latter shall have been paid in full for the work they did, under penalty of forty pounds.

(7) A warden shall be elected annually to have charge of every lodge in the district for which he is chosen by the votes of the masters of the lodges of such district and the consent of the Warden General if he happens to be present; otherwise the Warden General shall be notified of the election that he may send to the warden-elect necessary directions.

(8) No master shall take more than three 'prentices in his lifetime, without the special consent of all the wardens, deacons, and masters of the sheriffdom in which the to-be-received 'prentice resides.

(9) No master shall take on any 'prentice except by binding him to serve him as such for at least seven years, and it shall not be lawful to make such 'prentice a brother or fellow of the craft until he shall have served other seven years after the completion of his 'prenticeship, without a special license granted by the wardens, deacons, and masters, assembled for that

purpose, after sufficient trial shall have been made by them of the worthiness, qualifications and skill of the person desiring to be made a fellowcraft. A fine of forty pounds shall be collected as a pecuniary penalty from the person who is made a fellow of the craft in violation of this order, besides the penalties to be levied against his person by order of the lodge of the place where he resides.

(10) It shall not be lawful for any master to sell his 'prentice to another master, nor to curtail the years of his 'prenticeship by selling these off to the 'prentice himself, under the penalty of forty pounds.

(11) No master shall take on a 'Prentice without notice to the warden of the lodge where he resides, so that the 'Prentice and the day of his reception may be duly booked.

(12) No 'Prentice shall be entered except according to the aforesaid regulations in order that the day of entry may be duly booked.

(13) No master or fellow of craft shall be received or admitted without there being present six masters and two entered 'prentices, the warden of the lodge being one of the six, when the day of receiving the new fellow of craft or master shall be duly booked and his mark inserted in the same book, with the names of the six admitters and entered 'prentices, as also the names of the intenders [intendaris-instructors] which shall be chosen for every person so entered in the book of the lodge. Providing always that no man be admitted without an essay and sufficient trial of his skill and worthiness in his vocation and craft.

(14) No master shall engage in any mason work under the charge or command of any other craftsman who has undertaken the doing of any mason work.

(15) No master or fellow of craft shall accept any cowan to work in his society or company, nor send any of his servants to work with cowans, under the penalty of twenty pounds as often as any person offends in this matter.

(16) It shall not be lawful for any entered 'Prentice to undertake any greater task or work for an employer, which amounts to as much as ten pounds, under the penalty just mentioned, to wit twenty pounds, and that task being done he shall not undertake any other work without license of the masters or warden where he dwells.

(17) If any question, strife, or variance shall arise among any of the masters, servants, or entered 'prentices, the parties involved in such questions or debate shall make known the causes of their quarrel to the particular warden and deacon of their lodge, within the space of twenty-four hours, under penalty of ten pounds, to the end that they may be reconciled and agreed and their variances removed by their said warden, deacon, and masters; and if any of the said parties shall remain wilful or obstinate, they shall be deprived f the privilege of their lodge and not permitted to work thereat

unto the time that they shall submit themselves to reason according to the view of the said wardens, deacons, and masters.

(18) All masters, undertakers of works, shall be very careful to see that the scaffolds and gangways are set and placed securely in order that by reason of their negligence and sloth no injury or damage [hurt or skaith] may come to any persons employed in the said work, under penalty of their being excluded thereafter from working as masters having charge of any work, and shall ever be subject all the rest of their days to work under or with an other principal master in charge of the work.

(19) No master shall receive or house [resset] a 'Prentice or servant of any other master, who shall have run away from his master's service, nor entertain him in his company after he has received knowledge thereof, under penalty of forty pounds.

(20) All persons of the mason craft shall convene at the time and place lawfully made known to them [being lawchfullie warnit], under penalty of ten pounds.

(21) All the masters who shall happen to be sent to any assembly or meeting, shall be sworn by their great oath that they will neither hide nor conceal any faults or wrongs done to the employers on the work they have in hand, so far as they know, and that under penalty of ten pounds to be collected from the concealers of the said faults.

(22) It is ordained that all the aforesaid penalties shall be lifted and taken up from the offenders and breakers of their ordinances by the wardens, deacons, and masters of the lodges where the offenders dwell, the moneys to be expended ad pios usus (for charitable purposes) according to good conscience and by the advice of such wardens, deacons, and masters.

For the fulfilling and observing of these ordinances, as set down above, the master convened on the aforesaid day bind and obligate themselves faithfully. Therefore they have requested their said Warden General to sign these ordinances by his own hand in order that an authentic copy hereof may be sent to every particular lodge within this realm.

(Signed) WILLIAM SCHAW,
Master of the Work
[Maistir o/ Wark.]

If there is to be discovered in modern Freemasonry of English origin any direct influence from the craft guild, it is probably to be found through the London Masons' Company of the fifteenth century which received its Crown charter in 1481 but built is first hall in 1463. Therefore, the next chapter will be devoted to that company. In London in 1677 an operative masons' lodge used the last money in the lodge's chest to purchase a banner before the speculatives broke away to form their own lodge.[2] This company will be discussed in Chapter 5.

NOTES

1. Albert B. Mackey. *History of Freemasonry, Volume One.* (New York: The Masonic History Company, 1895), p. 29.

2. R. A. Leeson. *Traveling Brothers; The Six Centuries' Road from Craft Fellowship to Trade Unionism.* London" George Allen & Unsin Ltd., 1979, p. 68.

Chapter Four

Rough Mason, Mason, Freemason, Accepted Mason

We do not know exactly how Freemasonry began despite the apparent wealth of material which suggests or hints otherwise. This lack of solid evidence—documentation—has caused historians to softly smile at the claims of many Masonic writers regarding the origins of the institution noting that few similar organizations have attempted to make comparable historical claims. But these Masonic writers were sincere in their contention that their craft had existed since *time out of mind* or had its beginnings in a period *whereunto the memory of man reacheth not.* J. G. A. Pocock notes that the purpose of an *ancient constitution* was to prove that the existing institution, or some part of it, was immemorial in nature and custom, and therefore its present status was legally derived. This utilitarian approach to an institution's history also provides moral and practical support for current practices as well as examples of what should be imitated and should be avoided.

There are two approaches to Freemasonic history. There is a scientific, historical approach in which a theory of origin is developed using verifiable, documented facts which can be tested and the theory refined by diligent researchers as new material is discovered and new interpretations of existing material explored from a variety of perspectives. This approach includes a studied examination of the legends and myths regarding the origins of the fraternity prevalent since at least the fourteenth century and includes an analytical approach to Masonic custom, practice, esoteric tradition, ritual, psychology, governance, and ethics, as well as public opinion. A second approach is a less-authentic approach which focuses on myth, legend, and open-ended speculation.

One of these discarded purely speculative theories of origin, notes John Hamill, Librarian at the United Grand Lodge of England and concurred with

St. Hedwig and the new convent.

by Robert Cooper, curator of the Grand Lodge of Scotland, is that Freemasonry is a direct descendant of the medieval Knights Templars of the twelfth and thirteenth centuries in Outremer or overseas as the Crusader states established after the First Crusade were known. These states included the Counties of Edessa and Tripoli, the Principality of Antioch, and the Kingdom of Jerusalem; but more about the Templars at the end of the chapter. Part and parcel of this myth of direct association is Rosslyn Chapel, a medieval edifice abounding with carvings and sculptures and through which Dan Brown uses his vivid imagination to demonstrate the link. The chapel's handbook published in 1774 "makes no mention of any Masonic connections."[1]

One fact remains, the history of any institution—and Freemasonry is an institution—which has existed for centuries in various places is that of both constancy and change. Freemasonry is no different from any institution currently in existence in that it was founded and it persisted, but, as with others, it has changed in form, scope, and purpose as well as reputation. To search the records of the past for a *direct link* between some ancient organization and that institution which arose in the seventeenth century and has evolved into twenty-first century Freemasonry is unreasonable. It is reasonable, however, to examine the records and other evidence of related institutions just as we examine human genealogy for answers about an individual's origins. But the existence of a given institution, belief, or practice in the present day is not a sound indicator that it existed *as it does now* at any point in the past. It is the historian's role through careful examination of the evidence to document past practices and to show how, if at all, they relate to the current institution.

DEFINITIONS

Essential to any scientific or historical study of an institution is the establishment of clear, concise definitions. For this analysis, the original meaning of *freemason* is accepted as that found in the London Assize of Wages of 1212 as an individual who *wrought in freestone*.[2] Freestone is so named because it is a fine-grained sandstone or limestone which is easily worked in any direction and lends itself to undercutting and carving. It was and is generally cut into window and door frames, vaults, and ornaments. Freemasons were thus differentiated from layers, wallers, pavers, dikers ("dykers" in some texts), hewers, scalpers, carriers, and rough masons although the term appears at times to have been used interchangeably with hard hewer. The term *operative* is accepted to mean stone masons who engaged directly in the construction trade. *Speculative mason* is accepted as those non-operative individuals who joined the fraternity to engage in thoughtful reflection and meditation. *Freemasonry,* from a Masonic historian's perspective, is accepted to mean "the organization and practices which have from time to time prevailed among medieval working masons and their 'operative' and 'speculative' successors, from the earliest date from which such an organization is traceable down to the present time."[3] Finally, *accepted mason* is customarily agreed to mean a more general class of non-operatives who became guild members to fulfill certain administrative functions and to participate in fraternal relations, and later to engage in speculative endeavors.

An established part of Masonic history has been the attempt to demonstrate a connection between the medieval operative guild and the modern fraternity. A problem rises, however, when it becomes apparent that there was more than one such organization of masons and that not all masons were members of a guild. In France, we find the *corps de meiters* and *compagonnages*; the *Comacines* in Italy and Gaul; the *steinmetzen* in Germany; and other assorted lodges and guilds in Flanders, Scotland, and various European countries. While the *Comacine* masters give a point of departure for Masonic history and appear to relate to Bede's reference to masons from Gaul, it is only the Scottish, English, and Irish lodges which can be shown to have had a connection to modern Freemasonry in the United States and other nations.

One singular problem when "connecting the dots" of masonic history is that of vocabulary. The most ancient records tend to be written in Latin with words such as *cementarius, lathomus, lapicida*, or the French *masoun* or *mazon* used interchangeably. The first reference to a *free mason* in England is found in the City of London Letter Book-H dated August 9, 1376, which shows Thomas Wrek and John Lesnes as *fre masons.* In the *Constitutions of Masonry* as well as the *Regius* and *Cooke* manuscripts, the term is always *mason* with *freemason* completely absent. Most building accounts of the fifteenth through the seventeenth centuries use *mason* and *freemason* interchangeably, with the preponderant term being *mason.*

The surviving records of medieval construction in England indicate that masonry functioned under a direct labor system. The employer (usually the crown, church, or municipal government) appointed officials referred to as master, master or surveyor of the work, or clerk of the work who directed the complex operation of finding, quarrying, shaping, finishing, carrying, placing, laying, and finishing stonework in addition to the preparation work necessary such as the surveying of the site and the digging of foundations as well as housing, feeding, and clothing the workmen, providing their tools and, most importantly, paying their wages. This led to a dual administrative system at the quarry and the construction sites. One group of administrators provided financial and logistical management while a different group handled the technical aspects of the project. At a royal building site, the *clerk of the works* generally provided administrative supervision while the various *masters* oversaw different technical or construction aspects under the overall guidance of the *master of the works.* Most of the *clerks* in England were either king's clerks or officials from the Exchequer. They were often given the title of *keeper of the works* or, as noted, *surveyor of the works.* These men were not operative or working masons. The rolls at Vale Royal Abby, Caernarvon Castle, and Magdalen College list the names of those given the title *master of the works.* Elizabeth, mother of Henry VIII and wife of Henry VII, notes in her privy purse account for 1502-1503 that she replaced the house of Nicholas Grey, *clerk of the works at Richmond* after it had burned. [4]

A master mason was one who "has taken upon himself to be continually laboruing and diligent . . . and to do all care concerning the said work that accords to a master of work, both in labouring of his own person, in devising, and in supervising the masons and workmen under him." [5] The master mason tended to be one who had risen through the ranks much like Richard Beke who is listed as *master mason* at Canterbury Cathedral in 1435, but who had worked at London Bridge as a *mason* in 1409, and as *Chief Bridge Mason* in1417. Among the many duties of a master mason was the *devising of plans* for the work. It is clear from the record that kings, bishops, and abbots delighted in architecture and may have taken some part in the design process, but early building contracts often included details that imply that the master mason, mason contractor, or master of the works oversaw *both design and the drawings necessary* for the execution of the work *as well as the contacting and subcontracting.* The position of master mason was often a full-time appointment even though there were in many contracts provisions for masters to work at more than one site or to supervise more than one project.

Stone-workers tended by be classified thusly: fewers or freemasons dressed or finished the stones cut from the quarries by the quarrymen. They might also be listed as setters when engaged in placing the prepared stone into a vault or building a rose window. Layers or rough masons laid ashlar and "rockes", rough dressed stones with an axe, and may have laid pavers. Quarriers uncovered the stone, broke or split it into ashlars (generally two feet in length, one foot in height, and one and a half feet in width or breadth), and did a rough dressing. Other stone workers included cutters, scalpers, and layers. Cartagemen transported the stone from the quarry to the construction site and, because they were paid by weight, were often at the top of the pay scale. Cowans were dry wallers or drydikers who built stone walls without mortar and usually of a limited height. In more general terms, a cowan was one who attempted to do the work of a mason but who had not been regularly prepared, apprenticed, or bred in the trade and is a term utilized by the modern Fraternity to indicate an interloper.

TRAINING AND CONDITIONS OF EMPLOYMENT

The medieval quarry tended to be the prime recruiting site for new masons. A study of building accounts shows the names of men working in the quarries with those same names appearing in later accounts at construction sites listing them as layers or, even, masons. At the same time, the excessive cost of cartage presupposed as much dressing and finishing at the quarries as possible. This offered ample opportunities for unskilled quarrymen to work their way to rough mason, mason, and freemason. In addition, by performing the finishing work at the quarry, if a piece was damaged or otherwise spoilt, it could be immediately replaced and considerable savings made in cartage fees. There is ample evidence of this practice to be found in the leavings at every quarry site.

The second method for training new masons was the promotion system whereby a servant, family member, or friend of a mason worked for the master for a set number of years or until the master considered him *well as a sufficient mason*. Under this method a father could teach his son or grandson, an uncle a nephew, or a friend a friend.

The third system for training new masons was the apprentice system common throughout the guild system. The records suggest, however, that this was not that common among masons since the term *apprentice* or its equivalent does not appear until 1382 in the fabric roll of Exeter Cathedral. Most masons listed in these early rolls are journeymen with no job security and only a daily or piece-rate wage. There are records, however, of monastic authorities apprenticing craftsmen both lay and ecclesiastical. Monastic apprentices appear in the rolls of various Cistercian Abbeys. If the construction trade had been required to utilize the apprentice system only, the pool of skilled workmen would have been extremely small and stone building would not have progressed as it did during the thirteenth through fifteenth centuries. It was, in fact, the various alternative methods that provided the bulk of the labor force.

Wages were generally paid on a daily basis, with more skilled freemasons being paid by the piece or project. Labor contracts tend to spell out the set daily wage; the number of holidays both paid and unpaid; and the length of the winter season when construction work was virtually impossible. The general wage was about four pence per day in the fourteenth century increasing to about six pence per day in the fifteenth century. Wages did not, however, match inflation or changing conditions. Using a base 100 as the average wage of a mason in 1501, by the year 1702 the base had increased to about 346 or about three and a half fold. At the same time, food prices increased from a base 100 in 1501 to 682 in 1702 or more than six fold.[6] Winter rates were reduced in England by about a sixth while in Scotland the reduction was closer to thirty percent.

Working hours in the summer were usually 5 a.m. to 7 p.m. with several breaks during the day including an hour and a half for the midday meal. In the winter—November through February—labor generally commenced when the workmen could see and ended when the light had failed. During those months, there was a single noon or midday break. Saturdays received special treatment, however, with the work day ending at 4:00 p.m. to enable the mason to participate in vigils in preparation for Sunday. Many masons at Rochester Castle in 1368 were paid for 252 working days, but no layer was paid for more than 180 days which suggests interior work continued during the winter months with the those whose labor would suffer because of frost or extremely cold weather being paid for fewer days.

Impressment of laborers was common throughout the medieval period and masons were not exempt. Sheriffs throughout England were issued orders to produce from their counties a specified quota of skilled workmen for royal or government projects. This method was common during the construction of fortifications on the Welsh frontier and the construction of Windsor Castle. In other instances, master masons or clerks of the work were authorized to *take masons wherever they could be found*. Based on the surviving records, this was a more common method than utilizing the county sheriff. Finally, in London, the impressment responsibility fell directly on the London Masons' Company. Impressment would continue as a customary practice well into the seventeenth century and in the British Navy it continued into the nineteenth century.

Holidays were common, especially for those engaged at ecclesiastical sites where it was necessary to honor the numerous saints' days and church festivals, but workmen were not paid for all holidays with the average being about nine annually. The first records of what are now known popularly as "Monday holidays" come from this period. Generally, however, if two holidays fell within the same week, the mason received only one with pay, but some rolls indicate that at various sites there were no pay for holidays.

The two earliest accepted Masonic documents—the *Regius* and *Cooke*--do not use the term *freemason* instead simply using *mason* with no difference noted between operative and accepted. There are ample records, including the two immediately referenced, which indicate that masonic assemblies were not restricted to operative masons and were attended by a variety of people to include county sheriffs, mayors, and other elected officials as well as bishops and members of both the merchant class and the aristocracy. There is also evidence of royal support for and involvement in the various medieval guilds of which the masons were one. Marguerite, wife of Henry IV, *lately named Queen,* joined the London Skinners Fraternity, and Richard III and his wife were members of the Guild of Corpus Christi at York.[7] Royal patronage and money were essential to guild existence and the exercise of their prerogatives. But where did the institution begin and how did it become what it is today?

BEGINNINGS

A survey of the physical world indicates that for millennia mankind has engaged in organized activities which resulted in the erection of monumental structures. Such organization required a sophisticated level of communication; a strong organizational structure; and a purpose which could be visualized or understood by most of its members. The first villages appeared in the Neolithic age about 9,000 B.C.E. Still extant are stone structures from that period which, based upon the size and weight of the stones, indicate that they were constructed by numerous individuals who could plan; execute the plan; and who had a common goal. Gobelki Tepe, a ceremonial or ritual site in Turkey, was constructed more than 11,500 years ago and abandoned some 2,500 years later. Almost as soon as man settled into villages, he began to construct cities. The oldest continuously inhabited city is Jericho of Biblical fame dating also to about 9,000 B.C.E. Damascus, Syria, dates to about 4,300 B.C.E. And monumental structures went hand-in-hand with human civilization. By 4,000 B.C.E. mud-brick ziggurats were being constructed in Mesopotamia which may account for the Biblical story of the tower of Babel. Millions of mud bricks were stacked row upon row, terrace upon terrace to heights of a hundred feet or more. In pre-dynastic Egypt, similar structures were common prior to 3,000 B.C.E. and by the Old Kingdom (third millennium B.C.E.) mud brick mastabas were used for the internment of royalty. Mud brick quickly erodes and this building material was soon replaced with more durable stone as Egyptian religion began to focus on the afterlife with the ramifications of such a belief system noted in both construction techniques and materials.

This development of monumental architecture did not happen miraculously or overnight. The Egyptian dessert is dotted with unfinished, broken, and finished smaller mud-brick structures and stone pyramids. This suggests that the development from the earliest mud brick mastabas to the Great Pyramid at Giza was neither short nor smooth. It further suggests that the progress was not always one of contemplation or prior planning based on a thorough understanding of mathematics and engineering, but rather one of trial and error. The Bent Pyramid of Sneer, about twenty-five miles south of Cairo which is dated to the Old Kingdom, demonstrates the trial and error approach taken to these early construction efforts. On the other hand, the massive temples at Karnack (1500 B.C.E.) and Abu Sambal (1400 B.C.E.) indicate significant advancements in planning, organization, and engineering.

The Parthenon (447 B.C.E), the Colosseum (70 A.D.), and the Pantheon (126 A.D.) [from this point forward all dates unless otherwise noted are A.D.] demonstrate even more significant advances in engineering, but more especially in design, mathematics, structural analysis, art, and aesthetics—all elements of architecture. One of the best documented organizations of early architects is the *Comacine* Masters who appear, in both practice and organization, to have been forefathers of the master builders of the twelfth and thirteenth centuries. The very existence of the great cathedrals of Europe supports the contention that there existed, shortly after the fall of the Roman Empire, an organization for governing workers which operated under the approval of both church and state. It further supports, through the similarity of basic design elements, the existence of some form of brotherhood of architects, contractors, builders, and sculptors which maintained common aims, techniques, aesthetics, and knowledge. Since this great era of cathedral building flourished at the beginning of national governments as well as commerce, it further suggests that it did not spring forth as did the mythological Athena, full formed and fully clothed.

Pliny the Younger (61-112) in his letter to Mustio appears to confirm the existence of some form of guild structure in Rome in his time[8] , and Theodor Mommsen and Gustv Haenei note in *De collegiss et sodaliciis Romanorum* that even though the Roman emperors prohibited guilds from meeting, architects and artists were permitted to continue to work prior to the fall of the empire with their guilds dedicated to the arts, mutual assistance, aid for the sick, and burial of the dead.

An edict found in the Roman archives issued by Rotharis, King of the Lombards, and dated to 643 specifically uses the title *magistri comancini*. *Magister* identifies the architect who designed and then executed his design. He is the *operator ipse magister.* To be called *Magister,* Cassiodorus writes, is "an honor to be coveted, for the word always stands for great skill."[9] The master was one who had completed his education and risen to that stage of perfection in which he was qualified to teach others. Rotharis decreed first that masters who sign contract to restore or build a building and that if the structure should fall killing a person, the owner of the structure *shall not be cited* because, having entered a contract, the master assumed full liability. Secondly, he decreed that if a laborer was killed during the construction phase, the owner of the building was not liable nor the master but rather the subcontractor who hired the workman.

During the reign of the Holy Roman Emperor Otto (931-999), a writ issued in 962 exempts the inhabitants of the Comacine Island, specifically masons, from military service, taxes, and service on councils. For centuries prior to Otto's reign, the Comacine islands were considered safe cities and it is there that Leader Scott [a.k.a. Lucy Baxter] suggests "the guild of Architects would fly for safety to almost the only free spot in Italy; and there, though they could no longer practice their craft, they preserved the legendary knowledge and precepts which, as history implies, came to them through Vitruvius from older sources, some say from Solomon's builders themselves."[10] Scott goes on to note that Theodolinda, Queen of the Lombards, converted the Frankish ruler Agilulf from the Arian heresy to orthodox

Christianity and "it was under these Christianized invaders that the Comacine Masters became active and influential builders again.'[11]

Such decrees and other laws suggest that by the seventh century the construction guild *magistri comancini* was both well organized and politically powerful. In the vestibule of the Chiesa dei Santissimi Apostoli in Florence, founded reportedly by Charlemagne in the year 800, and among the oldest churches in the city, a slab on the façade notes its foundation and another inscription uses the wording *Magister Vassalecti* denoting Master Vassalecti as master at this site. Similar inscriptions may be found to other *magisgter* in the Church of St. Clemente, the lowest level of which dates to before the fourth century, and in St. John Lateran which is the most ancient basilica in Rome dating to 324. The fresco in St. Clemente clearly shows a Roman master as well as workmen dragging a column and lifting it with a lever. The mason's mark was common throughout Hellenistic Greece and Rome with its first appearance being at Knossos on Crete about 1900 B.C.E., but the designations in the churches noted above are the first recorded instances of the specific word *magistri* or master and often associated with a specific name.

Evidence that the guilds or colleges possessed some political power may be found not only in the edicts of Rotharis noted above, but also in edicts of the Emperor Otto who declared that they would not be called for military service; were not required to pay taxes on bridges, roads, beasts, land, ships, or land; nor were they required to attend to civic duties other than service on general councils. These master architects were active and significant builders. Christian philosophy had sharpened their minds and with that came a marked appreciation of the arts which enabled them to use the skills of the builder to glorify their religion and expound their faith. It is of note that the *alpha* and the *omega* so familiar in modern Freemasonry were also common in the art of this Roman guild. This does not indicate, however, a direct link to the modern Fraternity but only a commonality of focus and symbolic meaning. The guiding principle of ancient masonic law was, as with all Roman and Lombard architecture, the erection of strong and lasting edifices. Freemasons took this literal edict and transformed it into the symbolic language and teaching necessary to make strong and lasting men.

All early Roman guilds associated themselves with the mysteries of the various deities, a customary practice among the Greeks, as well. A mystery was a personal and secret introduction into a system of knowledge that promised some form of eternal reward and, according to the *Tablet of Hipponion*, a fourth century B.C.E. gold leaf tablet found in the Greek city of the same name, a *sacred way* to the afterlife. These mysteries required personal participation in set rituals, and involved both secrecy and a nocturnal setting, but there were no visible outward changes in those who experienced the mysteries. In the Christian era, the mysteries became highly allegorical ranging from the mass and baptism to the enormously-dramatized York Mystery Plays or York Corpus Christi Plays which consisted of forty-eight pageants beginning with creation and ending with the Last Judgment. They were performed in the city of York in May or June from the middle of the fourteenth century until 1569. The mysteries plays did not survive, however, and parts of them were subsumed into other institutional.

The mystery plays were most prevalent in England and other western Christian kingdoms. They first began inside the church or cathedral itself in those preliterate times when the congregation needed additional instruction beyond the Latin-language liturgy. The church provided everything needed for a dramatic presentation: narrative, dialogue, chanting, processions, a building with a fixed entry way, costumes (vestments), dramatic lighting, and symbolic structures such as altars and shrines. The plays first appeared when the priests acted out certain scenes from the liturgy in the vernacular language usually at the various stations within the cathedral as an instructional tool to enable the congregation to understand the lesson. In several situations, the congregation participated in the experience by responding to the priest as did the congregation in the Book of Amos. As their popularity grew and attendance increased, the plays were moved first to the cathedral steps, then to the courtyard or plaza, and finally to a larger venue such as at York. All of this dramatic activity had a liturgical foundation and though the Church for centuries endeavored to abolish what it deemed the pagan and unsavory dramatic practices of the late Roman empire, it was under the auspices of that very institution—the Church—that those practices were revitalized.

During the late Roman and early Christian eras, the guilds involved themselves in the mysteries by supplying the funds and manpower necessary. By the fourteenth century, the plays had become extraordinarily elaborate requiring both trained actors and substantial material support. To meet this need, each guild generally assumed the responsibility for producing one part of the cycle. For example, the carpenters or shipwright's might perform the Noah mystery; the fishmongers and bakers might work together to perform the mystery of the loaves and fishes; and the goldsmiths many times performed as Magi. Each guild provided aid in parallel with its nature as a craft thus enabling the guild not only to demonstrate its support for the Church and community but also to showcase the skills of its members and advertise its abilities and wares.

Beginning in the early sixteenth century, these dramatic activities went into sharp decline and eventually were banned by the government. In 1542 Edmund Bonner, Bishop of London, issued an edict forbidding "common plays, games, or interludes to be played" in or near the sanctuary.[12] Further bans came during the reign of Henry VIII and an almost total ban was put in place during the reign of Henry's son, Edward VI. After Edward's death and during the reign of Elizabeth I, some parish plays were revived, but the shift to Protestantism, and eventually Puritanism, ended even those small efforts. The last recorded performance of a mystery play was in Chester in 1575 though there is some evidence of a performance at Coventry in 1599. The influence of the tradition did not cease nor did guild involvement in mysteries stop completely. The guilds simply morphed themselves and their presentations into the friendly societies or fraternities that sprang up in force during the seventeenth century such as the Freemasons. One of the most popular of the mystery plays was that of Noah as found in Chapter I which was later subsumed into Masonic ritual.

LEGALITY AND AUTHORIZATION

Guilds, both craft and merchant, were a fixture in the medieval world well before the fourteenth century with some originating in pre-conquest England. And while they claimed in their poems and charters to have been created *out of time*, modern scholars recognize their establishment at various times in various countries based upon a combination of chronicles, guild account books and records, royal or Crown charters and regulations, and Church financial and building records. As noted in Chapter I, Bede writes about masons being brought to England as early as 675 and the *Regius Manuscript*, though apocryphal, dates the mason's guild to 926. There is, however, a more solid basis for documenting the medieval trades such as masons in England.

Political developments and cultural changes brought about by the conquest of England in 1066 as well as older Saxon and Welsh laws required the population to provide suitable housing for their rulers. The same obligation was felt by the population in relation to the Church. Throughout the Middle Ages both government and Church required construction and repair of manors, castles, cathedrals, fortifications, store houses, and a variety of other public buildings. As time progressed, these structures became larger, more elaborate, and more solid. As Bede suggests, prior to the importation of masons to construct his priory, churches and other buildings were made of wood, and even during the first century after the Conquest, most fortifications were of the mote-and-bailey type constructed of wood and earth. It will not be until the reign of Henry II (1133-1189) that elaborate stone structures began to mark the countryside, and the efforts of Edward I (1239-1307) to refurbish Henry's fortifications and further strengthen the Welsh border furthered the development.

During the reign of Henry III (1207-1272) and Edward III (1312-1377) vast expenditures were made on stone buildings such as Windsor Castle and a revitalization of the Tower of London. A fund of information about building activities during this period come from the Liberate Rolls of Henry III which contain orders to renew, alter, paint (white-wash), roof, wainscot, glaze, excavate, and furnish royal residences and government buildings. On the ecclesiastical side, still extant stone structures speak to the construction carried out across the land. At the same time, surviving and very detailed records kept by both Church and Crown provide documentation of the expenses incurred and the services rendered. Finally, as municipalities developed and expanded (in 1380 it is estimated that London had a population of thirty to forty thousand, York about eleven thousand, and Bristol about ten thousand), the need for accompanying government building grew. Town and guild halls originally constructed of wood were torn down and stone structures erected. Bridges were constructed and permanent markets established. City walls required strengthening. The city government at York in 1478 contracted with *Robert Davyson, mason,* to survey the city's walls and report defects. He and his men were then paid "such wages as belongeth to a mason to take by day" along with a rent-free house and a gown.[13] Davyson was succeeded by Thomas Briggs in 1485 as "common mason of the city." As crown, church, and municipality led, the public followed. Wooden manor houses were reconstructed in stone with *magister operacionum* and *custos fabricate* or master masons listed in extant household accounts.

By 1388 the English Crown had required all guilds to set down their rules for approval by the civil authorities. Norfolk alone listed some 160 guilds. The most numerous were social guilds or *friendly* societies, but also on the list were parish guilds, poor guilds, and the more traditional trade and craft guilds. These men *and women* had banded together originally for security and support. Many of them maintained their own plot of land for the interment of their members. Each guild maintained strict rules about decorum, behavior, annual gatherings, church processions and attendance, feasting, and attendance at regular meetings. They also fined members for missing meetings; refusing to serve the guild as an officer; being *foul-mouthed*; dozing during meetings; drinking too much, and for *taking another's rope*—appropriating the work of another. Each guild was associated with a church or parish and provided the wax or tapers or other aids for services. In the case of masons, the churches were usually dedicated to The Four Crowned Martyrs (see Chapter I). In turn, the Church provided the guild spiritual aid and guidance, medical care, help with writing, and in many instances the clerical assistance necessary to guild functions. Several guilds, among them masons, list ecclesiastics as what would now be secretaries and note that they were paid a wage for their duties.

One set of guilds particularly important to the English Crown was those associated with building: masons, carpenters, painters, plasterers, and the like. From Edward I to Henry VIII, the Crown conscripted laborers for some 1,500 royal building projects. At one time, Edward III employed more than 1,600 masons at Windsor Castle alone. Some of the more highly skilled journeymen masons moved about the country performing tasks at a piece or day rate for various masters, but life-spans coupled with difficulties in traveling great distances and the length of time necessary for the completion of a massive construction project suggest that most medieval masons ended their careers where they began them. By 1356, and possibly because of the labor shortages caused by the Black Death, the need was felt in London to establish a more stable institution and London masons petitioned the Mayor to allow them to establish a guild *as other trades do.* The *Regius* and *Cooke* manuscripts, dating from between 1390 and 1430, describe the rules established for the fellows and approved by authority. These *old charges* contain fanciful accounts of the creation and history of the craft, but the regulations accurately indicate the rules which governed the behavior of both masters and laborers, and stipulate the obligations each had to the other as well as to the customer. There is no documentation from this period, however, of any *national* organization, but it must be noted that in 1360 Parliament specifically banned *alliances and covens* of masons and carpenters, a ban that was repeated in 1425 under Henry VI.

Even though the Crown had banned the mason's craft organization, it was compelled to utilize their skills and, in turn, assist them to organize at the local level by providing funds and patronage. Notable change took place after 1350 and the introduction of the Black Death into England. *The people died wonderfully* wrote the Holinshed chronicler, and as the plague hastened an already evident trend of falling population, agriculture production decreased and wages increased because, as the population fell, the number of skilled workers was significantly reduced. Government then acted. Statutes were enacted setting wages for specific tasks and to prevent the migration of competent workmen, but the Peasants' Revolt of 1381, which many viewed as a direct result of these government restrictions, made it obvious that change was necessary.

Change came, but over time and in an uneven manner. The London Masons' Company was officially chartered in 1481 with the Carpenters Company following in 1487. Between 1514 and 1516, the twelve major guilds or companies in London formed The Great Twelve. The Great Twelve were the Worshipful Companies of Mercers, Grocers, Drapers, Fishmongers, Goldsmiths, Skinners, Taylors, Haberdashers, Salters, Ironmongers, Vintners, and Clothworkers. The Court of Alderman of London established the order of precedence in 1515 based on economic and political power. The 1515 list includes sixty-one minor companies, many now extinct. The Worshipful Company of Masons was number thirty on the list immediately behind Curriers (tanners) and before Plumbers and Tavern Keepers. Some of the ancient companies still exist with several providing professional accreditations similar to the American Bar Association and the American Medical Association. The modern Scriveners' Company recognizes senior legal professionals; the

Apothecaries' Company provides training and certification in medical specialties; and the Hackney Carriage Drivers' Company licenses taxi drivers. Other modern versions of British guilds or companies restrict membership to designated professionals. The London Solicitor's Company admits only attorneys and the Worshipful Company of Engineers is restricted to individuals with university degrees who are licensed in engineering.

In theory, the companies were chartered to regulate trade, prices, employment, and education. Craftsmen were to serve a set apprenticeship—usually seven years—and then be allowed to pay the company the *upstart* or *upset* fee which would allow them to take on apprentices and employ journeymen. The companies also generally established a fee to *pass or repass* into or out of a jurisdiction for work purposes: that fee usually being one penny. Further restrictions enacted by the companies included devices to prohibit a journeyman or apprentice from setting up as a master for three years after his *servitude* and establishing an age of responsibility. In the 1563 Statute of Artificers that age was *twenty-four*.

Further regulations imposed through the new charters limited the number of saints' days as paid holidays commonly known as 'Saint Monday" holidays. By 1547, restrictions appeared that specifically addressed the employment of women. As the powers of the liveried companies were assumed by the state, the old fraternities began to disappear and, accompanied by the suppression of the monasteries, the guilds began to seek a new reason for being. Faced with these changes, the companies turned their attention to charity and security as well as fraternity. In London in 1677, "the 'operative' masons used the last of the money from the 'acception lodge' to buy themselves a banner, before the 'speculatives' broke away to form their own lodge, the forerunner of freemasonry in the sense now understood."[14]

TRAVELING MEN

With these radical changes, especially after 1666, came even more initiative to travel. Masons, from the beginning, because of the nature of their craft, had been, to some extent, traveling men. Though some lodges were set in place at the quarry and did not move until the quarry played out, other lodges moved from construction site to construction site. These fellows or *felaus* made themselves known as they moved from town to town by passwords, signs, and handshakes. In Staffordshire, a perceptive observer noted in his diary that masons could identify themselves to the local lodge by "signs as potent as any document" and that a traveler's sign could bring a "fellow mason down even from the top of a steeple."[15] And as the castle construction phase waned and the country house phase rose, the network grew. Based upon the *old charges* as well as the nature of the profession, it is probable that masons were the first to utilize the traveling system. They established rules for their craft which coped with rather than attempted to deny mobility. They learned to adapt, to innovate, and to change. The Statute of Apprentices was strengthened, and laborers, including artificers and freemasons, were required to show a certificate from a previous master establishing their skills and education. Masons established a search procedure to identify and exclude *foreigners* or *cowans.* The regulations also covered those who had been suspended or expelled from the trade. Finally, the crafts reserved the right to *break and deface* the work of an outsider.

The confusion and disorder of the English Civil War increased the number of traveling men, but the Great Fire of 1666 enabled King Charles II (1630-1685) to use his power of conscription to stimulate the reconstruction of the City and limit movement or traveling for a time. The reconstruction, supervised by Christopher Wren (who may or may not have been a Freemason) and other great architects, took decades rather than centuries and the fire, destructive though it was, destroyed only about one third of the London standing before 1666. Thus, by the early eighteenth century traveling men were again common. The marked difference during reconstruction and in the years that followed was that the new city was made of brick and only occasionally stone, while around it a larger area remained timber-framed awaiting future generations of layers and masons willing to travel to those sites. The need for highly skilled *freemasons* was significantly reduced with an accompanying marked increase in the demand for layers and pavers working mainly in brick. In turn, friendly societies began to appear throughout the cities and elsewhere as offshoots of the older guilds, and many of the journeymen migrated to the new world to provide the seed for the revolutionary ideas that would arise in America.

Modern Freemasonry arose, then, as the operative guilds eroded during the seventeenth century. Much speculation has been focused on this change from operative to speculative ranging from assertions of association with the Jacobean Rebellion (see Mackey's *The History of Freemasonry)*; the restoration of the British monarchy after the Commonwealth (for example, is the Legend of Noah used in early Freemasonic ritual an allegory of the death of Charles I and the restoration of Charles II); the rise of Deism; and other conspiracy theories. John Robinson (1739-1805) is often quoted in his contention that the rise of Freemasonry was for the expressed purpose of rooting out all religion and existing governments. While some authors appear to support Robinson's contention, modern Freemasonry is not a government nor is it a religion. It is not a conspiracy to overthrow or subvert. It is good men gathered together supporting each other through brotherly love, relief, and truth. It is democracy at its perfection and spirituality at its best. It requires its members to be good, peaceful citizens, just to their governments and true to their countries. It is explicit that Freemasons should do unto others as they would have others do unto them.

> The real Freemason is distinguished from the rest of Mankind by the uniform unrestrained rectitude of his conduct. Other men are honest in fear of punishment which the law might inflect; they are religious in expectation of being rewarded, or in dread of the devil, in the next world. A Freemason would be just if there were no laws, human or divine except those written in his heart by the finger of his Creator. In every climate, under every system of religion, he is the same. He kneels before the Universal Throne of God in gratitude for the blessings he has received and humble solicitation for his future protection. He venerates the good men of all religions. He disturbs not the religion of others. He restrains his passions, because they cannot be indulged without injuring his neighbor or himself. He gives no offense, because he does not choose to be offended. He contracts no debts which he is certain he cannot discharge, because he is honest upon principal.[16]

Operative masons have been traveling men from time immemorial. But that travel was as much internal as it was external. They adjusted their craft to meet the ever-changing demands of culture, politics, economy, philosophy, and history. The operative builders' unions survived into the nineteenth century and in the twentieth century adapted themselves to modern trade unionism. Speculative Freemasons separated themselves from their operative cousins in the seventeenth century but maintained their connection with the deep past through a shared history and some shared ritual. The question of continuity or connection between old and new forms, between craft guilds and modern fraternities, intrigues historians, but this history is as incomplete as is the historical record. Whatever its history may be, modern Freemasonry is entitled to its legends and allegories when understood as just that. It is their prehistory as surely as is Malory's *Le Morte d'Arthur* that of England.

THE TEMPLARS AND FREEMASONRY

John Hamill, Librarian and Curator for the United Grand Lodge of England, wrote "a long-standing, though now discarded, theory saw Freemasonry as the direct descendant of the medieval Knights Templars . . . [who] gathered at the mysterious Mount Heredom (or Heredon) near Kilwinning and, fearful of further persecution, transformed themselves into Freemasons, turning the supposed secrets of the Templars into those of Freemasonry."[17] Initially, concurs, Peter Partner, noted British historian, Freemasons claimed no link with the Templars but by the middle of the eighteenth century they introduced first in Germany then in England the idea that the Templars were a prime example of a secret society that was destroyed because it was rumored to possess secret wisdom and magical powers learned at the Temple of Solomon in Jerusalem and handed down through a secret line to modern masons. Susan M. Sommers, professor of history at St. Vincent College and a noted historian of Freemasonry is explicit: "there is no historical connection between the Medieval Knights Templars or Knights Hospitallers, and the Masonic Degrees and orders of the same name."[18]

Both Malcolm Barber and Helen Nicholson, noted scholars of the Templar movement, as well as Masonic scholar Angel Millar, agree that the development of the Templar myth in association with Freemasonry is an eighteenth-century phenomenon which largely came from the writings of Andrew Ramsay (1696-1743) in his capacity as Grand Chancellor of the Grand Lodge in France. Ramsay, who styled himself the Chevalier Ramsay, was a Scottish-born writer who lived most of his adult life in France. He was a Baronet in the Jacobite Peerage even though his father was a baker. He converted to Roman Catholicism about 1710 and remained in France until 1724 writing political and theological essays. He was dedicated to the Jacobite claimant to the English and Scottish thrones and supported James Francis Edward Stuart known as The Old Pretender or James III. In January 1724, Ramsay was sent to Rome to tutor James' two sons, Charles Edward and Henry. He died in France in May 1743. Ramsay's association with the Jacobean cause and the restoration of the Scottish monarchy has led some to attempt to associate Masonic ritual with that political movement, but there is no evidence to support that speculation.

Yet Barber notes also that there is a certain attractiveness to Ramsay's explanation of the Templar/Freemasonry link which, when coupled with modern media (television and fiction), appears to provide clues about origins. He writes that "lack of evidence has never been a serious problem for such writers"[19] who, during the eighteenth, nineteenth, and subsequent centuries, attempted to verify their theories by making seemingly miraculous discoveries of ancient documents and artifacts to support their contentions to include caskets, coins, medallions, and documents with attribution no earlier than their own period and which have not withstood the scrutiny of serious scholarship.

So, what became of The Order of the Temple? About 1340, Ludolph of Sudheim, a German priest traveling near the Dead Sea met two elderly men who informed him that they had been Templars captured at the battle of Acre by the Mamelukes.[20] These two were a forgotten remnant of what at one time had been some seven thousand knights, sergeants, serving brothers, and priests who, by the end of the thirteenth century, had constructed about eight hundred and seventy castles in the East with members and pensioners living in France, England, Germany, Spain, Italy, Cyprus, and Mallorca. But their wealth and power was now long gone along with their archives. It is possible that those archives survived the fall of Acre in 1291 and were taken by the Order of St. John Hospitallers. Subsequently, it is possible that these archives were moved to Malta about 1530, but the existing Templar documents from those archives specifically addresses only Hospitaller business with the Templars not Templar history, ritual, or philosophy. The Ottoman Turks overran Cyprus in 1571 and with that the final destruction of whatever Templar records from the East probably occurred. [21]

The Templars did have much to offer Freemasonry in terms of their history and their dedication to a cause. And while books about the organization tend to fall into two distinct categories--orthodox and speculative—with the former camp being represented by the works of Barber, Nicholson, and other historians, it is the speculative writers who have created a flourishing trade in books that contain theories ranging from the barely plausible to the humorous. The facts reveal that the Order was founded at some time prior to 1119 in Jerusalem by the French or Frankish knight Hugues de Payen. De Payen drew up what became known as the Latin Rule of the Templars based on the *Rule of St Augustine* which included seventy-three clauses and regulated every aspect of Templar life from dress, to food and lodging, to how many horses a knight might possess. These were celibate knight-monks similar to the Cistercians being sworn to poverty, chastity, and obedience. By the 1260s, *The Rule* had grown to six hundred and eighty-six clauses covering the minutiae of daily Templar life.

The Order of the Temple very early in its history developed a solid reputation for being reliable bankers. They were Europe's first international bank with a credit system that allowed money deposited in one Templar preceptory (or bank) to be withdrawn at any other upon producing a proper note. The funds deposited were demonstrably safe as the Templar castles were formidable buildings. Sadly, this financial expertise and the wealth it created contributed to the Order's fall in the early fourteenth century.

Templar masons also built numerous churches throughout Outremer, as the Crusader states were then known, and were involved in the construction of a new Church of the Holy Sepulcher, dedicated in 1149, as well as the renovation of the Church of the Nativity in Bethlehem. In addition, they erected an ornate tomb for Baldwin IV, the leper King of Jerusalem, who died in 1185. In the West, where most of their men were located, their churches and buildings were simpler except at the major preceptories in Paris and London with the London church adorned with the distinctive round Templar design.

It was probably the myth of the Templar *secret* or *mystery* that first attracted eighteenth century antiquarians to attempt to establish a link between the Order and then emerging Freemasonry with it similar focus on the mysteries of life. It is also possible that the Order's concentration on building, the magnificence of the Templar castles and churches, and, above all, the Templar Rule provided then emerging Freemasonry with sound guides for ritual, symbolism, behavior, philosophy, and ethical decision making. What-

ever the motivation, as Pocock suggests, such linkages to a historical past
were often used to establish precedence for organizations and governments,
and were motivated not to perpetuate a ruse but to indicate that what existed
in the present had its legal and structural foundation in *time immemorial*.

THE TEMPLAR RULE

The statutes of the Order of the Temple included not only specific regulations governing daily life and religious practices to include charity; they also
covered procedures for military action. Templars met at least weekly as a
Chapter and dealt with Order or House business, corrected the faults of
members, and assigned relatively rigorous punishments. This weekly meeting was restricted to Knights only, and did not include sergeants or serving
brothers. The Rule required that the Knights live a life of obedience, silence,
humility, and poverty, and that they participate in both daily observances and
individual study. The Templar Day never really ended with Vigil all night
then Matins after midnight followed by Prime at first light and Mass at 6:00
a.m.; Terce at 9:00 a.m.; Sext at noon; Nones with Vespers for the dead and
vigils for the dead at 3:00 p.m.; Vespers at dusk; and Compline at dark.

The statutes, being those of a hierarchical order, gave explicit instructions
on how a Knight or Brother should make camp; march in line; form a squad-
ron; and charge the enemy (the modern Knights Templar drill manual is a
dim vestige of this part of The Rule.) The cavalry charge was the prime
feature of the Order's military tactics so there is no indication in The Rule of
how foot soldiers or archers were to be deployed. A squire's duty was to
assist his Knight, not to fight, but the very nature of medieval battle often
required that the Knights dismount and engage in direct hand-to-hand combat. The question arises, then, why do the statutes place such extraordinary
emphasis on mounted combat. The answer is that such combat was extremely
complicated and required intense organization, coordination, discipline, planning, and practice or drill. This level of discipline, planning, and coordination was not seen again among western armies until the rise of the British
army in the eighteenth century and Napoleon's campaigns in the early nineteenth century.

This coordination, discipline, and dedication was attractive to the organized minds of the enlightenment and furnished modern Freemasonry something to emulate; and, along with the Order's focus on charity, service to
God, and to their fellow man, provided a solid foundation for proper conduct
for future generations.

NOTES

1. Amanda Ruggeri. "The Lost History of the Freemasons" located at http://www.bbc.com/travel/story/20161209-secret-history-of-the-freemasons-in-scotland.

2. Douglas Knoop & G. P. Jones. *An Introduction to Freemasonry.* (Manchester, UK: Manchester University Press, 1937), p. 9.

3. Knoop & Jones. *The Genesis of Freemasonry*, p. 11.

4. Alison Weir. *Elizabeth of York: A Tudor Queen and Her World.* (New Work: Ballantine Books, 2013), p. 201.

5. Knoop & Jones, *Genesis,* p. 21.

6. , Knoop & Jones, *Genesis,* p. 116.

7. Sarah Gristwood. *Blood Sisters: The Women behind the Wars of the Roses.* (New York: Basic Books, 2013), pp. 113 & 136.

8. H. R. Heatley, *A Selection of Pliny's Letters with Notes, Maps, and Plates.* (London: Rivingtone, 1889), p. 60.

9. Heatley , p. 15.

10. Leader Scott. *The Cathedral Builders: The Story of a Great Masonic Guild.*, 2nd Edition. (New Orleans: Cornerstone Book Publishers, 2013), p. 29.

11. Scott, p. 33.

12. R. Beadle & A. Fletcher. *The Cambridge Companion to Medieval English Theatre.* (Cambridge, UK: Cambridge University Press, 1994), p. 21.

13. Douglas Knoop & G. P. Jones. *The Mediaeval Mason.* (Manchester, UK: Manchester University Press, 1933), p. 37.

14. R. A. Leeson. *Traveling Brothers; The Six Centuries' Road from Craft Fellowship to Trade Unionism.* London" George Allen & Unsin Ltd., 1979, p. 68.

15. Edward Conder Junior, Master of the Masons Company of this present year. *Records of the Hole Craft and Fellowship of Masons, with a Chronicle of the History of the Worshipful Company of Masons of the City of London.* London: Swan Sonnenschien & Co., 1894, p. 4.

16. *The Farmer's Almanac for 1823* published at Andover, Mass.

17. John Hamill. *The Craft: A History of English Freemasonry.* (London: Crucible Press, 1986), p. 21.

18. Susan Mitchell Sommers. *The Revival of a Patriotic Order: Knights Templars in England and New York.* Located at http://www.knightstemplar.org/KnightTemplar/articles/patroits.htm.

19. Malcolm Barber. *The New Knighthood: A History of the Order of the Temple, 12th Edition.* (Cambridge, UK: Cambridge University Press, 2015), p. 320.

20. Ludolph of Suchem. *Liber de Itinere Terrae Sanctae,* ed. F. Deycks, Stuttgart, Germany, 1851.

21. Malcolm Barber, *The New Knighthood*, p. 1.

Chapter Five

The London Masons' Company

Mason's Mark

Modern Freemasonry, as an organization, is generally dated from 1717 and the creation of the Grand Lodge of England in London. Yet the legends associated with the Masons' Fraternity in London suggest an existence from at least 1202, but those guilds were not the lineal predecessors of the London Company. English masons were not as well organized as other societies until the middle of the fifteenth century. There were strong local guilds with significant religious and social activity, but it was not until 1481 that the London Company was recognized by the Crown and granted a livery. The Constitution of 1481 notes that the company was chartered to the fellowship of the Freemasons enfranchised in City of London. That charter required members to attend mass officially once every two years and to hold an extravagant dinner with their wives invited. Membership into the company was granted in one of four ways: (1) seven-year apprenticeship; (2) the rule of patrimony which allowed sons *and daughters* "freedom of the company" even if not engaged in the craft; (3) purchase of *freedom of the company* for non-operative people; and (4) transfer from one guild to another.[1] This charter is also listed in *The Inventory of Constitutions* from the mayoralty of John Brown, City of London, in 1481.

The Reformation during the sixteenth century decreased the power of the companies as the Crown took control of their possessions, but the various guilds continued their social, charitable, and industry/trade regulation functions. The Masons' Company was among the most affected and by the middle of the seventeenth century had changed its name from 'The Company of Freemasons of London" to "The Company of London Masons." The first Hall of the Worshipful Company of Masons of the City of London was built about 1463 in the Ward of Bassishaw (prior to receiving a Crown Charter) and destroyed by fire but rebuilt on the same site in 1668. Speculative Masons continued to use the structure until it was sold in 1865.

In seventeenth century London, the rebuilding of the city after the Great Fire was governed primarily by two statutes passed in 1666 and a third in 1670. The purpose of these acts was to prevent in the future the problems that contributed to the conflagration and to insure for the city uniformity and gracefulness in building as well as to provide for properly arranged streets and the use of brick or stone rather and the more common wood and dab. The Lord Mayor, Aldermen, and Common Council were given the authority to select surveyors to ensure that the regulations were followed and to require that structures be erected within a stipulated time. The regulations also fixed the prices of materials and set wages for workers. Finally, the various Acts provided a source of revenue for the improvement of the city with a sizeable portion going to the completion of St. Paul's Cathedral.

In the seventeenth century, the London Masons' Company was still performing the traditional tasks associated with the old *mistery* or craft guild to include search for false work and preservation of the trade's monopoly in the city. The practice of trade monopoly was fourfold: (1) prevent or restrain foreign masons; (2) discourage masons from functioning outside the company (obtaining their freedom); (3) challenge any impostor who appeared to hinder a mason's work; and (4) stop mason's work from being done by men from other guilds or trades. The most acute of the problems seems to have been the question of *foreign masons. Foreign* did not mean of another nationality but rather simply from another town or county—someone outside the jurisdiction. The first ordinance in 1481 essentially forbid *foreign* masons from working in the city, but by 1521 that stance had softened and *foreign* masons were allowed but not as masters and only after having paid three pence quarterly to the common box. *Foreign* masons did work in the city, however, and in searches between 1640 and 1645 money was regularly received from these *foreigners and aliens*.

The reconstruction of the City that followed the Great Fire in 1666 markedly changed the situation. To facilitate rebuilding, Parliament passed legislation that allowed masons, bricklayers, carpenters, and other construction trades to work in the city "until the rebuilding was completed and further, that if they worked at such rebuilding for seven years, they were to enjoy the same liberty as freemen."[2]

THE COMPANY

The London Masons' Company was the first official unified guild of operative masons in England. Its formation was the result of an original dispute between the Hewers (stone cutters) and the Layers and Setters in 1356. The contenders went before the city's Council which ruled that the Company would be created to supervise work in the city and to create ordinances —a Code of 10 Rules—to govern the trade. The Company was formally incorporated and chartered by the city in 1481 and remained purely operative in nature until the mid-seventeenth century, but most records for the period prior to 1620 have been lost. The surviving records do indicate that by that timeplas there existed within the guild an *inner working* or a*cception* which *made* masons."

Medieval masonry continued to exist in some forms even after the great age of castle and cathedral building ended. Masons remained in their lodges and in London, the Masons' Company evolved to meet the demands of changing political, religious, and economic conditions. As noted above, a prime concern of the Company was *foreign* masons meaning anyone from outside the City, but there is evidence in the Company's records that prominent *foreign* masons were readily accepted into the craft. Of equal concern was how to deal with ex-apprentices who had not received their *freedom* as well as methods for discouraging unqualified masons from obtaining *their freedom* or, in modern terminology, their license to practice. In addition, the Company was faced with developing clear rules for the inclusion of non-operative masons into the guild. A 1678 list of masons working in London indicates that eight were members of the Haberdashers Company; three were Joiners; two were Clothworkers; and one each were Stationers, Fishmongers, Vinters, Barger/Surgeons, Weavers, and Tallow Chandlers.

It was not uncommon for the Company to clash with other guilds such as Plasterers, Joiners, and Carpenters to preserve its trade monopoly with most of the focus seemingly being on plasterers who were accused of covering rotten or ill-laid stone work with plaster to deceive the public. Other recorded disputes were with carvers and carpenters who often undertook work originally assigned to masons. This led the Company to establish strong rules regarding false work as well as guidelines for proper search. These rules indicate that in the City there were at least six classes of masons: shopkeepers, stone merchants, overseers, contractors, journeymen, and apprentices.

Shopkeepers were yeomen. They *kept shop* and received money from persons on account as well as made search for irregular goods and work. They were primarily administrators who had little or no operative background though some of these shopkeepers may have previously engaged in carving and tomb making. Stone merchants were exactly as described; they provided the raw material necessary for construction. Among the most popular products were black and white Nicholas Stone, Purbeck marble, Portland Stone, Taynton Stone, and Portland pavers. Based upon existing records, Portland stone was more useful that Purbeck and by 1663 required a special license to quarry. This type of stone was transported into the city in large quantity. Between 1674 and 1700 more than fifty thousand tons of Portland was moved into London along with more than twenty-five thousand tons of other types of stone with the cost of freight or cartage equaling that of the stone itself.

Overseers were responsible under the contractor for the work at the site. This title could refer to a contractor's partner or to a salaried supervisor at a site such as London Bridge. Some overseers also functioned as stone merchants, or at least as middle-men between the contractor and the quarryman. Contractors were prevalent throughout the period since most stone work was done on a contract basis from the construction of new buildings to the repair of ancient buildings such as Old St. Paul's. The direct labor system then in favor worked well with the contract system enabling the employer to hire only those workers needed at any given time on the site thus saving costs and improving profits. At St. Paul's Cathedral, for example, there are at least fourteen different contractors listed on the rolls and at Windsor, Winchester, Whitehall, Hampton Court, and Kensington Palaces at least twelve different contractors are listed. At the parish, municipal, and, even, personal level, contractors were prevalent.

Journeymen dressed and laid the stones, but, because of their place in the hierarchy, we know little about them. They were hired by the day or piece, and there was little or no job security. These were the traveling men of the period. Some are listed on the rolls as masons and seemed to have performed the tasks assigned to that trade, but lack of information about their backgrounds prevent further understanding of their training or expertise. The number of apprentices listed on the rolls in London suggests that the apprenticeship system was strong in the London Company, but the records also show that only about forty-five percent of the apprentices ever "took their freedom" or advanced to journeymen. A review of the records of those apprentices traceable through the rolls at Masons' Hall indicates that by the middle of the seventeenth century, if not earlier, the practice of utilizing an apprentice only in the presence of his master was no longer enforced.

The various masons' companies, to include the one in London, provided the rules and history which became indispensable to modern Freemasonry. Through these companies, the traditions of the craft were maintained even though, as Plott notes, men who were not directly association with the operative craft were readily admitted into the Society. And while the evidence is far from conclusive—the very nature of Craft trade secrecy worked against the preservation of records—by the mid-seventeenth century, Masonry was satisfactorily transitioning from operative to speculative, from *freemasons* to *accepted masons*. Men who were not operative masons had been made part of the Craft for centuries and by the late 1590s their number appears to have become dominant. By the mid-seventeenth century, accepted masons were outnumbering operative masons with men like Elias Ashmole being *made a Mason* in 1646 in Staffordshire. The operative mason had learned how to hue, square, mold-stone, lay a level, and raise a perpendicular; the speculative mason assigned symbolic meaning to these operative terms and tools, but secrecy was still directly associated with the Craft. The Fraternity and its excellent tenets would survive to be celebrated and loved by future generations.

NOTES

1. Edward Condor, Jr. *Records of the Hole Crafte and Fellowship of Masons: With a Chronicle of the History of the Worshipful Company of Masons of the City of London; Collected from Official Records in the Possession of the Company, the Manuscripts in the British Museum, the Public Record Office, the Guildhall Library, Etc. Et.* London: Swan, Sonnenschein & Company, 1894, various pages.

2. Douglas Knoop & G.P.Jones. *The London Masons in the Seventeenth Century.* (Manchester, UK: Manchester University Press, 1935), p. 10.

Chapter Six

Operative to Speculative

Master and apprentices

England, and with it the rest of Europe, changed dramatically during the seventeenth and eighteenth centuries. Large-scale production replaced the smaller, cottage industries prevalent during previous centuries. Technology improved, and the transition from medieval to early modern social, political, and industrial systems moved quickly forward. Transition in the building industry did not occur, however, in a fashion similar to that in, for example, the weaving industry where technology exemplified by the introduction of Kay's fly-shuttle marked the beginning of the industrial revolution. There was no similar drastic or sudden break with the past for the building trades,

In the medieval world, there was no clear demarcation between ecclesiastical and secular masons. There was interchangeability of function and responsibility. Walter of Hereford is listed as Master Mason at Vale Abbey in 1278 and then as Master of the Works at Caernarvon Castle; Henry Yevele was both Master Mason at Westminster Abbey and Disposer of the King's Works at Westminster Palace; and Richard Beke was Chief Bridge Mason at London Bridge and, later, Master Mason at Canterbury Cathedral. While the Dissolution of the Monasteries under Henry VIII markedly slowed ecclesiastical work, a similar decline in Crown building activity followed at the end of the sixteenth century. With this decline went profound change in the industry accompanied by transformation in public taste. Classical architecture began to replace the Gothic and that change was accompanied by the rise of professional architects who supplanted the medieval Master Mason. These architects preferred brick to stone because of lower costs; ready availability; and the ease with which it could be worked. They also expressed an advanced interest in all things Greek and Roman which was accompanied by a new interest on the part of scholars in architecture. This may well account for a part of the transition from operative to speculative Masonry.

This new age of inquiry was characterized by the revival of classical learning and style. The Italian style was adopted throughout Europe with a renewed focus on the classical orders of architecture. There already existed at this period, according to William Dugdale, author of *A History of St. Paul's*, a fraternity of *adopted masons.* The men responsible for the great medieval buildings were not professional architects note Knoop and Jones, rather they were "freemason[s] which can draw his plat, work and set cunningly."[1] The men who reconstructed London after 1666 were of the likes of Christopher Wren, more architect and designer than stone layer. A close study of the records of the Masons' Lodges indicates that, along with working and ex-masons, people of high social standing or wealth as well as those who were not trained as masons were on the rolls as members of the guild. William Suthis, listed as King's Master Mason, was a member of the Goldsmith's Company and Samuel Fulkes, a renowned mason-contractor, was by guild membership a Haberdasher. Since membership in the London Masons' Company granted holders no special or definitive privileges why, then, did non-operatives associate with the guild in the first place?

Reasons for becoming an *accepted free mason* obviously varied. The main ones, based on diaries of such members, appear to include a sincere desire for knowledge about art and architecture; a fascination with and a desire to share in the Masons' *secrets*; and personal curiosity about the admission ritual and mysteries. Fraternal or friendly relations also played a significant part as did moral and spiritual endeavors. Non-operative clerks of previous generations had been closely associated with the Craft, but the renewed interest in classical architecture on the part of scholars and the gentry led many to seek the trade secrets possessed by the fraternity as well as to gain access to the technical and geometrical knowledge operative masons possessed. As noted in Chapter I, these men were simply *made a mason.*

There appear to have been four main categories of men who sought membership in the speculative fraternity: landed gentry such as Col. Henry Mainwaring who was associated with Elias Ashmole; professionals, academics, clergy, and scholars such as Ashmole and Gotthold Lessing; men already connected with the trade such as goldsmiths, sculptors, and tomb makers; and other tradesmen such as tailors, bakers, and beer-sellers who had a product to offer the guild. Yet others were attracted to the Craft because of their interest in heraldry and antiquarianism with these men also indicating a strong interest in the *mysteries* of the craft and its association with ancient mystery religions. The probability is strong, therefore, that what is now purely speculative Masonry arose out of the non-operatives who attached themselves to the guild especially in the seventeenth century.

This group of emerging speculative Masons focused on the legends of the craft and developed ever more elaborate symbolism to include expanded uses of grips, words, signs, and spiritual or moral meanings for the working tools of the operative mason's trade. They also began to shorten or, even, eliminate, the recitation of operative rules and regulations which were the main portions of the *Old Charges* (see Chapter III). They instituted in their place moral teachings *veiled in allegory and illustrated by symbols.* From the latter part of the seventeenth century into the early part of the eighteenth century, the ceremony of gaining admission was significantly elaborated upon and expanded, eventually developing by the mid-eighteenth century into the three-degree system familiar today (see Chapter I for a description of an early *acception* ceremony). These rites and ceremonies did not, however, any more than the Fraternity itself, emerge fully formed. They evolved as the members innovated to meet changing demands and interests.

Speculative Masonry, or what Murray Lyon calls *symbolic* Masonry, was soon synonymous with *Freemasonry.* A speech delivered at Trinity College in 1688 notes that a "Society of Freemasons, consisting of gentlemen, mechanics, porters, parsons, ragmen, hucksters, divines, tinkers, knights"[2] had been formed at the college and that a collection had been made to provide charity for a reduced brother. There existed in England, Ireland, and Scotland in the seventeenth century, lodges of Accepted Masons that functioned in parallel with the traditional operative lodges, but there was no central authority and only lose control of the fraternity's legends or the *Mason's Word.* A document dated 1686 attributed to Robert Padegett gives his title as "clerke to the Worshippful Society of Free Masons of the City of London," but it appears to relate only to a single company or lodge not some larger organization. And while the evidence is far from conclusive, English lodges appear to have derived their work in some way from Scotland and may even have looked to that nation's lodge system for guidance. The result of this transition was the formation of the Grand Lodge of England in 1716-1717.

Other evidence for the existence of some form of Freemasonry or Accepted Masonry prior to the creation of the Grand Lodge of England may be found in Plott's 1686 *Natural History of Staffordshire* where he wrote of the existence of a Society of Free-Masons which consisted of five or six members of the *Ancients* order who wore gloves and communicated with *secret signs* that they were Fellows of the society otherwise called *accepted masons*. And John Aubrey in *A Natural History of Wiltshire,* also dated 1686, refers to a *fraternity of adopted-masons* whose manner of *adoption* is formal with an oath of secrecy included. A 1691 addition to Aubrey's text states that "a Fraternity of Accepted Masons was to be held at St. Paul's Church, where Sir Christopher Wren and certain others were to be adopted as Brothers."[3] Also in existence are references to a lodge at Warrington based upon Elias Ashmole's diary and a comment by Randle Holme III in his *Accademie of Armory* that he was a "member of the Society called Free Masons."[4]

GRAND LODGE OF ENGLAND

The formation of the Grand Lodge of England is wrapped in as much mystery and speculation as are the rites and history of the Fraternity itself. There are no minutes from the inception of the Grand Lodge in 1717 until 1723. Neither are any minutes from individual Lodges in London from that period extant. The principle source for information about its formation is James Anderson. Anderson, educated at Marischal College in Aberdeen, was a minister in the Church of Scotland. His father was a non-operative Mason in the Lodge of Aberdeen and was its Master on two occasions, but there is no record of the son being *made* a Mason in that lodge nor is there any record of his participation in the formation of the Grand Lodge in 1716-1717. It is possible, however, that a statement in the *Constitutions* which notes that several gentlemen of the best rank to include *clergymen and scholars* joined the Society under Lord Montagu's leadership may refer to Anderson. If Anderson was present at the formation of Grand Lodge, he would of necessity have been a Master or Warden of a regular lodge, but there is no record to support this contention.

Anderson's main claim to fame comes from his authorship of the *Constitutions*. By his own account, he was appointed to produce a first edition, but it is possible, according to Walter Begemann, that Anderson volunteered for the job. However the assignment came about, in December 1721 Montagu appointed fourteen *learned Brothers* to review Anderson's work and, after some amendments, it was approved and printed. In 1735 Anderson sought approval from the Grand Lodge to create a second edition of the *Constitutions* based on his contention that one William Smith had pirated the original work in such a manner as "to the prejudice of the said Br. Anderson it being his Sole Property."[5] The problem with the 1738 edition, though, is that Anderson gives the impression of being unable to copy exactly from his earlier work. That being the case, Anderson's account of the history of masonry in England does appear to rest on the facts as *then known and accepted,* but he was also in the habit of assigning to men throughout all ages grand Masonic titles when no such titles had existed. Anderson wrote much like the Renaissance artists who depicted Biblical events in Renaissance attire and with Renaissance architecture.

The minimal evidence available suggests that the account of the establishment of Grand Lodge of England was not an invention of Anderson and that some of the facts in his interpretation are accurate though some details are in doubt. For example, Christopher Wren is named by Anderson as a starting point referring to him as Grand Master, but at Wren's death in 1723, only two newspapers made reference to his association with Freemasonry and they most probably were using the term in its operative sense as was then common, though Aubrey appears to suggest otherwise. Secondly, there is some confusion regarding the number of local lodges that met to form the Grand Lodge with Anderson listing four and the *Multa Paucis* noting six but giving no specific names.

Both accounts of The Grand Lodge of England's formation do agree that Anthony Sayer was elected Grand Master. Anderson refers to him as *a gentleman* which suggests that he was of the landed gentry. By the end of his life, however, his circumstances had severely diminished when he petitioned Grand Lodge more than once for *relief.* Sayer was followed in the office of Grand Master by George Payne and John Desaguliers. Sayer, Payne, and Desaguliers were commoners who were succeeded by a long line of aristocracy and, ultimately, royalty as Grand Master and becoming Past Grand Master upon assuming the throne. These included George IV (1790), Edward VII (1874), and Edward VIII (1936).

In the United States, while there is no single Grand Lodge System, many of the nation's founding fathers and presidents were Freemasons. Among the founding fathers were George Washington, Paul Revere, and Benjamin Franklin. Presidents who were Freemasons began with Washington and included Andrew Jackson, James Garfield, William Taft, Theodore and Franklin Roosevelt, Harry Truman and Gerald Ford—fourteen in all. President Truman was Grand Master of Missouri in 1940 and President Taft was *made a Mason on sight* at Kilwinning Lodge No. 356 in Cincinnati, Ohio. President Ronald Reagan was an Honorary Scottish Rite Freemason and President

William Clinton was a member of the Order of DeMolay and inducted into the DeMolay Hall of Fame in 1988. President Abraham Lincoln applied for membership in Tyrian Lodge in Springfield, Illinois, in 1860. He withdrew his petition noting that he did not want it to be construed as a political move to obtain votes. He commented that he would resubmit his petition when he returned from the presidency. Sadly, Lincoln was assassinated in 1865. He was followed in the office by Andrew Johnson who was a Freemason.

Early English Grand Masters, especially those of *conspicuous birth,* lent distinction to the Craft but apparently exercised little authority. The most prominent officer in terms of influence on the Fraternity in England appears to have been the Deputy Grand Master with the existing minutes strongly suggesting that these men were active Freemasons and the moving force within the organization. The current Grand Master of the United Grand Lodge of England is Edward George Nicholas Paul Patrick, Prince Edward, Duke of Kent a grandchild of King George V and Queen Mary and first cousin of Queen Elizabeth II.

OPERATIVE TO SPECULATIVE CHARGES

The *new* or *speculative* Freemasons focused their attention on issues of charity and morality while specifically excluding politics and religion from the Lodge. The *Constitution* of 1723 notes that

> if you discover him to be a true and genuine Brother, you are to respect him accordingly; and if he is in want, you must relieve him if you can, or else direct him how he may be reliev'd; You must employ him some Days, or else recommend to be employ'd. But you are not charged to go beyond your Ability, only to prefer a poor Brother, that is a good Man and true, before any other poor People in the same Circumstances. [6]

Masons have throughout their history practiced charity in its many forms from providing food, clothing, and housing to needy Brothers to caring for widows and orphans, and establishing cemeteries for the interment of members of their Fraternity. This mandate for charity fits perfectly with the Craft's principle tenets which are brotherly love, relief, and truth. In putting this clause into his constitution, Anderson was affirming an ancient and honorable tradition not establishing a new precedent.

Throughout their history, Masons had been charged to be loyal to their king (or president) and their country, and if aware of any treason to properly report it to the civil authorities. In Anderson's constitution, this mandate is modified somewhat and political discussion within the lodge is prohibited.

A Mason is a peaceful Subject to the Civil Powers, wherever he resides or Works, and is never to be concern'd in Plots and Conspiracies against the Peace and Welfare of the Nation nor to behave himself undutifully to inferior Magistrates; for as Masonry hath been always injured by War, Bloodshed, and Confusion, so ancient Kings and Princes have been much disposed to encourage the Craftsmen, because of their Peacefableness and Loyality, whereby they practically answer'd in Times of Peace. So that if a Brother should be a Rebel against the State, he is not to be countenanc'd in his Rebellion, however he may be pitied as an unhappy Man; and if convicted of no other Crime, though the loyal Brotherhood must and ought to disown his Rebellion, and give no Umbrage of Ground of political Jealousy to the Government for the time being; they cannot expel him from the Lodge, and his Relation to it remains indefeasible.[7]

Anderson goes on to note that private quarrels are not to be brought within the Lodge "far less any Quarrles about Religion, or Nations, or State Policy . . . we are also of all Nations, Tongues, Kindreds, and Languages, and are resolved against *all Politics*."[8] Regarding religion, Anderson charges Freemasons to "obey the moral Law." Later authors have argued that Anderson's reference to Freemasonry as being the Center of Union suggests a strong association with deism if not a direct affiliation with that philosophy. Considering what is known about him, however, it is improbable that he would attempt to impose his personal belief system on others, something deist philosophy and Freemasonry prohibit, as well. Based on both Masonic and non-masonic writings from the period, there is nothing to suggest that these new Anderson charges in any went against established attitudes or that he introduced into the Fraternity any unusual innovations. Many influential men of the age were identified with the deist movement or had deist leanings to include Adam Smith, Benjamin Franklin, George Washington, Thomas Paine, Gotthold Lessing, and Voltaire. A considerable number of these individuals were also Freemasons.

DEISM

Deism is a philosophy that derives its name from *Deus* the Latin word for *God.* It came of age during the Enlightenment in Europe among Christians who believed in One God but had become disillusioned with organized religion. Classical Deists did not necessarily conceive of The Deity as non-interventionists, but rather as the creator of the natural world and of all that it contained. They sought the Deity through reason and the observation of nature, but included within their philosophy spiritual elements which included a personal knowledge of God through nature. They rejected dogma and were skeptical of miracles yet they strongly espoused the existence of God and that He gave to man the singular ability to reason thereby raising him above all other creatures. They believed that God could be experienced and that man, through reason, could partake of His perfection though they themselves were imperfect creatures. They tended to hold a variety of beliefs about immortality, with a sizeable number espousing the belief that the soul existed and that in the afterlife there would be reward or punishment for their behavior in life. They commonly used terms such as *Grand Architect of the Universe* and *Nature's God* to refer to the Supreme Being with Benjamin Franklin specifically referring to Him as the *Father of Light.* These eighteenth-century Deists were not believers in a cold, impersonal, non-interventionist creator. They inculcated a strong moral order and were wholly committed to intra-personal and inter-personal relationships with the Deity. They prayed what we now call Affirmative Prayer and were consistently appreciative to God saying *we thank you* rather than *please, God, grant unto me.*[9]

MASONIC RITUAL

As noted in Chapter I, Masonic ritual has evolved significantly since the first references to it are found in the seventeenth century. No longer are Brothers simply *made Masons* in a single ceremony. To find the origin of current practices, we must look at the legends as well as the history of the craft as recounted in the various *Old Charges* and at how the *Word* was transmitted. The earliest rituals suggest that a catechism was an integral part of initiation as was the imparting of *words* and *signs* accompanied by a demonstration of proficiency in both. In addition, some form of Craft history was recounted to the initiate, similar to the lectures given in modern degree work. All of this ceremonial activity was utilized to form a link with the operative past or *time immemorial* as well as between the Brothers.

Virtually all evidence currently existing relating to Masonic ritual and its inherent secrets is of Scottish origin which focused on the passing of *The Word* or tenets from generation to generation. This was done mouth-to-ear using a memorized catechism similar to religious instruction. Included in the ritual were set prayers for before, convening, and dismissing a Lodge similar to those found in the *Book of Common Prayer*. Evident as well in the evolution of the Grand Lodge system is the introduction of trigradual Freemasonry.

Early Freemasonry utilized a single ceremony to *make* a Mason which included parts of the current Entered Apprentice and Fellow Craft Degrees (see Chapter I). There is some evidence to suggest that as early 1696 in Scotland there were two ceremonies—one for Entered Apprentices and the other for Fellow Crafts/Master Masons, and that each propounded its own secrets. It further appears that at some point after 1726 in England, the three-degree system evolved, but the reasons behind this modification are unknown with the evidence supporting the contention that the evolution of the three-degree system in both English and Irish Lodges after 1730 may have originated about 40 years earlier as an attempt to expand Masonic education through more elevated moral and ritual instruction. This much is for sure, the work of *speculative* Masonic Lodges was significantly different from that of their operative ancestors and their manner of adoption or acceptance had become much more formal.

NOTES

1. Douglas Knoop & G.P. Jones. *Introduction to Freemasonry.* (Manchester, UK: Manchester University Press, 1937), p. 53.

2. Knoop & Jones. *The Genesis of Freemasonry*, p. 152.

3. Knoop & Jones, p. 148.

4. Knoop & Jones, p. 150.

5. Knoop & Jones, p. 164.

6. James Anderson. *Constitutions of the Free-Masons.* New York: Masonic Publishers, 1855, pp. 55-56.

7. Anderson, p. 50.

8. Anderson, p. 54.

9. For more information on Deism see *Encyclopedia Britannica; The Encyclopedia of Christian Civilization;* and Wilson and Reill's *Deism; English Deism: Its Roots and Its Fruits.*

Chapter Seven

Ritual, Experience, and Meaning

Ritual is a dynamic cultural experience that has been central to research in religion and society for at least one hundred and fifty years. Ritual is not just a tool for understanding social occurrences and dramatizations; it is also a window into the human experience. Ritual impacts upon both social cohesion and equilibrium as it contributes directly to understanding through experience. It enables the integration of belief and behavior; tradition and change; the real and the ideal. Ritual is a form of consecrated behavior which, through moods and motivations utilizing symbols, encourages men to formulate an order of existence.

All humans and many animal species engage in ritualistic behavior from how we dress or undress to courting practices, how we greet each other, and, even, how we fight. A great deal of human behavior can be explained and comprehended in terms of ritual because ritual is an essential part of communication, meaning, and understanding. At the same time, all animals are dominated by feeling, especially humans, but human feeling is special. Human feeling embraces conceptual processes which involve symbols, language, and, through them, ritual.

At issue in any consideration of ritual is its role and purpose in society, and its place in our social institutions. Ritual, notes Durkheim, is the method whereby individuals are brought together to "strengthen the bonds attaching the individual to the society of which he is a member."[1] Ritual shapes our perception of both the human and the divine as it serves a socializing function. The very structure of the ritual, notes Taylor, Robertson, Smith, and Frazer, is intrinsic to how the ritual functions in society. [2] Rituals facilitate the means by which human beings live together in an orderly social relationship by maintaining the unity of the group. Ritual also transmits through generations the basic sentiments of a society thus serving to reduce anxiety,

distress, fear, doubt, and, even, sorrow.[3] But Huxley notes that the modern
world fails to ritualize effectively which leads to a high propensity toward
flawed communication as well as a weakening of personal and social bonds.[4]
The question arises, then, how does ritual communicate.

COMMUNICATING INSTRUCTION BY SYMBOLS

Suzanne Langer notes that a symbol enables people to think about, understand, and react to something apart from its immediate presence. A symbol is
"an instrumental thought." [5] We assign to the symbol meaning which results
in an emotional response to the object. However, that meaning and response
may differ and, even, change from society to society, age to age, and person
to person. The swastika—a cross with four bent arms—is common to many
ancient civilizations especially those of the Indus valley where it represents
auspiciousness. The word "swastika" is literally translated as "to be good."
Consider how much that changed during the twentieth century when the
swastika was appropriated by the Nazi movement in Germany. The assigned
meaning of the symbol and our emotional response to it underwent a radical
and drastic reversal.

The meaning of symbols is transmitted through discourse with meaning
being the complex relationship among symbols, objects, and the person. In
discourse, it is not the words alone that create meaning but rather how the
words are grouped together through grammatical structure that enables us to
learn and transmit meaning. In this sense, language truly makes us human. In
order for language to function successfully, there must be some level of
shared meaning. We must agree upon *what we are talking about.* When we
use the word *dog,* the listener creates a mental image of the object. That
mental image may vary in detail—a German shepherd in one person's mind,
a poodle in another's. What is critical to communication is shared meaning:
that we agree upon the proposition—dog, a domestic animal with four legs, a
tail, a head—not necessarily the details.

A great deal of human behavior meets symbolic needs and symbolic acts
(speech for verbal symbolization and action for nonverbal symbolization)
result in ritual. Ritual not only enhances the quality of meaning and facilitates our understanding of objects, events, and people; it also serves to generate more penetrating questions about the meanings of the symbols involved.

The foundation of symbolic interaction (communication) is found in the
work of George Herbert Mead primarily in his book *Mind Self and Society.*
In order for humans to cooperate, they must first come to an agreed upon
understanding of each other's intentions. Symbol-using interaction serves
that function. Humans are biological creatures possessing a brain capable of
rational processing who, by mental processes, plan and rehearse their sym-

bolic behavior so as to better prepare themselves for social interaction. And while Kenneth Burke[6] is noted for his explanation of the use of dramatic metaphor in communication, he also distinguished how individuals present themselves to others through ritual and role-playing. Finally, Hugh Duncan stresses the importance of the symbol in transmitting meaning.[7] He also stresses the roles people assume noting that "Social order is created and sustained in social dramas through intensive and frequent communal presentations."[8]

Symbols function to synthesize the tone, character, and quality of human life by giving it a moral and aesthetic style and mood. They provide a picture of how things should be. Symbols represent sets of acts; establish powerful and long-lasting moods and motivations; formulate conceptions in general; clothe perceptions with an aura of factuality; and establish moods and motivations that seem uniquely realistic.[9]

Symbols are used as vehicles for conception—meaning—and are abstractions fixed in perceptible form with concrete embodiments of ideas, attitudes, judgements, longings, and beliefs. They are the key to understanding culture and cultural activity. A symbol is a plan for a house, not the actual house. It is the drawing, not the structure. Symbols provide templates for a process external to themselves but which lead to a definite form. In man, his genes do not speak to his ability to engage in the building trade, that needs a conception of what is to be built and that conception is done in symbolic form. Symbols are blueprints or textbooks not buildings. The proper manipulation of significant symbols gives them graphic power and enables man to attain his destiny.

In Freemasonry, symbols are intertransportable. They mean different things at various times and on various levels. And while they do shape our ritual into a distinctive set of tendencies, capacities, propensities, skills, habits, liabilities, and proneness, they give character to the flow of our activity and the quality of our experience. The legend is learned by heart with the moods the symbols induce ranging from melancholy to joy; from confidence to pity; from exalted to bland. Communication, then, is a complex process that utilizes symbols to transmit meaning and to socialize the individual. A primary form of this transmission and socialization is ritual.

ESOTERICISM IN RITUAL

The practice of the indirect communication of information through symbols is neither unorthodox nor relegated to any one age, civilization, or organization. "The world," says Sherlock Holmes in chapter three of *The Hound of the Baskervilles,* "is full of obvious things which nobody by any chance ever observes." Ancient philosophers had double doctrines; one external or exoteric the other internal or esoteric; one vulgar, the other secret. The esoteric was that which was suitable only for those who were serious seekers of knowledge and truth. Esoteric writing served to preserve this knowledge for a select audience with the "wits of such sharpness as can pierce the veil."[10] Esoteric writing was also employed as a restraint to avoid political and religious persecution with Thomas Aquinas noting in 1258 that "certain things can be explained in private which we should keep silent about in public"[11] and Maimonides, writing about a century later, reiterates Aquinas by stating that "these matters [he is referring to theology] are only for a few solidary individuals of a very special sort."[12] In the tenth-century Arabic philosopher Abu Nasor al-Farabi comments on Plato that "he followed the practice of using symbols, riddles, obscurity, and difficulty, so that science would not fall into the hands of those who do not deserve it and are deformed, or into the hands of one who does not know its worth or who used it improperly."[13]

Freemasonry is a complex and, even, contradictory marvel which has stood for different things at different times in different places. Throughout its history there are noted among its members many serious thinkers of each period who were dedicated to the use of the fraternity to advance progressive ideas and to counterbalance the institutions of church and state and, later, universities. Freemasonry was integral to the spread of the Enlightenment and the development of social order out of the chaos of the various revolutions that plagued Europe. In what was to become the United States, a number of the nation's founders were Freemasons and, according to Reinhart Koselleck, there were two social structures that left a "decisive imprint" on the Age of Enlightenment, "the Republic of Letters and the Masonic Lodge."[14] The use of esoteric writing and practice to transmit *enlightenment* in these lodges is found in the vast literature associated with the organization which used pseudonyms and anonymity as it illuminated the character of modern philosophy. The very creation of our modern open society required many changes in Europe and North America, the success of which also required esoteric secrecy.

Of the four forms of esoteric writing—defensive esotericism, protective esotericism, pedagogical esotericism, and political esotericism—protective esotericism comes closest to describing the Freemasonic motivation to protect its mysteries. It is also the most profound and meets the most resistance. Essentially, it is assumed that some truths may be harmful or dangerous if in the hands of the initiated. *A little bit of knowledge is a dangerous thing* goes the old adage. Ancient writings are filled with stories which enable the reader to reflect upon how humans have reacted when they came into possession of information they were not prepared to understand or utilize. The Tree of Knowledge, the Tower of Babel, the myth of Prometheus or the Sirens, as well as Plato's *Republic* and the *Ernst and Faulk* dialogues of Lessing dramatize the dangers of the acquisition by the unprepared of certain forms of knowledge. Truth does not always turn out to match our hopes and dreams, nor does reality always conform to the demands of the human heart or psyche. Seeing the truth, suggests some philosophers (and these stories), is often exalted above the capacity of the common man and requires special initiation and instruction.

The Jewish Kabbalistic tradition makes no secret of its use of esotericism. It is open about its secretiveness. The assumption that some knowledge may confuse some people is not rare. The Talmud, the primary text of Judaism after the Torah, requires that certain information be not "expounded" before other than "a Sage," and Maimonides writes that ancient sages "enjoined us to discuss these subjects privately . . . and then only if he be wise and capable of independent reasoning" finishing the paragraph by stating that "it is left to him to develop the conclusions for himself and to penetrate the depths of that subject."[15]

Christianity has a similar tradition of protective esotericism or *the discipline of the secret.* An entire article is devoted to it in the *Catholic Encyclopedia.* This tradition is molded on the parables and words of Jesus who, in Matthew 13:10-17, states that he would speak plainly to them (the disciples) but in parables to others. Thus Aquinas, commenting on Boethius, supports Paul's comment in I Corinthians 3: 1-2 that he could not give them the highest wisdom concerning God because it is only for the truly spiritual man to understand. Aquinas then explicitly states that "certain things can be explained to the wise in private which we should keep silent about in public."[16] Science, profane and divine, is hidden in riddles and parables.

The Masonic Craft has undergone a long, gradual development both in doctrine and ritual, but it is only recently that scholars have become interested in those initiatory societies which utilize esotericism to transmit information and mysteries. Much of Western esotericism has been transmitted through rituals of initiation which are, these scholars suggest, the sum of ancient religious practices. The candidate in these ceremonies is between an old and a new state. The mystery or sacred knowledge is intended to transform the candidate at an internal level into a new person. The candidate usually acts in a passive and humble manner, obeying his conductor and instructor, and fearing no danger. These initiation rituals are intended to develop intense fellowship or comradeship as well as egalitarianism or equality.

Freemasonry is generally described not as a secret society but as a society with secrets, and ritual is the manner in which Freemasonry, and other societies, transmits those secrets from generation to generation. Treating secrecy ritually removes it from the ordinary and implies a spiritual dimension. In Freemasonic ritual, the veil constitutes the message. A ritual (and a symbol) always has more than one meaning—a primary or immediate one, and an allusive or hidden one. The idea that the veil constitutes the message is considered by many ritualists as of utmost importance. Though esoteric rituals do not appear to have entered the world of Freemasonry until the mid-eighteenth century through the high degrees, but the evidence does suggest that early Craft masonry was moral rather than ritualistic in character, the link between ritual, esotericism, and Freemasonry was well established by the 1650s.

RITUAL AND MEANING

For humans, the meanings of symbols are often elusive, vague, and convoluted, but that meaning is capable of being discovered and understood through investigation and explanation. Just as language is constituted of units—phonemes, morphemes, words—so too is ritual constituted of discrete symbolic acts, and the meaning of both the symbols and the ritual are grasped only through cultural transformation or initiation. Yet while ritual may appear to exalt the outward or the contrived, when fully understood, it becomes an inward expression of an external reality.

Humans are cultural animals and prefer to live in societies. From the beginning of the human race, there has been a communal conception of the right way to live and a shared view of morality and the sacred. The basic concept was that we needed to join together. People are, Aquinas wrote in *City of God,* "bound together by a common agreement as to the objects of their love."[17] The flaw in human reasoning, though, is that while the lowest levels of life described in Maslow's Hierarchy of Needs as physiological and safety (air, water, food, personal security, and health) are self-evident, higher requirements such as love, esteem, and self-actualization, because they are elevated, are less clear and less understood. At these upper levels, there is a weakened sense of certainty and stability, a condition feared by many. In the modern world, communities or societies of common interest serve to ameliorate that concern by bringing into harmony through philosophic interchange questions about higher certainties. Thus, while authority is often rooted in tradition and custom, reason and custom may also provide guidance for human thought and action.

Humans are complex entities with a variety of illusions, beliefs, perceptions, questions, faculties, and desires. Most of the questions humans have about life and the world are practical and not of an academic nature. They do not require an abstract or complex answer. Instinct, habit, custom, laws, traditions, and mores generally suffice to address most of our issues. A crucial element of human interaction is our moral commitment to each other's welfare as well as that of the community; and while traditional virtues may vary from the austerity of Spartan society to the openness of modern

America, their intent is to create cohesiveness within the society or institution.

In *Laws*, considered Plato's most political writing, he tells the parable of the Athenian stranger with the stranger saying, "let our race be something that is not lowly, then, if that is what you cherish, but worth of a certain seriousness."[18] Many, however, using a Platonic metaphor, can only "stare reality in the face [and] the truth is too strong for most eyes."[19] A natural response to this has been through the use of esotericism and ritual. Ritual, which is natural in form and content, is often highly elaborate and filled with symbolism and allegory. Ritual tends to be celebratory in nature and is experienced at various levels through different senses. It can be a therapeutic and cathartic tool. It can be a formula that enables us to interpret our drives and motivations in terms of brotherly love and respect for tradition and others. It is not necessarily to be understood, however, but to be felt and experienced. Ritual is a celebration of life and its experiences as well as of human striving and motivation. It may well be a higher route to the understanding of the human and the divine.

RITUAL

Originally, *ritual* referred to the Roman judicial concept of the proven or correct way to perform. It was also considered as that which was normal, natural, and true. Ritual functions by facilitating the human brain's ability to focus on the question or object in such a way as to lead the individual and the group to a shared meaning that serves the best interest of those involved.

Our ancient brethren worked long and hard to develop and understand their Craft, and to perpetuate its history, knowledge and identity by initiating novices through a system of ever higher levels of knowledge (degrees) imparted through ritual. By the early eighteenth century, Knoop and Jones note, our more recent brethren had expanded their practices (ritual) by assigning to their working tools special moral and spiritual meaning, and by utilizing those symbols in their ritual. This enabled the brethren to conceive of something apart from the immediate or practical nature of the object. The symbols had become *instruments of thought* that required further study and contemplation to reach a full understanding of their meaning.

Ritual employs shared meanings to transmit to the audience and from generation to generation the concepts of the institution. It comes to us in at least six forms: formalism, traditionalism, invariance, sacred, sacrifice, and performance. It may further be categorized by genre: rites of passage, commemorative rites, rites of communion, rites of affliction, and rites of festival. Above all, ritual enhances meaning and understanding as it furthers learning. We first learn the basic principles—memorize the catechisms and degree work—and then we progress to the utilization of that information in our search for and attainment of higher, more significant knowledge.

In Freemasonry, our rituals or forms and ceremonies perform not only as formal, institutionalized exercises that create an *esprit de corps* as well as a shared experience and language, but they also serve as the means to transmit our traditions and to establish for the brethren the higher meaning of the signs, symbols, allegories, and landmarks of our craft as well enabling them to grasp those special meanings. The functional aspect of the ritual is important—opening and closing of the Lodge, the conferral of Degrees, the installation of officers, the interment of the dead and should be uniform utilizing an agreed-upon language, symbolization and action—but it is the meaning of the ritual that is paramount.

Ritual enables the participants to order the world that surrounds them in an agreed upon manner. It simplifies the chaos of events and communications by imposing thereon a coherent system that enables us to catalog, categorize, and understand experiences. Not only is seeing believing, doing is believing.

Humans also seek predictability in their lives in a very unpredictable world. When you step on the gas pedal, you have the firm expectation that the vehicle will begin to move and, even, gain speed. When this does not happen, your expectation is not fulfilled—you are frustrated. The same is applicable to the human communication. When we say *good morning* to another person, we anticipate that we will receive a similar greeting in return. When that does not happen, our expectations are defeated and, again, we become frustrated.

Human life is also a series of choices in an unpredictable world, and the more choices that confront one; the easier it is for that person to become stressed. Ritual fulfills a psychological function for humans as they go through their daily lives by addressing issues of choice. It is predictable and that predictability has a calming effect. It also serves the human psychic by enabling the individual to accurately predict what will happen next and, when it does happen, to feel a certain degree of ego fulfillment and self enhancement by having predicted correctly.

Most our fears can be dealt with through ritual. Young children, for example, engage in certain ritualistic behaviors such as saying certain words, prayers, or stories at bedtime. This fulfills a child's need for routine and structure. A constructive ritual provides the same peace and order to daily routines. The difference between healthy rituals or routines and those that suggest a psychological malady is that a healthy ritual may be interrupted and resumed at pleasure without losing its impact.

Normal routines and rituals have a calming effect on humans by reducing fear. For example, most humans fear loss—of parents, objects, and friends. We overcome this fear through the ritual of collecting be it photographs, rocks, dolls, coins, or baseball cards. A healthy ritual (or hobby) does not interfere with one's ability to function or take up too much time or space; it is a normal human activity utilized to deal with the uncertainty of existence.

Ritual enhances learning by connecting the inner emotional experience of the presenter to that of the audience through a systematized set of words, gestures, and movements. This is accomplished through an understanding of how humans behave when responding to various emotional and real life situations and transferring those observations to the structure of the ritualistic experience. These ritualistic gestures, movements, and words must not, however, be stereotyped or melodramatic, but rather they should be performed in such a manner as to result in an emotional connectivity between the presenter and the audience.

Ritual also serves the interest of the performer. Humans respond to actions more than they do to words. Telling a child to do as you say, not as you do, is not going to produce the behavior you desire. Behavior (ritual) is a much stronger driving force than is simple verbal communication. In conjunction with this, when actions are coupled with words, the learning experience works faster and with better comprehension and retention.

Ritual further serves learning through observation and imitation. Experience is definitely a great and wonderful teacher, but you cannot experience everything yourself. You can, however, observe the actions of others engaged in a ritualistic experience and through that observation learn and imitate.

Psychologists sometime refer to ritual as a form of repetitive behavior engaged in by persons to neutralize or prevent anxiety and to help the human address that which is new, strange, and different. At the same time, and important to Freemasonry, ritual contains content and centrality. It is both a form of communication and a means for both outward communication and inward reflection. Rituals are to be both performed and contemplated. To perform any ritual at its most impressive and instructional, especially on of a Masonic nature, we should understand the symbolization involved and be able to interpret it utilizing our physical and oral skills. The performance and content of the ritual may vary, as it does between Masonic Jurisdictions and, even, Lodges, but that does not reduce the impact or intensity of the ritualistic experience, the centrality of ritual to our Craft, or the ability of those rituals and symbols to link us together through a common belief system and a shared communication experience.

We perform spiritual ceremonies or rituals because they comfort us; because they possess innate power; because they are engaging; because they are familiar; because they teach; because they illustrate; because they reduce anxiety; because they enhance performance; because they require personal involvement; because they make us part of a community; because we receive physical and psychological benefits; and because they have a direct influence upon what comes after as well as our interpretation of what came before. Ritual provides us with a safe place, free from the worries of daily life. It is an anchor line—*a cable's length*. It provides us a link to a sound foundation. For some of us, notes Elizabeth Gilbert in *Eat, Pray, Love*, it helps us fix our own broken down emotional system.

Ritual gives shape and order as well as identity and direction to our lives. Much religious ritual is oriented to the calendar and enables us to celebrate and acknowledge the passage of time. Other religious rituals, communion, for example, link us to our past and, since done with other people, make us part of a larger community. The power of ritual is linked to the number of participants and, as with a wedding or funeral, celebrates life events common to all humanity.

Ritual is not meaningless repetition. Each time a ritual is performed, we discover something new. Each time we participate, we hear a new word, discover a new physical movement, or experience a fresh emotional response. Ritual, like a good play or drama is cathartic: it provides us with an emotional release (sometimes strong). But ritual is not, as some describe it, *mumbo-Jumbo.* It engages us physiologically and psychologically because it enables us to utilize space and time to express ourselves and demonstrate our involvement in the process. It can, however, lose its power if too protracted or too esoteric.

COMFORT, POWER, ENGAGEMENT, FAMILIARITY

Ritual is not easy. It requires dedication, thoughtfulness, and concentration. When engaged in ritual, we are able to shut out the intrusions of daily life and focus on internal rather than external matters. The clear intent is to make us fully aware of the moment and mindful of the situation. Stage fright is a well-documents phenomenon. Even Helen Hayes, the first lady of the theatre, is said to have experienced it. Essentially, however, stage fright or communication apprehension, as it is termed in scholarly circles, is the fear that, for lack of skill or self-control or an accident the actor (ritualist) will show through the part and the aesthetic distance will be lost. The "willing suspension of disbelief" would dissolve. Such fear is overcome, however, through regular practice and review of the ritual and its content as well as its meaning.

A perfectly performed ritual is similar, in emotional response, to a perfectly performed musical composition. The sour note, the misplaced beat, the break in rhythm draws attention away from the intended goal. The perfectly performed composition moves us to transcend the mundane and respond at an emotional and intellectual level. Ritual works in an identical manner: the closer to perfection, the greater the impact of the ceremony.

In some ancient societies, the power of ritual was inherent to its perfection. It was deemed essential to the well-being of the people and the favorable reaction of their gods. In Aztec culture, the exact performance of certain ritual practices, especially that of the drummer, was considered essential to success in warfare. The failure of the drummer to perform exactly led to swift and sure punishment because it was perceived to predict defeat. In a comparable manner, imperfection in the performance of ritual was considered a direct factor when the rains did not come on time or came too forcefully; when the animals necessary to survival disappeared; or when the illness did not abate after treatment by the priest or shaman. Even in the Christian faith, the failure to perform a ritual correctly—a marriage ceremony, for example—is perceived by some as rendering the outcome invalid.

Ritual is most comfortable when we have mastered it. The mastery of ritual is directly related to our personal concept of accomplishment and well-being. We strive for perfection, though we settle for excellence or less. We are not perfect creatures, but when we perform ritual in a proper manner and are fully confident in our performance, our level of comfort increases. This level of comfort is transmitted to other participants as well as to spectators and becomes an expression of the power of the performance. When great actors appear on stage, their confidence in their performance contributes to the willing suspension of disbelief and enables the audience to participate in the dramatic event to the fullest extent. So, it is with ritual, the more confident the ritualist, the more compelling the ritual.

Ritual is familiar, and that familiarity adds to its comfort level. Ritual is predictable whereas the world around us is chaotic. When an individual leaves for work in the morning there is an unpredictable aspect to both the journey and all probable future events which may be discomforting. With ritual, we know what is coming. It is not a surprise. It does not change and, while change may be the one constant in life, it is disconcerting. Through ritual we neutralize anxiety.

ENGAGING, TEACHING, PERSONAL INVOLVEMENT

Ritual requires us to participate either directly as an actor or indirectly as an observer. In both roles, we are engaged in the event. As in sports, both the player and the spectator participate in the game and, in turn, in the win or loss. For both the participant and the observer of ritual, there is a type of mystical inspiration. It is a shared experience. The level of involvement determines the degree to which the observer partakes of the experience.

There are many motives for engaging in ritual: eustress (positive stress), escape, entertainment, group affiliation, self-esteem, and, even, peer pressure as well as family needs. In ancient times, we lived in relatively small groups or tribes. The leaders—performers of ritual—were representative of *the people*, and the performance of ritual was perceived to be directly related to future events. In the modern world, ritual enables the observer and participant to feel a deep emotional response in a protected, safe environment in which there may be no real-world consequences. It gives us something that we can value without requiring from most of us too much overt physical or mental action.

Ritual serves a distinct teaching function. In Masonry, we learn the signs, symbols, allegories, tokens, and the meaning of the Craft through various degrees and Lodge ritual. This learning is enriched by our physical performance during the ritual. Learning through a single sense—hearing—is possible, but it is enriched when pictures and action are added to the words. As a young surveyor, the author memorized the various geometrical theorems and trigonometric functions. But he did not fully understand them until he went into the field with a survey crew and made practical application of that information. That practical application—the doing—enhanced and completed the learning experience as well as the understanding of the mathematical equations. Ritual functions in a comparable manner.

COMMUNITY AND RENEWAL

Ritual is an organized communication performance within a shared experience. It is repeated on a regular basis. It is familiar and routine. Ritual is important because it provides for a renewal of our shared or common experiences and gives legitimacy to what we are doing. In a very real way, ritual makes us free men while enabling us to interact with others.

Ritual helps us remember, renew, and refresh. Repeated tasks help us do our jobs; engage with family, friends, community, and strangers; and participate more fully in a social setting. Ritual is storytelling at its most sincere, austere, and complete. Consider the rituals of the three degrees of Freemasonry as an example. They tell a complete story—the allegory of the building of King Solomon's temple and Hiram Abiff. They refresh for us the meaning of power and personal strength as they orient the newcomer to our organization while they reaffirm for all the meaning of their involvement. Further, our ritual introduces and refreshes our sense of group identity as it teaches us the courtesies and obligations of our Craft. It also teaches us the culture of the organization by enabling us to *learn the ropes* through a series of performances. Although this may be accomplished by direct instruction, engagement in ritual enables us to interpret the event in terms of the organizational perspective—to be part of the group. Ritual, therefore, contributes directly to understanding the cultural meaning of Freemasonry.

Ritual utilizes symbolic acts which involve speech and language as well as various methods of nonverbal symbolization. All of these play a direct part in the human response we call "life": the better the ritual, the better the response and, in turn, the better the quality of meaning, understanding, and life.

SOLEMNITY OF RITUAL AND DEGREE WORK IN THE LODGE

Joseph Campbell notes that ritual is meant to convey an inner reality, though it is now, for many, merely form. Society without ritual, he suggests, lacks the method to introduce the young into the tribe. Children in order to function rationally in society need to be twice born, notes Campbell. Masonic ritual serves that exact function.

Ritual or degree work in the Lodge is an essential element of Freemasonry. It takes the man from the outside world—the profane—and transforms him into a Brother, a Freemason. Our ritual is designed to impact directly on the inner life of the candidates and brothers. It is not an empty, meaningless ceremony and should not be treated as such. Thus, there is no place for mirth in our ritual. There is evidence in ancient records and charges of some level of frivolity in Masonic Lodges, but by the early 1700s and the establishment of modern Freemasonry, that type of behavior is specifically addressed and prohibited. Tricks, jokes, gestures, even side-line whispering are strongly discouraged. The focal point of all our work is the *Holy Bible* and, as such, it deserves our respect as it serves to temper our actions.

Along with the issue of frivolity or mirth during ritual arises the issue of applause. Nothing that a Brother does during the ritual merits applause. The candidate has come to us of his own free will and accord and we, in turn, are welcoming him to our fellowship with a specific time assigned at the end of the Communication for more personal expression. The same admonition applies to applause for the ritual and degree team. There is ample opportunity within the Closing for the team to be properly recognized for work well done. To engage in applause during ritual or exemplification destroys the illusion and significantly reduces the impact of the event on all involved, especially those at its focus—the candidates or Brothers. Our degrees are an allegory of good and evil, of life itself. Death is prominent throughout the Third Degree and specifically referenced in the First Degree. Applause in our ritual is no more appropriate than would be applause during a religious service or a funeral. Ritual is intended to speak directly to the inner life of the candidate. All outward incursions impede that intent. Should levity, mirth, or applause interrupt or disturb the fellowship and working of our ritual, its intent is destroyed and those involved "simply miss the point."

DECORUM

Decorum refers to the proper or appropriate style for a presentation or ritual. It is a proper or right social behavior fitting to the situation. It is a standard of behavior as well as a as an adherence to proper procedure. It includes not only correct or proper behavior but also a certain level of dignity in both speech and dress. Decorum is essential for the proper performance of ritual. In Freemasonry, proper decorum is not something to be determined by the individual Brother according to his own tastes. It manifests itself by showing respect for the Craft, and it is a courtesy to the Brethren. *The Regius Manuscript* or poem, which dates from the late fourteenth century, as well as succeeding constitutions and charges, required those who were *made a Mason* to pay due respect to the Craft through their proper behavior and appropriate dress.

How a person dresses is a significant factor in the establishment of first impressions. It is the right of the individual to dress and live as he pleases so long as he does not infringe on the rights of others. Freemasonry, however, is a collective effort and, like a sports team, standards of dress are not inappropriate. Based on the photographic record present in most modern Lodges, Brethren in the nineteenth and first half of the twentieth centuries exercised a high standard of dress in the Lodge—Sunday best, if you will. During Masonic ritual, especially degree work, it enhances the overall experience when an elevated standard of dress is maintained. The general rule, outside the United States, is that a dark suit and appropriate tie are required. Attendance at Lodge should be as special as attendance at a wedding or a church service. Why dress differently for Lodge than you would to attend your house of worship? The question a Mason should ask himself is this: "In terms of showing reverence and respect for the Craft, is that my best, and is that what my best should be?"[20]

We should also consider that appropriate dress *sets the stage* and strengthens the ritualistic experience as it solemnizes and honors the experience. Consider a priest at Mass: would the service have the same impact if he was not wearing liturgical vestments? Military chaplains, even in combat zones, strive to maintain some level of appropriate, liturgical dress to formalize and solemnize the ritual. The author often observed chaplains, Catholic and Episcopal, in chasuble and stole standing on muddy firebases in Vietnam bringing comfort to soldiers. And those same priests always wore a stole, muddy at times, when giving Last Rites during a firefight. Part of the comfort offered came from the soldier recognizing the priest by the clothes (vestments) he wore. Those vestments were what set him slightly outside the profane and the reality of the moment. Appropriate attire, especially for degree teams, can accomplish the same.

Essential to proper decorum in the Lodge is the minimization of whispering or talking on the side lines. The focus should be on the work (ritual) and the degree candidate. Verbal and even non-verbal interjection serve only to disrupt and disturb the intent of the ritual. The same goes for prompting. Even the greatest, most professional theatres have a designated prompter. So should our Lodges. It should be that prompter alone who assists with the ritual and then only upon request prearranged through specific predetermined signals. Extraneous or multiple prompts serve only to reduce the importance and impact of degree work and ritual.

PACING, REPETITION, MEMORIZATION, PRACTICE, AND FOCUS

Great musical compositions have much in common, but especially rhythm or pacing. It is the rhythm that enhances the emotional response as is suggested in the lecture for the Fellow Craft Degree. Rhythm can impact directly upon human psychology and, through a pattern of regular or irregular beats, make for either a strong or weak response. Rhythm is the pattern of the flow of both sound and action in ritual. The proper use of rhythm serves to enhance the ritualistic experience as it enables the brain to more fully comprehend the situation through a pattern of regular stresses. It also serves to facilitate memorization.

Ritual is by its nature repetitive. Repetition is the most intuitive learning technique and is documented in both Chinese and Egyptian records dating to 3,000 B.C.E. or before. It requires us to do the same thing several times in the same way. In teaching, an ancient maxim is to say and/or do the same thing three times and so it is with our ritual. This repetition not only provides for better retention but it also marks those parts of our work which are to be remembered. Repetition enables us to efficiently store information and guides to action in our memory. Repetition strengthens skill at both the conscious and subconscious level. When a skill has been set through repetition—riding a bike—it is possible to quickly recover that skill at a later date.

The majority of rote learning is based on repetition but repetition alone does not lead directly to understanding, it is the first step. We memorized the letters of the alphabet and then used them to form words and sentences to express our thoughts. We memorized the *rules of the road* to pass the driving test and then formalized that learning through practice. In the military, one memorizes the functions of his weapon so that, when in combat, he does not have to "think" but is enabled to instinctively lock, load, fire, and reload. Memorization facilitates the human experience by removing the necessity to think about and analyze each individual step or function. *Practice makes perfect* goes the old saying. It is true. Professional golfers hit thousands of balls each week on the range to perfect their game. Professional football quarterbacks throw thousands of passes, often at moving targets, to strengthen their arms and to hone their delivery. Masonic ritual requires the same type of practice, probably not as intense or extensive, but never-the-less it is essential to the proper performance of ritual and the ritualistic experience.

Finally, focus is essential to successful ritual. A great actor is able to focus his attention on his performance thus shutting out the audience and its responses. Most great actors tell us that, once on the stage, they do not see the audience. The same happens for great athletes, they are able to focus on the game and their performance, thus excluding from their perception distracting, outside events and people. Think about the basketball player who is about to shoot a free throw. He prepares to shoot facing the spectators, some of whom may be hostile to his intent. His successful performance depends upon his ability to focus. Proper performance of Masonic ritual requires no less. We should focus on the ritual, on our work, on the candidate, and on our experience thus shutting out external events.

TEACHING RITUAL

Ritual is often perceived as incredibly difficult, but it can be taught whether it is the public rituals of church and state, or the private rituals of families and fraternities; and since ritual makes people feel their group solidarity, it is best taught to groups. Yet, ritual must to be taught with a level of mind-body interdependence unusual to most education settings. You cannot teach ritual sitting down nor can you teach ritual from books. Anciently, ritual was exclusively oral and physical and is still very much so.

In ritual, action holds the most prominent place. Details are important with repetition and redundancy essential. Ritual is for the five senses. It is a way of articulating ideas that enables us to connect content and action as it deepens understanding. When ritual is properly taught, it permits the members of the group to pass their traditions to future generations because it requires a significant level of rehearsal of those doctrines which aids memory and understanding as it motivates participation.

MAIMONIDES' PARABLE

A wise ruler of a very large empire erected a magnificent palace of immeasurable dimensions and extraordinary architecture. He gathered around him assistants qualified to produce the work and provided them with the high-quality instruments to pursue their labors. This magnificent structure, though not of ordinary construction, was pleasing to the eye and served its purpose. It was durable and functional—it inculcated the mysteries of the kingdom to its subjects. From outside it was perplexing, but from within it was full of light, knowledge, and coherence.

There were those in the country, especially wise men skilled in architecture, who were offended by its very structure. It had few windows and it was not easy to gain entrance. The doors did not seem well placed, and the gates were guarded. These learned men could not grasp that each apartment received its light, as did the whole, not from without but from above. They could not comprehend that those summoned to the palace went of their own free will and that the entrance provided them with the surest route to their objective.

Accordingly, these wise men explained the words, symbols, and architecture as they saw them according to their preconceived ideas of the plan. They paid no heed to those who worked within the palace and had neither the time nor the inclination to discuss with them the plan, even denouncing those who supported the edifice as despoilers of the palace itself.

One terrible night, the night watchman called "Fire! Fire!" and everyone leapt from their beds scurrying through the darkness squabbling with each other about how best to save the edifice. Each said that they had the proper plan to save the palace based on his experience and expertise. But none sought to find a bucket of water to throw on the reported flames. If there had, in fact, been a fire, the palace would have lain in ruins at dawn, but the watchman was wrong. He had mistaken the northern lights for a conflagration and the flowing interior light confused the experts. What each quibbler failed to acknowledge or accept was that the great and wise ruler had built his magnificent palace on a sound foundation based on ancient plans give him by his ancestors and that it was infused with interior not exterior light.

True Freemasonry strives to promote brotherly love and affection, and it exemplifies these attributes through its ritual. Masonry provides light through rituals which represent the letter and the spirit of the Craft's ancient beliefs. It ceaselessly strives to promote human brotherhood and is inevitably put at risk when social, political, or religious divisions are permitted to intrude. Freemasonry is not dogmatic and through figurative language endeavors to illustrate and amplify that which is self-evident. Freemasonry has its riddles and paradoxes that often seems to use ellipsis and aposiopesis to deny the casual viewer a definitive statement or definition. Our ritual fills those ellipsis and aposiopesis not with words but through action with meaning.

The Lodge is to Freemasonry what the church edifice is to religion. No conclusions should be drawn from the external prosperity or inner trappings of a church building as to the faith of its members. Sometimes the two do not go together. It is the internal, not the external which has enabled Freemasonry to survive and even prosper for more than 500 years. Ritual is the single most important aspect of our observance of the Craft. Human history has been enriched through the extensive use of ritual by all societies. Ritual appeals to us because it provides us with a window into our shared culture. It is central to both religious and secular society because it generates an emotional response and because it is understandable. It is a physical manifestation of an internal, emotional experience.

Ritual appeals to us because it is experiential and analytical. It engulfs the total person, transporting him into another mode of existence. It has persuasive, even mystical power, and is filled with extraordinary personalities. It enables us to do what we are thinking about, and, at the same time, reflect more fully upon the experience. Masonic ritual enables us to understand our symbols and history. It may be *scary* to some and misunderstood by others, but proper performance and appreciation of our ritual serves to facilitate full development of the Symbolic Lodge and the Brotherhood. It was our ritual that attracted great and learned men to Freemasonry in the seventeenth, eighteenth, nineteenth, and twentieth centuries, and it serves the same purpose today.

In 1986 and 1987 Bill Moyers interviewed Joseph Campbell for the PBS series *The Power of Myth.* Part of their discussion focused on the Great Seal of the United States. Moyers asked Campbell: "Aren't a lot of these Masonic Symbols?" Campbell replied: "They are Masonic signs." What followed is here noted. Moyers: "What explains the relationship between these symbols and the Masons, and the fact that so many of these founding fathers belonged to the Masonic order?" Campbell: *"This [Masonry] is a scholarly attempt to reconstruct an order of initiation that would result in spiritual revelation"* (emphasis by author). Moyers: "So when these men talked about the eye of God being reason, they were saying that the ground of our being as a society, as a culture, as a people, derives from the fundamental nature of the universe?" Campbell: "That's what this first pyramid says. This is the pyramid of the world, and this is the pyramid of our society, and they are of the order. This is God's creation, and this is our society."[21]

Earlier in the same interview, Campbell states "If you want to find out what it means to have a society without rituals, read the New York *Times. . .* destructive and violent acts by young people who don't know how to behave in a civilized society." Moyers responds, "Society has provided them no rituals by which they become members . . . of the community."[22] Freemasonry provides ritual and thus a firm foundation for our society as it transmits our values and customs through a succession of ages.

Ultimately, man can adapt himself to anything, but he cannot deal with chaos. Ritual is order and normality. One of the most important assets of Freemasonry is that symbolic ritual which orients our nature on earth by what we do. It reduces chaos and enables us to explain and demonstrate things which cry out for enlightenment. It is the foundation not only of our Craft but also of our very existence.

NOTES

1. Steven Lukes. *Emile Durkheim: His Life and Work: A Historical and Critical Study* (New York: Penguin, 1977), pp. 471.

2. Henri Hurbert & Marcel Mauss, *Sacrifice: Its Nature and Functions* [1898], trans. W.D. Hall (Chicago: University of Chicago, 1964), pp. 8-9.

3. Robert Segal. "The Myth-Ritualist Theory of Religion" in *Journal for the Scientific Study of Religion 19, No. 2, 1980,* pp. 173-185.

4. Julian. Huxley. "A Discussion on Ritualization of Behavior in Animals and Man" in *Philosophical Transactions of the Royal Society,* series B, 251, 1966, pp. 247-525.

5. Susanne Langer, *Philosophy in a New Key* (Cambridge, MA: Harvard University Press, 1942), 26.

6. Stephen Littlejohn, *Theories of Human Communication* (Columbus, OH: Charles E. Merrill Publishing Company, 1978), pp. 68-72.

7. Hugh Duncan, *Symbols in Society* (New York: Oxford University Press, 1968), p. 60.

8. Duncan, p. 60.

9. Clifford Geertz, *The Interpretation of Cultures: Selected Essays by Clifford Geert* New York: Basic Books 1973), p. 90.

10. Francis Bacon, *The Advancement of Learning,* edited by G.W Kitchin (Philadelphia, Paul Dry Books, 2001), pp. 132-133.

11. Arthur Melzer, *Philosophy between the Lines: The Lost History of Exoteric Writing,* (Chicago: The University of Chicago Press, 2014), p. 16.

12. Melzer, 16.

13. Melzer, 17.

14. Reinhart Kossellec, *Critique and Crisis: Enlightenment and the Pathogenesis of Modern Society* (Oxford, UK: Berg, 1988), p. 62.

15. Isadore Twersky (ed.), *Miishnab Torah, Bkk. 1,* in *A Maimonides Reader* (New York: Behrman House, 1972), p. 47.

16. Melzer, *Philosophy Between the Lines,* p. 167.

17. R.W. Dyson (ed.), *Augustine: The City of God against the Pagans.* (Cambridge UK: Cambridge University Press, 1998), p. 960.

18. Plato, *The Laws of Plato,* Thomas Pangle (trans.). (Chicago: The University of Chicago Press, 1980), p. 194.

19. Melzer, *Philosophy Between the Lines,* p. 190.

20. Andrew Hammer. O*bserving the Craft: The Pursuit of Excellence in Masonic Labor and Observance.* (San Francisco, CA: Mindhive Books, 2012), p. 85.

21. Joseph Campbell, *The Power of Myth.* (New York: Anchor Books, 1991), p. 38.

22. Campbell, p. 9.

Chapter Eight

Education

A Bold Imaginative Experience through the Liberal Arts

The Masonic life is symbolically described as a journey from west to east in search of intellectual and spiritual light. This journey requires not one but two distinct paths: one moral or spiritual, the other educational or intellectual. This is the result of a common misunderstanding of the ultimate objective—understanding. Both science (the intellectual mechanism) and religion (the spiritual mechanism) seek the same thing: an understanding of the totality of existence; a final definition of reality, the universe, and man's place in it.

In the oldest literature of Assyria (abt. 1300 B.C.E.), we find evidence of this spiritual quest. A half millennium later it is obvious in Pythagoras' search for the *meaning of life* through the divine understanding of numbers and their relationships, and two millennia after Pythagoras, Galileo, Pascal and Leibnitz echo him as they refer to mathematics as the *speech of God.* This search for the ultimate answer, the final authority, had as its most powerful impetus the search not only for the divinity, but also for the very nature of man—the meaning of life.

In the late seventeenth century, three English Protestants laid the foundations for physics, psychology, and biology as part of this spiritual quest. Isaac Newton saw God's speech in the great laws of physics and celestial gravitation. John Locke defined the self, theorized that the mind was a blank slate, and that knowledge is obtained logically through the senses and our perceptions of reality. And John Ray, a minister with no pulpit who is considered the father of English natural history, classified plants according to similarities and differences that emerged from observation thus advancing scientific empiricism. In this search for natural history, the perfection of the Divine Creator was deemed both obvious and benevolent.

But while most contemporary scientific and spiritual movements tend to make rear focused allusions telling us what *has* gone wrong and even hinting at some unbounded previous catastrophe, the Masonic quest looks forward. We endeavor to make good men better by looking to the future. We emphasize a stability and firmness of principle to fully discover ourselves and the world in which we live.

In the second or Fellow Craft Degree, the intellectual part of this quest is explained in terms of the liberal arts, the five senses, and the orders of architecture. The liberal arts, often considered synonymous with the introductory courses in the university curriculum, provide us with the foundation necessary to our intellectual quest. The five senses, as Locke noted, provide us with the information essential to the final objective—understanding--and the five orders of architecture speak to the orderliness of the quest as well as to the artistic and creative potential of man.

Anciently, the liberal arts (*artes liberales*) were considered the essential skills required for a free person--a citizen--to participate in public life. These arts made the citizen truly a *free man.* In modern times, the term most often refers to the disciplines of literature, language, philosophy, history and mathematics, as well as to the social and biological sciences.

In the classical world, the liberal arts were divided into the *Trivium* and the *Quadrivium*.

The *Trivium* included grammar, logic (also named dialectic), and rhetoric. The *Quadrivium* included arithmetic, geometry, music, and astronomy. Arithmetic and geometry along with trigonometry and other numerically based studies now fall under the rubric of mathematics, and astronomy, now based on observable, replicable science, was anciently known as astrology and included the auguries of that pseudo-science. Let us take a closer look, however, at the liberal arts and consider them as an experience essential to reaching the Masonic goal of enlightenment.

The first goal of the liberal arts is to give the individual the ability to reason well and to recognize when reason and evidence are not enough. The liberal arts give us the ability to be creative—to connect two previously unconnected concepts in a new and novel way or to find a previously unknown connection between already joined concepts. They encourage in us serendipity and analysis. The key to reason is to recognize fully when more evidence is needed.

Grammar enables us to read, write, and speak with some level of distinction and style. Reading the words alone is not sufficient to knowledge. Writing simple sentences does not create understanding on the part of the reader because it does not sufficiently express the thoughts of the author. Simply speaking words does not make one a great orator. Grammar is the set of structural rules that govern the way in which we speak and write. It consists of morphology, syntax, and phonology as well as phonetics, semantics, pragmatics, spelling, and punctuation. Grammar is the rules which make understanding and communication possible. Properly constructed language enables us to engage in probing analysis by enabling the mind to synthesize the information inherent in the written or spoken word. It is the key to understanding human communication which enables us to function in a societal framework, and it governs our thought process. *It is the primary skill which renders us truly human.*

George Herbert Mead, a social psychologist, contended that mind, self, and society are one—the social act—and that communication—the use of grammar—was part of that act. He described humans as far advanced creatures capable of rational thought. It is through language—significant symbols—Meade suggests, that man sees himself as others see him and, in turn, the individual internalizes these perceptions and structures his behavior to be consistent with them. The structure of our brains directly impacts on our perceptions and the grammatical structures of our language. Language may be created within the individual in terms of how an object is identified, but for that definition to be shared, it must be placed into an agreed upon grammatical structure.

Rhetoric or dialectic refers to the reasoned use of dialogue and the *art* of logical discussion. It is the ability to communicate effectively with appeal and impact. From ancient times, rhetoric has been valued in direct relation to its involvement in the political forum. The purpose of rhetoric is to *find the truth.* It requires not only that the speaker *speaks well,* but that the audience *listens well.* One of the oldest manifestations of rhetoric may be found in the Socratic Method which tests beliefs through questions as it examines the structure and reason behind the belief or idea. Rhetoric focuses not just on persuasion but also on truth seeking and requires that the audience reflect critically on the topic. Rhetoric, when properly and effectively used, can and does change opinions.

Propaganda is part of rhetoric but is most often examined as a threat to human society. It is, in fact, an objective human phenomenon which employs rhetorical tools to impact on public opinion (tendency to an action). Education employs propaganda as part of its tool-kit, but the issue arises as to how to differentiate falsehoods propounded through propaganda from truths propounded through education. Essentially, this is done through the human capacity to evaluate the propagandists—to reason. Who is he? What are his organizations, occupation, political position, prior statements, prejudices, and the like? What are his background, education, experience, and personality? What are his resources and his objectives? Can the listener, through deliberation and reflection, discern intentions and possible unforeseen consequences? For propaganda, is the message disseminated through media and, if so, what is the nature and agenda of that media? What are the underlying themes as determined through an analysis of frequency of usage and prominence of wording? Is the message received or perceived? What is learned, relearned, unlearned, or not learned? Rhetoric is intended to persuade; not to propagandize in the negative sense.

The liberal arts help us understand and utilize numerical data. This enables us to make sophisticated responses to arguments and positions which depend upon such information. Mathematics introduces us to risk, instability, orders of magnitude, confidence levels, and uncertainty. They give us the ability to grasp and analyze the information presented in a logical manner—not being deceived by appearances. Much in the modern world is expressed in mathematical terms and, without the ability to understand and analyze the propositions presented, we are unable to determine if the conclusions (or answers) are valid. There is a common saying in mathematics: *anything can be proven by the manipulation of numbers* especially when the audience lacks the basic computational skills implied in this part of the liberal arts. Even though the original Liberal Arts classified arithmetic, geometry, and astronomy into separate classes, an overview of the subject suggests that they are interrelated.

For Freemasons, both geometry and astronomy hold special significance. Geometry treats the magnitude, shape, size, position, and properties of space. The word comes from the Greek *geo* meaning earth and *metron* meaning measurement. It is the foundation of our Craft. As an academic study, it dates to at least the sixth century B.C.E. and by the third century B.C.E. it was a well-established part of the curriculum. Its practical applications far precede its study as is evidenced in such architectural marvels as the Great Pyramid of Giza, the Temple of Artemis at Ephesus, the Statue of Zeus at Olympia, the Mausoleum of Halicarnassus (destroyed by earthquakes between the twelfth and fifteenth centuries), the Colossus of Rhodes, and the Lighthouse at Alexander (felled first in 1303 with destruction completed in 1480). Archimedes used geometry to calculate areas and volume by displacement. "When I get into a tub," he reasoned, "water comes out. There must be a relationship between that outflow and the size of my body." He extended that observation as well as the importance of scientific control to the *case of the two crowns.* The king had a new crown. It looked like gold, it felt like gold, but was it gold? Archimedes solved the problem by obtaining a piece of gold and a piece of silver with the same mass. He placed the gold into a container of water and measured the outflow. He did the same with the silver. Both metals had the same weight, but silver, being less dense than gold, had a larger volume. Subsequently, Archimedes obtained a piece of pure gold of the same weight as the crown and placed both into water, one at a time. The crown displaced more water than the gold thus enabling him to rule that the king had been cheated.

Practically, geometry enables engineers to survey, measure, construct, evaluate, and create. Relationships common to circles, triangles, cylinders, spheres, and pyramids are demonstrated. It further provides evidence of the relationship between points, lines, and planes. Geometry is at the same time a function of numbers. Numbers provide coordinates as well as data about size, and through numbers, geometric shapes may be realized and analyzed by using their algebraic representation. Anciently, the focus of geometry was on relative position and spatial relationships. Modern geometry expanded the understanding of nature by demonstrating that Euclidean space is only one possibility and contributed directly to the development of Einstein's general theory of relativity. Geometry further considers the properties of dimension and symmetry. Symmetry is emblematical of the principle of duality in which points and planes meet with, lie within, and contain each other. Symmetry is classical Euclidean geometry of congruence and motion. It transforms straight lines into curves and suggests the duality of existence—space and time.

Astronomy is a natural science and possibly the first science known to man. The oldest known star chart is carved in Mammoth ivory dated to about 30,000 B.C.E. It is a drawing of what scholars accept to be the constellation Orion known in the ancient world as the heavenly shepherd. Also dating to about the same period is a drawing of the Pleiades found in the Lascaux caves in France. The Nebra sky disk, found in Germany, dates to the Bronze Age about 1600 B.C.E and is considered the oldest concrete depiction of the cosmos. Astronomy is the law or culture of the stars. It is the study of celestial objects, their physics, chemistry, evolution, and phenomena. It includes celestial navigation, chronology, and astrophysics. Its earliest manifestation was in observation of motions of celestial objects using the naked eye. It is found in all ancient civilizations including Mesopotamia, Greece, India, China, Egypt, and Central America. The earth, in these ancient cosmologies, was at the center of the universe. One of the earliest and most important astronomical discoveries was made by the Babylonians who, using mathematical and observational astronomy, noted that lunar eclipses occurred in a set cycle which repeated itself.

Until the later middle ages, the study of astronomy, hidden deep in astrology (a pseudoscience) was stagnant throughout Europe though it did flourish in the Islamic world. The Catholic Church in Europe contributed financially to the advancement of astronomy during this period, but the focus was on using the science to establish not the situation of the stars or the size or shape of the earth but the date of Easter.

During the Renaissance, Copernicus proposed the heliocentric solar system. His work was confirmed by Tycho Brahe, Galileo Galilei, and Johannes Kepler. For Copernicus, the Catholic Church was mainly silent. The main

condemnation of his work came from Martin Luther in his *Tischreden* or
T*able Talk Diary* when he wrote:

> There is talk of a new astronomer who wants to prove that the earth moves and
> goes around instead of the sky, the sun, the moon, just as if somebody were
> moving a carriage or shop might hold that he was sitting still and at rest while
> the earth and the trees walk and moved. But that is how things are nowadays:
> when a man wishes to be clever he must needs invent something special, and
> the way he does it most needs be best! The fool wants us to turn the whole art
> of astronomy upside-down. However, as Holy Scripture tells us, so did Joshua
> bid the sun to stand still and not the earth. [1]

And though Luther referred to Copernicus as "a fool who went against
Holy Writ," the general response to his theory was indecisive and the Catholic Church remained hostile but generally silent. The principle responses to
Copernicus came from Protestant theologians who, utilizing conventional
methods including conversations and sermons, organized essentially an anti-
Copernican campaign. It was Galileo, some 90 years later, was tried and
condemned by the Roman Catholic Inquisition which declared heliocentrism
heretical. On February 24, 1616, the Qualifiers speaking for the Church
unanimously held that the idea that the sun is stationary is "foolish and
absurd." And while Copernicus' works were not banned outright because of
their usefulness in setting calendars and establishing the date of Easter, Galileo's writings supporting Copernicus were condemned and banned. By 1758
the Catholic Church had dropped its general ban on teaching heliocentrism
and in 1835 Copernicus' *De Revolutionibus* and Galileo's *Dialogue* were
removed from the *Index Librorum Prohibitorum* or List of Prohibited Books.
In 1992, the Catholic Church finally vindicated Galileo noting "The error of
the theologians of the time, when they maintained the centrality of the Earth,
was to think that our understanding of the physical world's structure was, in
some way, imposed by the literal sense of Sacred Scriptures."[2]

Astronomy, speculative and scientific, has not answered, nor may it ever
answer, all the questions posed about the nature of the universe such as what
is its origin and nature of stellar mass? Is there life elsewhere in the universe?
What caused the universe to form and how does this impact on its demise?
What is dark matter and dark energy? What are black holes and how do they
relate to the formation and destruction of galaxies? And ultimately is the
universe eternal? It does, however, address the logic of universal structure
and attempts to provide understanding of the evolution of the heavens.
Astronomy has also contributed to the study of ancient cultures through
archeology, and anthropology. It works with the biological sciences to answer questions about the creation and evolution of biological systems in the
universe as well as on earth. Forensic astronomy utilizes astronomical methodology to solve problems proposed by law and history. Astrostatistics at-

tempts to analyze the vast amount of data available and to apply that analysis it to predict the future.

The sixth of the classical Liberal and Sciences is music or the study of sound which through pitch, melody, harmony, rhythm, meter, articulation, and the dynamic qualities of timber and texture impart meaning and impact upon emotions. Flutes—musical instruments—are among the oldest artifacts of human existence dating back 40,000 years or more. The ancient civilizations of the Indus valley display musical traditions, and the earliest and largest collection of musical instruments was found in China and dates to about 7000 B.C.E. The oldest notational music comes from Amorite city of Ugarit dating to approximately 1400 B.C.E. In ancient Egypt, the god Thoth was credited with the invention of music and harps, flutes and cymbals, and a form of clarinet that was dated to the Old Kingdom period. Genesis 4:21 identifies Jubal, seven generations removed from Adam, as the founder of music. His half brothers and sister created other mysteries or sciences: Jabel—husbandry and herding; Tubal Cain, metal work; and Naamah, weaving and cloth work (see Chapter I and the Legend of Noah). While the first five books of the Old Testament are virtually silent on the utilization of music in Jewish life and religion, I Samuel suggests the use of large, organized, trained musicians and choirs, and Amos is written with audience response as part of the rhetorical scheme with the figure Amos providing Yahweh's responses and admonitions to the peoples' questions—see Amos 6, 7 and 8. This is similar to the *sing out* camp meeting style popularized during the nineteenth and early twentieth centuries in the United States wherein the pastor or preacher *sang out* the words line by line to be followed by the congregation.

By the twentieth and twenty-first centuries, the impact and place of music in daily life had vastly increased, especially with the introduction of modern sound reproduction technology. Phonographs led the way followed quickly by movies, radio, television, and the internet. New rhythms became common with improvisation, syncopation, and other innovations leading to a fusion of styles and forms of expression. Basic to the philosophy and study of music, however are simple questions. How do we define music? What is the relationship between music, mind, and emotions? What does music reveal to us about the world and about ourselves? How does music communicate? Does music have meaning and how does that meaning relate to human life?

Music is a mathematical phenomenon with cosmological dimensions. It is about hearing and experiencing; about beauty and enjoyment; about sensory perception and revelation. It also delves into feelings and responses; excitement and exaltation; sadness and bewilderment. The central theme of music is its ability to express and excite human emotions. Music effects not only our emotions, but also our intellect and psychology. "It wraps us in melancholy and elevates us joy; it dissolves and inflames; it melts us with tenderness and excites us to war." Yet, "through its powerful charms the most discordant passions may be harmonized and brought into perfect unison." Plato in *The Republic* states that music has a direct effect upon the soul. It is an investigation of human skill, creativity, intelligence, psychology, and social behavior. It is lyrical and harmonic; it is hypnotic and emotive; it is playful and colorful; but above all it is a human expression of an inward condition. In music, each note has its distinctive message.

As humans, we must understand our history and the consequences of past actions as well as the uncertainty of human society. The more sophisticated our understanding of our past, the better prepared we are to deal with the complexity, ambiguity, and uncertainty of the present and the future. This is the intractable condition of human society. George Santayana wrote: "A man is morally free when, in full possession of his living humanity, he judges the world, and judges other men, with uncompromising sincerity."[3] He also wrote: ""Those who cannot remember the past are condemned to repeat it."[4] An understanding of our history—not just names, dates and events, but outcomes and long-term consequences—is essential to the full and productive public life of a free man.

What would the world be without the arts, letters, and sciences? Thomas Hobbes in *Leviathan* wrote:

> Nature hath made man so equal in the facilities of body and mind . . . and as to the faculties of the mind . . . I find yet a greater equality amongst men than that of strength . . . Hereby it is manifest that during the time men live without a common power to keep them all in awe, they are in that condition which is called war; and such a war as is of every man against every man . . . no knowledge of the face of the earth; no account of time; no arts; no letters; no society; and which is worst of all, continual fear, and danger of violent death; and life of man, solitary, poor, nasty, brutish, and short. . . Reason suggesteth convenient articles of peace upon which men may be drawn to agreement. These articles are they which otherwise are called the laws of nature. [5]

These laws become known to man through the liberal arts experience.

When man emerged from what Kant referred to as his *nicht alt* or *nonage* during the 17th century (which also saw the beginning of what we now commonly call Freemasonry), a new spirit permeated his thoughts. It was this spirt which led thinkers and philosophers in Europe and America to question every given from the past. In politics, religion, science, art, learning, even in government, new forms of thought were developed and new skepticisms appeared. This was, as the Germans called it, *Aufklarung* which translated perfectly into the English word *enlightenment*. It was a time in which the liberal arts impacted directly on human culture in the West.

The liberal arts imply, but do not explicitly state, that an understanding of the scientific method is essential to the individual's grasp of the reality of the world in which he exists. The use of the scientific method enables the individual to explain what he observes. It uses a system of techniques for investigating phenomena, acquiring new knowledge, correcting previous information, and integrating new observations with those previously made. It is based on empirical and measurable evidence, and is subject to repetition and confirmation. It has characterized the study of natural science since the seventeenth century. An individual using the scientific method seeks to let reality speak for itself and allows it to either support or disprove the proposition.

Francis Bacon (1561-1616) proclaimed the basic tenets of science which led to the understanding of the interrelation of all natural phenomena. His writings created a link between nature and science. He turned man outward to the stars and inward to the molecule. Although his association with and direct influence on Freemasonry is in doubt, Bacon is credited with being the first person to illuminate the scientific method and to use it to solve problems. Some authors have claimed that he was initiated and an active speculative Mason, but there are no known records except the spurious link made by Christoph Nicolai who wrote that Bacon had possibly read some writings of John Andrea, the founder of Rosicrucianism, and that his ideas heavily influenced Elias Ashmole.

The scientific method requires that the researcher observe some aspect of the universe; hypothesize an explanation of that observation; use this explanation to make predictions; test those predictions through experiments; repeat steps three and four until all discrepancies have been controlled; and report the results. A common criticism of the method is that it does not accommodate for those things which cannot be proved through observation and experimentation. This is a misrepresentation of the method. When a theory is adopted or accepted, it is done so because it has correctly explained the phenomena observed, but it is constantly in the mind of the researcher that old theories may fail, that new experiments may be developed, and that different observations may be made. The scientific method is not an issue of faith and does not present a single, incorruptible explanation: it is always open to its own analysis. Finally, the scientific method is cross-cultural. The method provides a theory of gravitational forces that apply equally to all. Jump and it is verified.

Throughout history science has served to enhance and clarify the liberal arts. The use of the scientific method increases our understanding of our world, the universe, and how it and we function. It has enabled man to arrive at specific solutions to world problems in medicine, energy production, and the improvement and increase of the food supply. At the same time, it enables us to identify and defend against scientific fraud (the spurious link between vaccines and autism, for example). To fully participate in modern civilization, the study of art, music, literature, history, and the humanities is assumed. Yet we gain a more in-depth understanding of the human condition through biological and physical sciences. We do not have to teach calculus, combinatorics, or mathematical physics to every student, but basic numeracy is essential to success. The scientific method teaches one to utilize observation rather than indoctrination to arrive at solutions to problems.

Yet knowing the science is not sufficient. Alexander Pope wrote "the proper study of mankind is man." It is not sufficient to know just the science. Let us consider medicine as an example. Ambrose Pare, was a French master barber-surgeon who lived in the sixteenth century and is considered the father of modern surgery. Pare wrote "I dressed him, and God healed him"[6] thus noting that part of the healing process beyond which no physician can take a patient. A good physician is a student of both science and humanity. The physician must understand not just quantity—how long we live—but must also understand quality, meaning, and enjoyment—why we live. That is why the liberal arts are essential. They enable us to go beyond science and find truths about how humans flourish because they speak to the human need for moral and spiritual meaning.

Inherent to the liberal arts experience is the ability to make ethical choices and to assume responsibility for those choices. Ethical choices are defined as those choices that enable us to live together as one family regardless of race, creed, national origin, or political persuasion (see Chapter IX). Ethics involves a methodical procedure for developing, systematizing, defending, and recommending concepts of correct behavior. Ethical decision making is essential to the survival of any society. Inherent also within the liberal arts is an understanding of values and the ability to use them to make sound ethical choices. We must learn how to make real choices. Yet, we must be comfortable with our personal behavior and, more importantly, know why we behaved in such a manner. Our vision must be bolder, more energetic, and filled with leadership. Values are everywhere; the liberal arts lead us to prevail in a new era. They provide us with sound guides for the future.

Inherent to ethical decision making is the ability to assume responsibility for one's actions, behaviors, and choices. In a world where a common excuse is *the devil made me do it,* the strength of character exhibited in the ability to assume responsibility is paramount to our success both in our individual lives as well as in our Masonic journey.

Art describes a wide range of human activity to include the visual arts--painting and architecture, for example--as well as music, theatre and dance. In the seventeenth century, *art* referred to any skill or mastery and was not differentiated from crafts or sciences. One essential of art is its ability to have a direct impact on our psychological as well as physiological responses as is so eloquently described in the lecture of the Fellow Craft Degree's explanation of the science of music. Through art, we are enabled to hear more, see more, experience more, and to do all at a significantly deeper level.

The liberal arts encourage sequential learning. As we learn to read beginning with simple three and four word sentences then progress to more complex expression, so all learning is sequential and based on the firm foundation of the liberal arts. Sequential learning is essential to the great leaps of imagination that generate new and great discovers from the structure of DNA to the complexities of the atom and the modern iPhone.

Along with sequential learning, we must also develop a grasp of the technological advancements that so rapidly overtake us. At the same time, we must understand how these advancements are to be applied in terms of their capabilities and limitations. The modern computer, for example, is a marvelous machine, but it still requires a significant degree of human input and imagination to function. It must also be managed by the human psyche so as not to become addictive or lead to destruction.

Finally, the liberal arts are guides to international understanding between men of every country, sect, and opinion. Freemasonry through the liberal arts provides insights and understanding of the human condition which enable us to better grasp that which is outside our immediate experience and comfort zone. They empower a wider comprehension of the universe as they prepare us for what is surely to come.

The totality of the liberal arts experience may be expressed in three related statements:

1. To create insights and understanding not only of our world but of the rest of the world as well;
2. To develop the ability to see the world as it really exists and to understand what we see; and
3. To understand that change comes not necessarily through innovation, but through new ways of seeing. The liberal arts give us those new ways.

At age sixteen, Joseph Lister, the pioneer of antiseptic surgical techniques, enrolled at University College in London to pursue his medical education. He received his Bachelor of Arts Degree from that college in 1847. Lister, a devout Quaker, had excelled at the Quaker schools he attended but, because the Society of Friends would neither take an oath nor subscribe to the Thirty-Nine Articles of the Episcopal (Church of England) faith, he was not eligible to enroll at universities such as Oxford or Cambridge. University College of London was called "the godless college" because it did not consider social rank or religious belief among its admission criteria.

Lister the younger was well versed in the Quaker world view of directness and honesty, and like many of his faith, was attracted to science. The Society of Friends waited upon the Lord and believed in the inner light *of God in everyone.* They were hardworking people adept at business, investing, education, and science. Rickman Godlee, Lister's nephew wrote that it was common to find the intellectual man of high science "serving behind his own counter." Joseph Jackson Lister, the younger Lister's father, wrote to his son in 1844 informing him of the importance of a sound general education prior to beginning his medical studies, counsel even more important in the twenty-first century than in the nineteenth.

How, then, do we utilize our educational experience to learn to live a virtuous life and to make sound ethical decisions? First, we define. We do this using grammar: *the key by which alone the door may be open to the understanding of speech.* We further define our terms and our propositions through rhetoric: speaking and arguing the proposition *eloquently* and without disparagement. This is aided by the science of Logic (which can be performed mathematically) and *directs us to form clear and distinct ideas of things, and thereby prevents us from being misled by their similitude or resemblance.* We then analyze our results using mathematical procedures common in both hard and social sciences. Analysis leads to conclusions based upon evidence—not on emotions—which, in turn, provides guidance for improvement. Finally, as in every scientific experiment or advancement, there must be a strong element of control. Control provides the reference point to determine what change (if any) occurred when some part of the process was modified. Control is essential to the ability to generalize the outcomes to a larger population. We evaluate our educational outcomes by controlling for each part of the process to determine which worked, which did not; which led to the desired outcomes, and which led elsewhere.

The Masonic journey or quest for *light* (enlightenment) is often described as a trek that culminates when the traveler reaches the *top of the mountain* and attains a significant degree of self-knowledge. It may, however, be better to describe it as the exploration of a dense and entangled forest where it is easy to walk at some levels and on some paths, and difficult at others. The traveler's problem is how to shift for himself. He is searching for direction rather than height. In this forest, some paths are tangled thickets, some overgrown from disuse, some fashionably clear and easy, and others interwoven. The challenge is created by this complexity and divergence.

Masonry, through its utilization of the liberal arts experience and its spiritual foundation, provides the guiding light essential to successful progress. It removes the ear-plugs and blinders. It enables the traveler to grasp and utilize the complexity and diversity to one's benefit. In that sense, the forest and the mountain are one. We all travel in the same land; the terrain is difficult, the routes varied; but the goal is common to all mankind, especially Masons.

The arts and sciences, especially the sciences, are not of human invention, writes Thomas Paine. All science has its basis in a system of principles as fixed and unalterable as is those which govern the movement of the heavenly bodies. Man cannot invent things which are eternal any more than he can prevent an eclipse. The principles which man uses to determine that eclipse are contained in trigonometry, astronomy, and geometry. And while a man may draw a triangle, a triangle is only the image of the principle, not the principle itself. In a like manner, man can make a lever, but he does not create the principle by which the lever functions. Man participates in and witnesses the effect, not the principle.

If man does not make principles, then, where does he gain his knowledge of them? It is through observation of the structure of the universe, Paine writes, that man has discovered these principles. The structure was pre and ever existing, but it was through mathematics that man learned its principles, harnessed them, and made them useful to himself. "It is only by contemplating what he calls the starry heavens, as the book and school of science, that he discovers any use in their being visible to him . . . but when he contemplates the subject in this light he sees an additional motive for saying, *that nothing was made in vain.*"[7]

NOTES

1. Richard Pogge. "An Introduction to Solar System Astronomy", The Ohio State University, www.astronomy.ohio-state.edu/~pogge/Ast161/unit3/response.html, retrieved July 3, 2015.

2. Pope John Paul II, *L'Osservatore Romano N. 44 (1264)* – November 4, 1992.

3. George Santayana & William Holzberger (ed,). *The Letters of George Santayana, Book Five, 1933-1936: The Works of George Santayana, Vol. V.* (Boston: MIT Press, 2003), p. 162.

4. Marianne Wokeck & Martin Coleman (eds). *The Life of Reason: Introduction and Reason in Common Sense: Critical Edition, Vol. 11.* (Boston: MIT Press, 2003), p. 172.

5. Thomas Hobbes, *Leviathan.* https://ebooks.adelaide.edu.au/h/hobbes/thomas/h681/chapter13.html, retrieved, July 9, 2015.

6. Sherwin Nuland. *Doctors: The Biography of Medicine.* (New York: Vintage Books, 1988), p. 107.

7. Thomas Paine. *Age of Reason: The Definitive Edition.* (Grand Rapids, Michigan: Michigan Legal Publishing, Ltd., 2014), p. 33.

Chapter Nine

Ethical Decision-Making

Freemason¹ , Soldier, Physician

The real Freemason is distinguished from the rest of Mankind by the uniform unrestrained rectitude of his conduct. Other men are honest in fear of punishment which the law might inflict; they are religious in expectation of being rewarded, or in dread of the devil, in the next world. A Freemason would be just if there were no laws, human or divine except those written in his heart by the finger of his Creator. In every climate, under every system of religion, he is the same. He kneels before the Universal Throne of God in gratitude for the blessings he has received and humble solicitation for his future protection. He venerates the good men of all religions. He disturbs not the religion of others. He restrains his passions, because they cannot be indulged without injuring his neighbor or himself. He gives no offense, because he does not choose to be offended. He contracts no debts which he is certain he cannot discharge, because he is honest upon principal.
—*A Farmer's Almanac,* 1823

Freemasonry has always existed . . . They allow good men and youths whom they consider worthy of their company to divine and guess at their deeds, to see them, in so far as they can be seen. These others find them to their liking, and perform similar deeds. . . And what exactly do they boast about? Only such things as one expects of every good person and every good citizen . . . and deeds speak for themselves. . . Their true deeds are their secrets. The true deeds of Freemasons are aimed at making all that are commonly described as good deeds for the most part superfluous.
—Gotthold Lessing in *Ernst and Faulk: Dialogues of Freemasons.*

Freemasonry is best described as a system of moral instruction taught by types, symbols, and allegorical figures. Consistent throughout its degrees is the reminder that a Freemason should always remember the rectitude of conduct essential to his and his Brothers' wellbeing and that this wellbeing, this rectitude of conduct, this morality is based on subduing one's urges and passions.

A real Freemason "restrains his passions because they cannot be indulged without injuring his neighbor or himself."[2] Every significant moral philosopher from Plato to Aquinas, from Voltaire to Durkheim, and from Gertrude Elizabeth Anscombe to even more recent thinkers share a focus on temperance and ask the same two questions: How ought we to live? And what is good?

Plato (abt. 427-347 B.C.E.) was much influenced by Socrates. Socrates (abt. 469-399 B.C.E.) was by trade and profession a *stonemason* as had been his father who used his analytical skills as a tool to ferret out the meaning of truth and to understand the world. The only reliable way to deal with an ever-changing world in constant flux is through reason and argument (rhetoric), he argued. The basis for this reason, Socrates (through Plato) suggests, is within the self. Both Socrates and Plato placed much emphasis on knowledge of what is good with Socrates expressing the belief that virtue is achieved only through knowledge. Socrates did not leave a written record of his philosophy but is reported to have suggested that a person should devote or appropriate his thoughts on philosophical matters to himself (contemplation) since writing was only an aid to memory.

Plato, a soldier and wrestler, emphasized two principle questions: how ought we to live and how can we know how we should live? Plato answered these by delineating, as did Socrates, the four cardinal virtues so familiar to all Entered Apprentices: fortitude (bravery or courage and forbearance including the ability to confront fear, uncertainty, and intimidation); prudence or wisdom (the ability to judge between actions and to determine appropriate actions at a given time; temperance or restraint (the practice of self-control, abstention, and moderation); and justice or fairness, the most extensive and most important virtue. A fifth virtue, alluded to by Plato and others is piety which includes religious devotion, spirituality, or a mixture of both, but the most common element of piety is humility. Plato further suggested that what is good is that which is most useful to man noting that we should refrain from wrongdoing; be watchful of the views of society; made good decisions based on virtues; and act upon those wise decisions so that others will imitate our actions and thus we are fulfilled. He further suggests in the *Republic* that those who make unethical decisions—who are unjust—are harmed by their injustice. He argues that even though they tell themselves that all is well, they are inwardly miserable, fearful, insecure, anxious, and suspicious. The bad guys, says Plato, may get away with it, may even have fun doing so, but they never regret the harm they have caused and ultimately pay the price for their actions.

As Socrates was mentor and teacher to Plato, so was Plato to Aristotle (384-322 B.C.E.). These three philosophers form the cornerstone of Western philosophy. Aristotle, the son of a physician and himself trained in medicine (the physicians' art was generally passed from father to son), was tutor to Alexander the Great. After Alexander's death, Aristotle, like Socrates, was charged with impiety, but unlike Socrates, Aristotle fled the country rather than stand trial. From these three ancient philosophers, we received the basic paradigms of ethics: deontological, consequentialism, and virtue ethics. Deontological ethics is the ethics of duty; consequentialism notes that an action is to be judged by its outcome; and virtue ethics makes moral excellence the proper topic for reflection. This theory suggests that ethical rules result in actions that are the derivative of virtues. The perfect example of virtue ethics is the letters *WWJD—what would Jesus do.* Follow the model of the virtuous person is the dictate. The problem, though, is how to identify the truly virtuous individual outside the divine.

Aristotle noted that good is the object of all human striving suggesting that a prime object for man should be to *know thyself* but to do so without excess. He also noted that what is good is that which is both useful to man and, more importantly, enables him to live at peace within society. Aristotle taught the Golden Mean--man should do nothing in excess and should use reason as the best way to direct his activities. He further offered the principle that tells us to follow appearances suggesting that appearances often match reality until we have excellent reasons to believe otherwise. It is not so much what people say, this principle notes, but how they act that counts. A person may profess to care about others, but unless he or she demonstrates this in daily life, their words are, at best, misleading and self-serving.

Aristotelian philosophy will dominate Western thought and practice for more than one thousand years though heavily influenced by Christian tradition and morality. But the universe of Aristotle and his successors was a closed system of crystal spheres developed first by Plato and refined by Aristotle and Ptolemy. It was fixed and unchanging with the stars and planets imbedded in several concentric spheres composed of a transparent fifth element. These fixed stars did not change their positions relative to each other because they were imbedded in the permanent surface of one of the spheres. The world of mankind, to include his actions and his intentions, was considered parallel to this crystalline universe, fixed and unchanged from the beginning.

By the eleventh century the notion of intent was incorporated into moral philosophy through the writings of Peter Abelard (1079-1142). Abelard suggested that man was neither good nor bad and that God considered our intentions as well as our actions. He further suggested that the determination of good and evil is dependent upon intent. Thomas Aquinas (1225-1274) expanded on Abelard and suggested that ethics is that which directs a person to appropriate behavior with happiness being the ultimate reward for virtue. He noted that man is naturally inclined to good and that doing what does right and ethical behavior follow each other. Once you *do the right thing,* you are more inclined to do the right thing in the future and this leads to others also *doing the right thing."*

Three hundred years later man found himself at the cusps of the age of reason and Francis Bacon (1561-1626), who may or may not have been a Freemason, the evidence is far from conclusive, recommended that in order to achieve moral and ethical fulfillment, man should apply the powers of reason to his decisions; exercise self-control over his appetites and passions; and find truth through the scientific method. This required, according to Bacon, a search for new knowledge and wisdom. Although Bacon did not always follow his own teaching, his influence on future generations is unmistakable.

One hundred years before Bacon (and in Italy not England), Niccolo Machiavelli (1469-1527) wrote *The Prince* in which he expounded a very complicated philosophy based on the ability to understand and adapt to change. He was the ultimate pragmatists. He noted the necessity of keeping up appearances while keeping others in awe. And while his name is synonymous with political machinations, his work focuses on the techniques necessary for success in politics and, in turn, in other endeavors. *The Prince* is a challenging treatise which has a high degree of intellectual integrity and stability, but its resolute teachings must be read alongside Machiavelli's more profound work *Discourses.* He had no time for tyrants, tyrannies, or their governments because of their instability, cruelty, and unpredictability. He strove for a government—a rule—that was esteemed by the population governed and relatively responsive to its needs. Much like Theodore Roosevelt, Machiavelli saw the need to be both feared and respected.

The period from the 1650s through the 1780s is referred to as the *Age of Enlightenment* or *Reason* and was highlighted by cultural and intellectual forces in Western Europe which emphasized reason, analysis, and individualism rather than traditional lines of authority. The most notable philosophers of the age were Voltaire, Rousseau, Spinoza, and Kant. François-Marie Arouet, better known by his *nom de plume* Voltaire (1694-1778), was a French philosopher who emphasized the use of reason to balance passion noting that man should act for the greater good of society. A Freemason and member as well as Master of the Lodge of the Nine Muses in Paris, he was a close friend of Benjamin Franklin. Though an aggressive critic of religious traditions, he was not opposed to the idea of a supreme being. As a deist, he held that God was a question of reason and wrote that "it is perfectly evident to my mind that there exists a necessary, eternal, supreme, and intelligent being. This is no matter of faith, but of reason."[3]

Jean-Jacques Rousseau (1712-1778) was of Swiss origin and believed that conscience, compassion, and reason combined to enable man to make sound ethical decisions. He contended that once people achieve consciousness of themselves as social beings, morality also becomes possible, but, he warns, humans can deceive themselves about their own moral qualities. Rousseau had profound impact on philosophers who followed him because of the ambiguities in his work that led to often incompatible interpretations of his writings. His greatest influence, however, is probably on the writings of Immanuel Kant (1724-1781) and Kant's concept of the categorical imperative. Rousseau also had a direct impact on the contemporary philosophy of John Rawls and his *A Theory of Justice.*

Baruch Spinoza (1632-1677) is considered one of the most radical and important early modern philosophers. Born in Amsterdam of Portuguese-Jewish origin, Spinoza in his book *Ethics* argued that happiness is not found in dependence upon our passions and the temporary pleasure we may receive from that, but rather in reason. Use reason, he admonished man, to determine the proper course of action. What is good? He asks. His answer: that which we know to be useful having set aside our emotions and rationally justifying what we did and why we did it. It is difficult, most philosophers suggest, to conceive a more reasoned and zealous defense of reason and toleration that that offered by Spinoza. For Freemasons, Spinoza's friendship with and influence on Gotthold Lessing, a German Freemason and philosopher, is of great interest.

Rousseau's greatest influence appears, however, to have been on the writings of the German philosopher Immanuel Kant (1724-1804). Kant's basic standard was that it was necessary for man to act on the principle that what you do should be generalized to all others. He argued that science, morality, and religious belief are mutually consistent because they rest on the same foundation—human autonomy. He is most associated with the categorical imperative which postulates that man occupies a special place in the world and that morality is an imperative or the ultimate commandment for reason. Duty, Kant suggested, requires man to act within the constraints of moral law. "Act only according to that maxim whereby you can at the same time will that it should become a universal law without contradiction."[4] The ability to reason and to act upon that thinking is what sets man apart and makes him a moral, ethical creature.

In the nineteenth century, John Stuart Mill (1806-1873), a British philosopher, wrote that man should act by the rule that whatever he does should be that which will bring the greatest good noting that *moral behavior* comes from within, not without. During the same century, Arthur Schopenhauer (1788-1860), writing in Germany, told his readers to think carefully about any action, to act with compassion, to respect themselves and others, and to use experience to achieve balance in thinking. All of the philosophers noted above are addressing the same issue: how to make ethical decisions.

Morals and ethics are not easily differentiated. Some philosophers and ethicists argue that morality is the common, everyday evaluation of acceptable behavior while ethics is the reflection of personal and social consciousness. Everyone, it is suggested (except some psychopaths), has a moral sense, but not everyone has the capability of thinking critically about his decisions, actions, and emotions.

The word *ethics* is derived from the Greek word *ethos* meaning character or personal disposition while the word *moral* is derived from the Latin word *more* or *mos* meaning custom. In this this chapter, ethics will be considered as the individual's ability to determine right and wrong and to act accordingly. Ethics will be accepted as being directly influenced by societal values which point to standards or codes of conduct or behavior expected by the group. It is assumed in these definitions that a person must learn how to follow ethical standards and that, as suggested by Socrates, Plato, Nietzsche, and more recent philosophers, "the righteous individual who is wrongly declared unjust and severely punished is happier than the scoundrel who bamboozles people and receives the honor of the local chamber of commerce."[5]

The basis for ethical or moral decision-making is more than societal mores; and they differ significantly from legal strictures. The law does not care about the basis of your actions as much as it does with its outcomes. Whether you paid your taxes with alacrity or bitterness is legally irrelevant. Ethics, however, considers the foundation of your actions or the spring of your wisdom to account for the worth of those actions. Strong ethics provide the standard for law, but the law does not measure that standard. Ethics is the consideration of *oughts:* how ought we behave; how ought we relate to our fellow man; how ought we understand human nature. "Our present study, unlike the other branches of philosophy, has a practical aim for we are not investigating the nature of virtue for the sake of knowing what is, but in order that we may become good without which result our investigation would be of no use."[6]

There is no agreed upon, universal definition of morality or ethics, but at the current time it is standard practice to differentiate four primary areas of moral philosophy: value ethics, normative ethics, natural ethics, and utilitarian ethics. Value ethics proponents strive to determine what is of value, what is worth pursuing? The Greek philosopher Epicurus and the English philosopher John Stuart Mills asked the same question. What is the ultimate good? Is it happiness or something else? Normative ethicists seek that supreme principle, that norm which defines right action. This is a philosophical and theoretical approach, similar to unified field theory in physics, which seeks a single principle to bind together the field of ethics and which will, in turn, explain fully why keeping your word, telling the truth, not committing murder, and not stealing are morally right. The problem with this theory, as Plato suggested in *Euthyphro,* is determining the authority. The Divine Command Theory advocated by Socrates more than 2,500 years ago attempted to address this issue. What if God is not the ultimate source of morality? Who are what is the ultimate authority? Thomas Aquinas, considered the greatest of natural legal minds, advocates this position and argues that natural law, our respective natures, should be the determining factor in ethical decision-making.

Utilitarianism, propounded most fully by John Stuart Mill (1806-1873) and earlier by Jeremy Bentham (1748-1832) and argued by modern philosophers such as J.J.C. Smart, asked the question: did the action yield the greatest happiness of all available actions? Right actions are to be judged by their consequences with the focus on action. The German philosopher Immanuel Kant (1724-1804) suggested that results are morally irrelevant and that acts are right because we are consistent in our behavior without involving ourselves in contradictions. Kant's categorical imperative held that humans occupy a special place in creation and that morality can be summed up as an imperative, an ultimate commandment of reason, from which man can discern his duties and obligations. To Kant, an imperative was a proposition that declared an action or inaction to be necessary. He solved the problem of man's acquisition of knowledge through experience by contending that the mind imposes principles upon experience to generate knowledge. This theory was of Greek origin and was discussed in the sixteenth century but not fully developed until Thomas Hobbes' *Leviathan* published in 1651. Kant's imperative was simple though difficult to follow: "act only in accordance with that maxim through which you can at the same time will that it become a universal law . . . as if the maxim of our action were to become by your will a universal law of nature."[7] Essentially, Kant's imperative, along with social contract theory and natural ethics, sought to answer the same question: what if everyone did that?

In contrast to Kant, Hobbes, and Bentham, British philosopher W.D. Ross (1877-1971) argued in his theory of *prima facie duties* that we have a standing duty to keep our word, do justice, not kill, and the like. The problem lies in that there is no fixed ranking for these duties. What happens when they are in conflict? Sometimes, Ross suggested, it may be less important to keep our word than to prevent harm. It may be necessary to kill to prevent the taking of an innocent life. It becomes even more complicated when it comes to final, conclusive knowledge that our actions, our duty, are not always situationally specific. Some duties, he noted, rest on our previous actions; some on the previous actions of other men; some, like justice, may not be in accordance with personal desires; some on the knowledge that others are benefited by our actions; some because they improve ourselves; and some simply because, they do no harm to others. Ross suggested that we can determine our prima facie duties through reflection and reason. "The existing body of moral convictions of the best people is the cumulative products of the moral reflection of many generations . . . The verdicts of the moral consciousness of the best people are the foundation on which he must build; though he must first compare them with one another and eliminate any contradictions they may contain."[8]

At this point, some 2,400 years after his death, Aristotle, considered by many as the greatest philosopher who ever lived, again came into play with virtue ethics. Virtue ethics, while not a single theory, can be traced from Aristotle's *Nicomachean Ethics.* We understand what is right by reference to what the virtuous person would do (*WWJD*). An act is morally and ethically correct because it is what the morally correct person acting in his normal character would do. And while we have a large set of moral duties—be honest, act loyal, be courageous, be just, show wisdom, compassion and temperance, free yourself from prejudice—when these rules conflict, what do we do? Virtue ethics does not accept a simple formula for determining the rightness of an action. Ethics is complex and often disorderly because it is based in decision- making and requires emotional maturity, sound judgment, and the capability of evaluating the outcome of an action as well as its motivation. Yet, as with all learning, we begin with the simple and proceed to the complex. The child learns the golden rule. It is rote learning to be acted upon accordingly and directly. A child, as Aristotle noted, does not possess full moral wisdom. Morality and ethics are like the laws and theorems and formulae of trigonometry or geometry or engineering. *Rules of thumb* may lead us into as well as out of error because rules often conflict and rules, like the laws that govern the rotation of the planets, are not influenced by human emotions. It is our emotional side which tempers our decision-making pro-cess.

Consider the parable of the Spartan boy. He was taught bravery, tenacity, and loyalty. He was taught how to behave based upon the example of his elders and to trust and respect them at all costs. He learned to strengthen his body and his memory, and make decisions quickly, even without thinking. But he was not taught to reflect upon his actions, to consider their outcomes, or to evaluate them in terms other than those of strict obedience. One day he stole a live fox in keeping with the Spartan tradition of stealing (for which young boys were praised). The fox, attempting to escape, gnawed a hole in the boy's chest killing him. The young boy abided by the societal rule—he stole. He further abided by its rules to keep it a secret and to deny the theft. He further abided by the rules by ignoring the pain. This is not the path to proper ethical decision-making. Blind obedience to the entire package does not work. No package created by man comes without the necessity for evalu-ation. Water is essential to human life, but too much or too little or water in the wrong place can be deadly. Man has the ability to discern when and how much to drink. So, too, with ethical decision-making, he has the ability to evaluate and discern.

The role of emotions (passions) in ethical decision-making must not be underestimated. With proper training and education, they can be controlled and subdued. Emotions aid us in determining what is ethically relevant by giving us *internal hints* about what matters in a given situation. Fear, guilt, and compassion are all emotional responses to a situation. A person who is compassionate, who is sympathetic, who is kind, will see things in ways that others who do not possess these qualities will not. But just like our minds, our emotions must be well and properly trained if they are to alert us to impending danger.

If we are soundly and virtuously educated and enlightened, we become anxious when certain actions are taken. We know which paths to follow and which to avoid. A good man takes pride in his actions; he has done well. Anger is a reliable indicator that something is wrong—I have not done something well. Our emotions aid us in determining the right thing to do, but knowing what is right is one thing, doing it is another. A person possessing sound virtuous education will have an easier time determining what is right in any situation. The morally virtuous person knows and does what is right. They are free of inner conflict and take internal pleasure in taking the virtuous action.

Sound ethical decision-making comes from not just from practical wisdom; it is both learned and experienced. Practical wisdom can help us fix our car because it requires knowledge of a set of facts and procedures, but ethical decision-making requires more than that. We need emotional maturity, worldly experience, and, most importantly, we must utilize a great deal of introspection, reflection, and thought to attain moral wisdom. We need to know not only how to read people but how to read ourselves. Ethical decisions come through moral wisdom which is an extremely complicated skill. Virtue—moral wisdom--is not genetic, we do not come preprogramed to be what we become. It takes wise teachers, the right environment, good role models, and, to a degree, luck.

We are to be praised or blamed, suggested Kant, only for that which we can control. Moral luck involves those actions or decisions that depend upon factors we do not control. We are, Kant noted, blamed rightly for what we can control, what we become, not what we were, yet circumstances and factors outside our control may impact directly on outcomes. Where we were born; to whom we were born; who influenced our early and middle years; our economic background; the circumstances of community and their beliefs; and even the history of our times, are not within our direct control. We may go through life on autopilot deviating little from our past—that is luck; but we are humans and possess reason and with it the ability to reflect, adapt, and change. That is the tension in moral reasoning. To reflect, adapt, and change, one must have clear guidance and sound principles upon which to proceed. Freemasonry offers its members and the greater society guidelines for good ethical decision-making.

The reason for moral education is simple—to help people acquire virtue and to enable them to make sound ethical decisions. The path to this development is straightforward. Children or apprentices are taught the complex skill—how to make sound ethical decisions using moral wisdom. We begin as apprentices. We follow the rules exactly. The rules are set down by our parents, teachers, and other role models. We learn and apply them by rote. These rules are often rather crude, however, and do not allow for much interpretation or wavering. When you see a snake, do not pick it up is the rule; it protects us from harm. As we mature, however, these rules are modified, expanded, and, even, changed through experience and education. Not all snakes are dangerous, but it takes education to tell the difference. We are loyal to our friends, but we do not cover for them when they commit a crime. Through virtuous education and wise experience, we learn the proper course of action.

The definitive outcome of moral education is to make a better person. Virtue is a character trait, not a habit. It becomes both an issue of motives as well as outcomes. Virtuous people are as they are not so because of their actions but because of their inner life. They are internally and externally different from unvirtuous people. Their understanding of themselves, others, and society is will integrated with their emotions. They are not ruled by their passions but rather use them to guide themselves to proper action. "Virtuous conduct gives pleasure to the lover of virtue."[9] As Lessing noted in 1778, "Their true deeds are their secrets. . . the true deeds of Freemasons are so great, and so far-reaching, that whole centuries may elapse before one can say 'This was their doing!'. . . the true deeds of Freemasons are aimed at making all that are commonly described as good deeds for the most part superfluous."[10]

The overview of various theories addressing ethical decision-making given above suggests that it is a diverse topic and that no one theory alone addresses all of man's concerns. When taken in combination, however, and with consideration of the various epochs involved, some combination of theories might best provide a sound guide to Masonic life. Immanuel Kant argued for the categorical imperative noting that an action's moral worth should be based on expected effects. "I ought never to act except in such a way that I could also will" that all others act the same. Social contract theory is based in the assumption that cooperation is a state of nature and essential to the success and survival of any society. This theory of ethical decision-making justifies obedience to law as a moral duty. It also explains why we are bound to keep our promises and the implications of breaking the same. Virtue ethics, on the other hand, looks to the virtuous example to assist us in understanding how to make sound ethical decisions. It addresses the issues of emotional maturity, honorable education, reflection, and training. Add these together, and we find a solid monitor which parallels a Freemasons' obligations and provides a sound guide to decision-making.

Ethical decision-making, then, *is* *accepted* as that process through which good men stabilize society and function successfully within a social setting. Their true good deeds render all other good deeds superfluous, noted Lessing. Sound ethical decisions are also those which serve the common good as they reduce fear within the individual and the group. Those decisions, based on wisdom, experience, and education are not ruled by passion or emotion and result in the proper action for the situation. Those actions do not divide, they join. They link mankind together by uniting persons of every country, religion, race, creed, or nationality by removing fear and encouraging equality. They are *on the level* and *upon the square.*

THE TEN COMMANDMENTS

A great deal of western tradition is based on the Decalogue or Ten Commandments as found in Exodus 20 and Deuteronomy 5. This set of biblical admonitions relates to both worship and ethics. They include specific regulations for the worship of God, the sanctity of the Sabbath, and a strong prohibition against idolatry and blasphemy. They also speak directly to societal issues such as murder, theft, dishonesty and adultery. The Decalogue is fundamental to both Christianity and Judaism, and the *Quran* speaks of Ten Commandments.

The first four Commandments specifically address religious practice: you shall have no other gods before me; you shall have no false idols; you will not take the Lord's name in vain; and, remember the Sabbath Day. The other six deal with practical, societal issues: honor father and mother; do not commit murder; do not steal; do not commit adultery; do not lie (bear false witness); and do not covet what your neighbor has. These last six are those most directly related to the above definition of ethical decision-making: those things necessary to the stability of society and the reduction or elimination of fear in others.

Let us consider, as an example, the prohibition against murder. The Hebrew words *lo tirzah* are commonly translated as *thou shalt not kill,* but textual analysis suggests that a more accurate translation would be *thou shalt not murder* or d*o not kill unlawfully and with intent.* Both the Old and New Testaments concur that murder is a grave evil and link murder to the question of blood guilt which often leads to revenge. When a person is in fear of being murdered-killed unlawfully-he will act in a manner consistent with that fear. Those actions may result in unintended consequences. Fear increases stress, both physical and psychological, taking a marked toll on the human psyche. Reduce the fear by a strong admonishment against the action and man is able to function successfully within a societal setting. Consider the soldier on patrol in a combat zone. His anxiety is enhanced and his stress level significantly increased because of the fear that he might be killed or injured at the next step. When we transfer that level of hyper alertness-- fear—to the civilian setting, the results are well documented in studies dealing with post-traumatic stress disorder. Reduce the fear and you reduce the internal cues that lead to psychological problem.

ETHICAL DECISION-MAKING

Ethical decision-making leads to ethical behavior. It requires that standards be set high and thusly maintained; that those standards be made known to all members of the group; that those standards be enforced in some manner; and that we understand that we are human and make mistakes. Ethical decision-making requires the individual to place upon himself a moral obligation to adhere to the standards of the group and to act as a guardian for those standards by keeping his moral code above reproach. Not only should one not do wrong, *one should not give the appearance of doing wrong*. Perception--what one thinks about you--carries as much or more weight than your behavior!

A person who makes good ethical decisions is one who possesses excellent character. Thomas Paine (who may or may not have been a Freemason, solid evidence either way is lacking) stated that "reputation is what men and women think of us . . . character is what God and the Angles know of us."[11] A man of principle is not a man who understands a principle, but one who understands, accepts, and lives by that principle. Thus, proper decision-making is based on having good judgment not influenced by passion and using common sense. The outcome of ethical decision-making is expressed through courtesy, compassion, and an appreciation of human dignity. Wisdom is knowing; virtue is doing.

Ethical decision-making is in the best self-interest of the individual since it impacts directly upon his interaction within society. Doing the right thing will, ultimately, serve us as well as it will serve our neighbor. To do the right thing, though, one must be honest with himself. Unreality is unreality and has no value in the decision-making process. Nothing, be it love, fame, or riches, is of value if obtained by fraud and deceit, internal or external. At the same time, one must respect himself, but pride is not to be confused with arrogance. Rational pride is the understanding that who you are and what you are is based upon your values and serves society by enabling you to treat all people in accordance with their actions and societal standards not your pre-conceived notions or opinions.

The public has high expectations of Freemasons who espouse a strong system of ethical decision-making and moral behavior. It expects good judgment, common sense, honesty, fairness, and equality. As Freemasons, we have become *lightning rods* for the indignation of those who do not understand our ancient and honorable Fraternity. If we, as Freemasons, make sound, ethical decisions and maintain clear moral standards, publicly and privately, defamation and character assassination from external as well as internal sources is rendered moot. Your actions and decisions reflect not only on you but also on your family, friends, co-workers, and Freemasonry.

MASONIC ETHICS

Sound ethical decision-making is based on the development of good character traits as well as on knowing the right way to behave and doing it, but such traits are not genetic; they are learned through sound, virtuous education, and exemplary role models. These character traits include courage, justice, compassion, and temperance (see the Entered Apprentice lecture). As a Freemason, our fundamental duty is to serve our brothers and mankind. We should keep our private lives unsullied and keep ever secret that which is confided to us unless that revelation is necessary to the proper administration of justice. We should be courteous to our brothers and act without favor, malice, prejudice, or ill-will. When making an ethical decision, one must avoid the obvious traps: everyone else does it; nobody will care; no one will know; that's close enough; and some rules are made to be broken. Ethical decision-making is the realization that knowing what is right is doing what is right. Acting ethically and making ethical decisions are not things that you turn on or off at will. It is part of your internal makeup. Sound ethical decisions mark the very character of a man. They can be summed up in five words: duty, honor, integrity, loyalty, and empathy.

General Douglas MacArthur, a Freemason, admonished the cadets at West Point in his farewell address to the corps to "never forget these requirements, these ethics. Rather, cherish them; keep them close to your heart. And hold them in reverence . . . for as long as you live. They will never fail you."[12] We would do very well to follow our distinguished Brother's advice.

Freemasonry offers its members and the world sound guidance on the proper way to make ethical decisions. If a Freemason follows the lessons taught in the various lectures, obligations, and rituals, he will find himself well prepared to serve as a role model. Freemasons, for example, are taught to keep their promises, no matter how small. Consider the public attention given to Masonic secrets and the Craft's demand that a Brother keep such secrets. In fact, Masonic secrets are few—recognition and some ritual—and even they are not that secret in the Internet age. At issue in the obligation to keep secrets is the ability to keep one's word. If you cannot be trusted with the small things, how can you be trusted with big things? "'Well done, good and faithful servant! You have been faithful with a few things; I will put you in charge of many things."[13]

Freemasonry also provides clear guidance on charity and conscience (taking care of others); doing what you say you will do when you say you will do it; abiding by agreed upon rules; maintaining a Brother's trust by not gossiping or revealing that which was revealed in confidence; not cheating, stealing, or defrauding; not engaging in illicit activities with a Brother's significant other or family; offering support to a Brother who is in danger but not violating the law in the process; and taking care of others by warning them of the incorrectness of their actions.

Above all, Freemasonry teaches loyalty, but loyalty is not blind. There are, as any infantry officer or enlisted person can tell you, orders that are not lawful and that should not be obeyed. Freemasonry teaches us to use our intellect and our reason to determine what is lawful as well as what is best for us, for our society, and for our Craft. Freemasonry gives us the tools to discern right from wrong and guidance on how to follow the proper path. Freemasonry is, as Wilmshurst writes, a philosophy. Freemasonry leads to a higher consciousness. The Masonic system is more than an elementary moral code. It is one that that leads to reflection and contemplation, and is a system which is useful to Mason and profane alike. While Freemasons are fully expected to improve in their external deportment, they are also expected to find within the Craft a deeper significance, an awakening. Freemasonry emphasizes truth, but the virtue of the truth comes not only in its possession but in the manner in which it is obtained. Understanding comes through knowledge of both perfection and imperfection—and the ability to discern the difference. Freemasonry provides those who seek, those who inquire, an answer about the purpose and destiny of human life. That path is not totally external, however, and requires a great deal of introspection—*under the hoodwink*—into the hidden recesses of the human heart and soul.

Freemasonry is transformational: that is inherent in the mysteries of the Craft. Freemasonry is universal. The end of one individual or period or epoch does not end Freemasonry. No edifice remains unfinished because of the demise of a single individual. The genuine mysteries of the Craft are perpetual; they are well known, and they manifest themselves in all societies. Freemasons are not seeking to restore some ancient, lost knowledge. That may be the allegory, but the import of Freemasonry lies in its search, not for what has been lost but for what we each of ourselves must learn as we *travel through the vail of tears.*

NOTES

1. A *Freemason* was originally an individual who worked in free stone or was a stone carver which may include the skills of a layer or mason. Modern Freemasonry assigns a more symbolic meaning to the word.

2. "Character of a Freemason." *A Farmer's Almanac.* Andover, Mass., 1823.

3. "Voltaire" at http://deism.com/voltaire.htm, retrieved, June 5, 2015.

4. Immanuel Kant (1785); translated by James W. Ellington. *Grounding for the Metaphysics of Morals, 3rd. Ed.* (New York: Hackett, 1993), p. 30.

5. Gordon Marino (ed.). *Ethics: The Essential Writings.* (New York: The Modern Library, 2010), p. xii.

6. Reginald E. Allen (ed.) *Greek Philosophy: Thales to Aristotle, 3rd Edition, Revised and Expanded.* (New York: The Free Press, 1991), p. 10.

7. Immanuel Kant (1797). "The Good Will and the Categorical Imperative," in Mary Gregor *Groundwork Of the Metaphysics of Morals.* (London: Cambridge University Press, 1998), p. 32.

8. W.D. Ross. "What Makes Right Acts Right?" in Russ Shafer-Landau (2015) *The Ethical Life: Fundamental Readings in Ethics and Moral Problems.* (New York: Oxford University Press, 1930), p. 121.

9. Rosalind Hursthouse. *On Virtue Ethics.* (Oxford, UK: Oxford University Press, 1999), p. 186.

10. Gotthold Lessing (1778). *Ernst and Faulk: dialogues for Freemasons to His Grace Duke Ferdinand,* in, H.B. Nisbet (ed.) *Lessing: Philosophical and Theological Writings.* (New York: Oxford University Press, 2005), p. 189.

11. Thomas Paine in "Common Sense," 1776.

12. Gen. Douglas MacArthur's Address to the Corps of Cadets, U.S. Military Academy, West Point, New York, May 12, 1962.

13. Matthew 25:23.

Chapter Ten

Once and Future Freemasonry

Philosophy and Meaning

"Even after his admission," writes W.L. Wilmshurst, "[a candidate] remains quite at a loss to explain satisfactorily what Masonry is and for what purpose this Order exists."[1] And Silas Shepherd notes: "It will be readily conceded that any person who desires to become a member of the Fraternity has little conception of its serious purposes."[2] Yet, it is clearly stated that Freemasonry is a beautiful system of morality, veiled in allegory, and illustrated by symbols with multiple layers of meaning. To truly improve oneself in Masonry a man must have a basic knowledge of the purposes of Speculative Freemasonry and, ideally, an even more comprehensive sense of his need to utilize the allegories and legends inculcated through the various degrees to address personal issues of fear, hate, greed, intolerance, envy, anger, prejudice, and selfishness. But above all, he should demonstrate his desire for knowledge and his willingness to be serviceable to his fellow creatures. If he does not do these things, he fails to comprehend the essence of Freemasonry—a spiritual quest.

Current research suggests that a significant portion of young people designated as *millennials*, those between eighteen and twenty-five years of age, consider themselves more spiritual than religious with a common response to survey questions being "we have dumbed down what it means" to be religious.[3] A Pew Research Center report states that "Gen Nexters say people in their generation view becoming more spiritual as their most important goal in life."[4] This generation interprets the Deity's wish for man as to be happy and to do good things. They also maintain closer contact with their parents than the previous two generations and feel removed from the political process.

They are more interested in world and national affairs than their predecessors and seek strong communal and social ties. They are more motivated toward learning with a marked percentage seeking education beyond high school. Finally, they are more inclusive than their parents or grandparents, and they find their heroes close and familiar.

This new generation possesses fewer prejudices and biases than their forefathers, and often looks with disbelief and pity on those who still profess such, especially racial, or act in such a manner. This should be nothing new to Freemasons. Theodore Roosevelt wrote that he neither disclosed nor revealed any Masonic secret when he stated that the Fraternity gives men of all walks of life a common ground upon which all men are equal and have one common interest. He also noted that Freemasonry teaches not merely temperance, fortitude, prudence, justice, brotherly love, relief, and truth, it also denounces ignorance, superstition and bigotry.[5] R.W. Gilbert Weisman, W. Grand Orator of the Grand Lodge of Florida, in the Grand Oration given in May 2015 states unequivocally that

> you could also define tolerance as freedom from bigotry . . . It is morally correct to encourage people to take a stand against everyday bigotry, apathy, and ignorance. It has no place in our society, our Fraternity, our schools, our place of worship, or our individual neighborhoods . . . your children, and their children's success depends on it. Success in today's world—and tomorrow's—depends on being able to understand, appreciate, and work with others of any race, color, or creed . . .treating others in the way that you would like to be treated.[6]

When asked to name a person they admire, these generations tend not to name past heroes. They list the names of teachers, mentors, people in their community that they respect, and family members with whom they have direct contact and who, to them, exemplify what it is to be a good person. What more fertile ground for growth could Freemasonry seek? The Fraternity offers spirituality without a denominational orientation and timeless guides to ethical decision making and upright action. It condemns prejudice and bigotry and is, as is the generations in question, inclusive. Above all, the Fraternity offers the example of good men made better through Freemasonry; men potential candidates know and interrelate with on a regular basis.

Freemasonry teaches through allegory and ritual that the human body is but a temporary, temporal edifice for an immortal being. This concept is firmly rooted in spirituality which resolutely acknowledges, as did the founders of Freemasonry, the existence of a Supreme Being but a creator who does not always intervene in the universe. This type of spirituality is the outgrowth of an intellectual movement that originated in the seventeenth and eighteenth centuries, parallel with the foundation of Freemasonry, and focuses on the existence of the Creator based on reason rather than supernatural activity.

"Get knowledge, get wisdom; but with all thy meaning, get understanding. Wisdom is supreme--so get wisdom. And whatever else you get, get understanding," writes The Teacher in Proverbs 4:7. The modern Craft of Freemasonry is a successor to the ancient mysteries in its spirituality and teaching technique as well as its ritual. For the millennial and nexter generations therein may lie the future of the Freemasonry. If the Brethren inhabiting the Craft do not seek knowledge, understanding, and wisdom and pass it "through a succession of ages," Freemasonry will fall to the fate of all human endeavors that have come before from which the spirt as well as intent was lost or ignored.

Cliff Porter writes in *A Traditional Observance Lodge* that "men entering the fraternity of Freemasonry in the 21st century generally have much higher expectations of their lodge and fraternal experience than did their predecessors. They are remarkably 'old school' in their spiritual aspirations."[7] He notes further that these young men have at their fingertips a wealth of information about the institution and have arrived, prior to the submission of their petition, at the conclusion that the Fraternity is dedicated to and focused on truth-seeking, self-development, education, and, above all, their spiritual nature and development. A problem arises, however, when their expectations are not fulfilled. Frustration results and with it goes the concomitant loss of an individual who could have been a dedicated Mason. Gotthold Lessing in the eighteenth century noted the same attraction to the Fraternity. He also reported the same frustration and, eventually, departure.

Freemasonry is, according to Andrew Hammer in *Observing the Craft*, "a philosophical society which demands of its members the highest standards in all areas of labor."[8] Tolerance of different opinions is paramount to the success of the Craft and should form the basis for all Masonic discourse. When a society fails to place sound value on the acquisition of knowledge from many sources, it is on the path to self-destruction. Each man who asks to join the Fraternity comes for his own reasons, but most come seeking the opportunity to explore innovative ideas and find new ways of looking at the past and themselves.

Freemasonry from its beginning has offered its members the freedom to determine their own destiny and reach their own understanding of the legends, allegories, and principles inculcated in the lodge. Freemasonry serves to better one's mind (simply memorizing the catechisms and ritual indicates soundness of mind and a retentive memory) as surely as it serves to better oneself. Freemasonry also requires more than insignificant improvements in a man's approach to life and his analytical techniques. It requires constant development through reading and self-discipline (see Chapter VII). The ultimate questions a Freemason must ask himself are *is this the best I can do? Is this the best I can be?* It is through proper decorum, reverence for the Craft, respect for one's Brothers, excellence in ritual, and sound Masonic Education that Freemasonry will survive into time immemorial.

WHY I BECAME A FREEMASON

I came to Freemasonry late in life even though my father had joined the Fraternity prior to World War II. I mistakenly thought that one had to be asked to join this elite organization so I waited. When I came of age, I spoke to my father of my interest in the Craft but received no response. I went on my way, joined the Army, fought in Vietnam, and came home. On my return, I again asked about his membership, and again received no response. Many years later I asked yet again about Freemasonry and was met with a much different response: "what took you so long." I learned later of the *three knock* rule then applicable in that jurisdiction. I did not immediately become a Mason, however, using profession and family as excuses. To my deep regret, I was not initiated until some seven years after my father's death, but I am now a Freemason. I will forever regret that my father was not present that night.

What originally attracted me to the Lodge of Freemasons in the small southern town where I grew up? First was probably the grandeur of the Masonic Temple. It was the tallest building in town at four stories and the only one with an elevator. It was situated in a prominent position on the town square, but, other than the architecture, it did not advertise its existence. That was not necessary. Masonry was well known and highly respected at that time and in that place. That building and its Lodge room on the top floor are now on the United States' Register of Historic Places. As I became more familiar with its members, I knew that what was represented there was the kind of man I wanted to be and the kind of men with whom I wished to associate. Two were past governors of my state with one of them having been appointed as Ambassador to the Court of St. James in the early 1940s. Others included elected state and local officials, judges, attorneys, businessmen, bankers, mill owners, ministers, professors, and teachers, and many, many others from a variety of backgrounds and professions.

What most impressed my young mind the was that these leaders in my state and community met with and welcomed my father and his friends. My dad was a policeman who worked as a carpenter in his off hours. His best friend was a butcher and his brother worked in a hardware store. I did not understand it at that time, but these men truly *met on the level"* with the butcher and the Ambassador sitting together. I did, however, sense that there was a special equality located in that place and that the past governors greeted the policeman and the butcher as Brothers.

My father became an adult during the depression and served in World War II. He was an honorable man who *walked the walk and talked the talk.* He was my hero and I wanted to be like him especially in the manner he treated his fellow man. He truly did unto them as he wished them to do unto him. He was dedicated to his God and his family as well as his nation. As a policeman, he went far beyond *the call of duty* in his community. He was what Gotthold Lessing referred to when he wrote "Their true deeds are their secrets." It was only after his death when I reviewed his life that I learned exactly what his true deeds had been and how secret many of them had been kept. Looking back, I think that review more than anything motivated me to finally become a Freemason. I wanted to be like him.

Seen through the eyes of those not familiar with Freemasonry, I seem to have accomplished so much more than my father. I left home at eighteen; obtained several academic degrees; fought in a foreign war (as did my father); held responsible positions in the military, the church, and the academy; and taught in foreign lands. My dad lived his life in that small southern town, but his deeds live after him. Among his effects were letters and notes from grateful parents, children, and so many others praising his compassion and his dedication to his duty and to mankind.

He was a sergeant and then lieutenant on the small police force in my hometown throughout the turbulent years of desegregation in the south, and he led by example. He selected as his patrol partners two of the African-American officers on the force and rode with them for several years. When he celebrated his eightieth birthday with a small family gathering, one of those patrolmen was an honored guest and, at my father's funeral, shed tears of loss. My father, true to his innate humanity and his Masonic obligation, treated all men equally, the high and the low, without regard to race, color, national origin, religion, or politics. All were equal in his eyes. Much like Scout and Jem in *To Kill a Mockingbird*, I learned my lessons at my father's knee—and he was a Freemason.

If I am half the man he was; I will be well satisfied. And as I look now with a new perspective, I discover each day how Freemasonry provided him with a guide to action and a strong foundation based on morality, brotherly love, relief, and truth; and that throughout his life, he displayed fortitude, prudence, temperance, and justice. If I leave the same legacy, I will have followed in his very big footsteps.

SEEKING A DEEPER MEANING

To begin the journey into the mysteries and allegories of Freemasonry that helped create my father and his companions, and, hopefully, will guide me in his paths, let us consider the story of Jephthah as found in the Second Degree as an example of the ancient mystery teaching technique of using allegories about problematic people to impart important lessons, which, upon analysis, contribute to our understanding of man's condition and serve to teach us how to better live our lives. The story of Jephthah as recounted in the book of Judges is one of the most complex and troubling accounts found in *The Bible*. It has been the subject of art and literature, and is the only instance in which human sacrifice, condemned so frequently in *The Bible*, is condoned. Many scholars suggest that this illustrates that in the ancient biblical tradition, extraordinary sanctity was given to a vow, especially when made to God and allowed no choice. Others suggest differently.

Masonically, the story of Jephthah is also significant because it includes the only biblical account of the use of a password. The word *shibboleth*, which originally meant *stream* or *flood* (the story of Jephthah includes a stream or river), was used as a test of tribal affiliation because the *sh* sound was obviously pronounced quite differently by the two tribes. Outside *The Bible* there are virtually no references to passwords. The phrase *open sesame* is found in the tale of Ali Baba and the forty thieves in *One Thousand and One Nights* and *swordfish* gains the Marx Brothers' entry into a speakeasy in *Horse Feathers*. But the story of Jephthah is much more problematical than the use of a password and has much to teach Masons about the human experience.

To understand the story of Jephthah and the Ephraimites, we must consider the history of Israel as well as the fact that a vow was considered to be a transaction between a person and a deity wherein the former devotes something valuable to the deity's use. The vow was an oath, with the deity being both the witness and recipient of the promise. The religious nature of the vow indicated that the petitioner's piety and spiritual attitude outweigh all other considerations.

THE AMMONITES AND THE EPHRAIMITES

Ammon was an ancient nation noted in the Old Testament that was located east of the Jordan River. The Ammonites were the descendants of the incestuous union between Lot and his youngest daughter (traditionally named *Aggadah*) thus making them related to the Israelites but with no tribal affiliation. In Deuteronomy 2:19, the Israelites are commanded to avoid conflict with them, yet, throughout *The Bible*, the Ammonites and the Israelites are described as mutually antagonistic. Jephthah lived among the Ammonites after he was expelled from Gilead (Israel).

The descendants of Joseph formed two of the tribes of Israel, Ephraim and Manasseh (Jephthah's home tribe). The Tribe of Ephraim was part of the loose union of Israelite tribes which was led in times of crisis and war by *ad hoc* leaders known as *Judges* who remained in tentative control until the time of the first Israelite king, Saul. When Rehoboam, the grandson of David, ascended the throne in about 930 B.C.E., the northern tribes split from the House of David to form the Kingdom of Israel under Jeroboam with Rehoboam remaining king over Judah in the south composed of the tribes of Benjamin and Judah. The northern kingdom or Israel was conquered by Assyria in 723 B.C.E. and the southern kingdom, Judah, fell to the Babylonians in 586 B.C.E.

JEPHTHAH, JUDGE OVER ISRAEL

Jephthah was a member of the tribe of Gilead which was a subgroup of the northern tribe of Manasseh. The Old Testament describes him as a "mighty warrior" and further notes that he was "the son of a harlot" (Judges 11:1). He was driven out of the tribe by his half-brothers and went to Tod east of the Jordan River in the land of Ammon (as in Ammonites) where "worthless [also translated as 'empty'] fellows collected round Jephthah, and went riding with him" (Judges11:3).

When the Ammonites made war on Israel, the elders of Gilead (the tribe of Manasseh) "went to bring" Jephthah to be their leader. Jephthah held out for a more stable position and the elders, who had earlier driven him out of the land, agreed that, when he defeated the Ammonites, his position would become permanent. On behalf of Israel as a whole and relying upon the might of God, Jephthah challenged the Ammonites vowing: "If thou wilt give the Ammonites into my hand, then whoever comes forth from the doors of my house to meet me, when I return victorious from the Ammonites, shall be the Lord's, and I will offer him up for a burnt offering" (Judges 11:30).

Jephthah defeats the Ammonites and upon his return is met first by his daughter, his only child, but he is bound by his vow to God: "For I have opened my mouth to the Lord, and I cannot take back my vow" (Judges 11:35). The daughter then says: "Let this thing be done for me; let me alone two months, that I may go and wander . . . and bewail my virginity." When two months had elapsed "she returned to her father, who did with her according to his vow which he had made" (Judges 11:39).

At this point in the account, the men of Ephraim come to Jephthah and demand to know why they were not included in the battle and threaten to "burn your house over with fire" (Judges 12:1). Jephthah responds by noting to the Ephraimites that they were the ones who did not answer the summons saying: "I took my life in my hand, and crossed over against the Ammonites" (Judges 12:3). He then gathered the men of Gilead and fought with those of Ephraim taking control of the *fords* across the river Jordan thus preventing

them from escaping and utilizing the word *shibboleth* to confirm tribal affiliation.

THE REST OF THE STORY

Many biblical scholars as well as the rabbinic tradition note that the death of
Jephthah's daughter is in direct violation of God's law and that this story is
meant to illustrate the terrible tragedy of human sacrifice. Others note the
complete lack of censure by God in the biblical account. The victory over the
Ephraimites comes after the death of Jephthah's daughter and "Jephthah
judges Israel six years" (Judges 12:7). Sacrifice of the first born is referenced
in Exodus 22:27-29 and there appears to be a possible reference to it in
Ezekiel 20:25-26. James Kugel, chair of the Institute for the History of the
Jewish Bible at Bar Ilan University in Israel and the Harry M. Starr Professor
Emeritus of Classical and Modern Hebrew Literature at Harvard University,
suggests that such sacrifice was done among the early Israelites otherwise the
later admonitions against the practice would not have been necessary.

Other scholars have expressed alternative views and more poetic interpretations of this sacrifice. One suggests that Jephthah's vow was in some way
modified and that the daughter's fate was perpetual virginity or solitary con-
finement. This is not supported by the biblical text. Another cites the semantics of the vow noting the word *and* ("shall surely be the Lord's, *and* I will
offer it up") suggesting that this is a mistranslation and should be properly
rendered as *or*. A third reiterates the perpetual virginity explanation and
suggests that the daughter was committed to the service of God (much like
Catholic nuns) rather than physically sacrificed.

These interpretations are in dispute with many scholars noting that the
Israelites were at the time a decidedly barbarous people and that there are
within *The Bible* several other examples of rash vows with similarly terrible
results such as Saul's vow in I Samuel 14, Solomon's in I Kings 2, and
Herod's to Salome in Mark 6. It is worthy of note, as well, that a biblical
narrator in the story of Joshua and Gibeon reports that vows were broken.
The previously referenced Ezekiel 20:5 may be interpreted to mean that
earlier issued laws—the solemnity of a vow, for example--were misplaced:
"Wherefore I gave them also statutes that were not good, and judgments
whereby they should not live." Scholars also note that nowhere in the Biblical text are there any negative comments associated with Jephthah's vow and
sacrifice. Be that as it may, the lesson to be learned from Jephthah's ordeal is
not about child sacrifice but about constraint and much more.

LESSONS FOR MASONS

Considering the complexity of the story of Jephthah and the Ephraimites, it is easy to lose the lessons offered in the horror of human sacrifice. This story has much to teach us as Masons. It speaks to equality, oaths, background, and the necessity of being ever watchful and thoughtful in what we say, think, and do. Jephthah was the illegitimate son of a prostitute and from a sub-tribe—a minority—Gilead. He was *thrust out*, disinherited, and forced to flee to a foreign nation by his half-siblings. Although surrounded by *worthless fellows,* Jephthah creates a reputation such that when threatened by the Ammonites the elders of Israel seek him out and bring him back be their leader. He was made equal with the leaders of the confederation and, subsequently, the leader of the confederated tribes for his lifetime. This teaches us that we are not bound by birth to a particular place or level of society but that we have within us the God-given ability to overcome even the most appalling circumstances and achieve by our own merits.

Secondly, this story teaches us that we are capable of overcoming poor associations and are not bound to follow the paths of our fellows when they adhere to ruinous causes and come to debased ends. We may be marked by those with whom we associate but we can we disassociate ourselves from them and we are not bound to follow their lead. Not only are we capable of achieving beyond our birth, we are capable of refusing to allow peer pressure to govern our lives and form our destiny.

Third, the story of Jephthah reminds us of the power of an oath or vow—our *word*, especially when made to the Deity. The power of the oath is in how Jephthah construes its meaning and his commitment to his faith. We can easily break a vow or oath if we assume it has no meaning and, even when the name of the Deity is included, that the oath has no power and is not binding. For Jephthah, his spirituality appears to have outweighed all other concerns and so it is with Masons.

Fourth, and directly related to number three, is our own tendency to speak before well considering our words; to think in narrow ways; and to act in a manner that is not pleasing to God or man. We are rash creatures. Let prudence and temperance govern our passions, our words, and our vows. The following story is told of Brother Harry Truman during his time as President of the United States. His daughter, Margaret, made her professional singing debut. Her performance was panned. Truman immediately wrote a scathing letter to the critic and the critic's editor. Truman, who had a strong temper, had assumed the habit of placing such heated missives in a desk drawer until several days had passed when, if he still felt as strongly about the topic, he would reword the letters and send them. In this case, the letter to the critic left the White House immediately. When the story broke in the newspapers, Truman was criticized for intemperate comments and poor judgment.

As Masons, we are taught to subdue our passions, to reflect upon our thoughts and words, and to act only after careful consideration. We are also taught that, once taken, an oath is for an indefinite period and covers all situations, even when what such an oath or obligation covers what may appear to be trivial things. Had Jephthah more wisely considered his words, he may not have been forced to exclaim: "Alas, my daughter! You have brought me very low, and you have become a cause of great trouble to me."

ONCE AND FUTURE FREEMASONRY

Freemasonry currently appears to be experiencing a downward trend in terms of membership numbers and, some suggest, that the quality of the Brothers initiated as well as the experienced gained through membership has slipped markedly. There are about half as many members in Florida Lodges (the author's Grand Lodge) in 2015 as there were in 1980. Lodges are struggling and Grand Lodges are retrenching and downsizing. A reduction in numbers may not be a bad thing. It is quality for which Freemasonry strives, not quantity. There has been a great deal of *hand-wringing* and predictions of Freemasonry's imminent demise. Many have questioned the prohibition against overt recruitment and others point a finger at what they consider the *distasteful* use of secrets, but as written in Proverbs 11:3, "a tale-bearer revealeth secrets; but he that is of a faithful spirit concealeth them."

The call is loud and clear, notes John Bizzack in *For the Good of the Order: Examining the Shifting Paradigm within Freemasonry.* "Freemasonry has been able to pass on its gift of fellowship and its central lessons from one generation to the next because it has held onto its core ideologies and each generation has adapted them to its own needs. . . To attract quality members, Freemasonry must provide a quality experience . . . it must stay true to its principles."[9] The twenty-first century and the generation of young men who refer to themselves as millennials with their spiritual and knowledge-seeking focus, offer the fertile ground necessary to strengthen the Craft through adherence to its core tenets and principles. But it requires quality to attract quality.

There is little doubt that the Internet has increased interest in Freemasonry. Baby Boomers and their children tended not to be *joiners,* and current generations seek quality in most of their doings rather that the quantitative aspect of being part of a large group. They are searching for meaning in an ever more complex and diverse world in which there appear to be no *heroes* and no sound guides to action. They, as did their forefathers, desire freedom and the right to determine their own thoughts and destinies. They seek to better their minds as they seek to better their understanding of the world. They are more educated than previous generations yet they strive to improve themselves, but they are not always focused on material gain. They are in many ways similar to the men who made the Fraternity great in previous centuries.

There is within the Craft a movement to return to what is commonly termed Observant Lodges. These Lodges focus on decorum to include dress and actions within the lodge; excellence in ritual work with the accompanying reverence for the lessons to be learned there; and the belief that they can become better than they are in both a temporal and spiritual sense. They seek an elevated level of unity with and understanding of the Deity which they perceive is not always available through organized religion as now practiced. Finally, they seek knowledge. The development of the modern middle class was dependent on the rise of higher education, but for many of those in the middle class in previous generations that education was financially beyond their reach. The Masonic Lodge provided that sought after education: it can again.

A Stated Communication in a Lodge of Freemasons should not function as does that of other social organizations and clubs. Yet too often Lodges have abandoned or forgotten through disuse what for centuries made them great and important. They have become good old boys' clubs rather than centers for spiritual and educational advancement and renewal. The lessons of the Symbolic Lodges would easily fill the curriculum of an undergraduate degree as well as several advanced degrees. They are worthy of a lifetime of study and analysis. In the seventeenth century, Accepted Masons gathered to discuss the latest advances in architecture, geometry, mathematics, and other philosophical pursuits. This attracted even more members and provided the Lodges and the world with new insights into the human condition as it contributed to the overall advancement of knowledge. These Accepted Masons made themselves better men through their focused pursuit of enlightenment and, influenced by the concept of the universality of man, they contributed directly to our modern democratic and educational systems. They noted the universal principle laid down in *The Book of Constitutions* that exclusion based on race or religion is not Masonic.

Freemasonry is not now nor has it ever been a mainly social institution. It has achieved its objectives by removing from the Lodge considerations of national allegiance, partisan politics, and sectarianism. Freemasonry cannot be all things to all people. It is not a religion or a political party but it was not fashioned to accommodate *all* ideas or *all* people. It was not created in man's image, no matter how much man has tried to change that. It is a privilege to be *Made a Mason* and so it should be treated. The nature of man is that he values least that which is easiest to obtain and comes at the lowest cost in money, energy, or time. He values most those things that are difficult to obtain and which few people possess such as a high-status profession—a physician--or a high rank in the military. He further values those things with markedly higher price tags; otherwise luxury automobiles would not sell as well as they do. Finally, he values most that which requires his skill to obtain. Freemasonry should not be *what you get out of it, it must require something of you to be of value.*

The key word in Freemasonry should be *excellence* which comes from the Latin for *to rise out from, to rise up,* or *to rise above.* It does this by initiating only those who seek its wisdom and who meet the full test of investigation and the ballot—or it should. In the ancient operative lodges, not all who sought admission were accepted with the records clearly indicating that only a small number were ever advanced beyond the most basic level. Freemasonry was not then nor should it be now, a product to be bought and sold. William Preston in 1861 warned that "the privileges of Masonry have long been prostituted for unworthy considerations. . . Many have enrolled their names on our records for the mere purpose of conviviality . . . but the evil stops not there. . . Persons of this description, ignorant of the true nature of the institution . . . are induced to recommend others of the same cast, to join the society for the same purposes."[10] The same can be written almost one hundred and sixty years later, and it is this ready availability, this lack of *specialness,* this open-door policy, that many suggest has contributed to the reduction in the Fraternity's reputation and the accompanying loss of good men seeking its wisdom.

Freemasonry should not be for the *faint of heart* or the over-committed. It is not a quick way to enlightenment or fulfillment. Like anything worth having, it demands hard work, dedication, focus, and a significant commitment of time. The essence of Freemasonry is that it must be sought by those willing to meet its demands. The new man coming into the Craft must be willing to give as much as he receives, but he must have sound guidance, solid education, and strong moral leadership. While the word is much overused in modern education, Freemasonry should be a truly *transformative* experience, but as with any craftsman, just because you possess the basic skills does not make you a master of the trade.

All Lodges operate under the laws, rules, and regulations of their Grand Lodge, but every Lodge can and should also uphold the highest standards of Freemasonry. A quick review of photos of Lodge activities from the last century and before indicate that, based on the clothing worn, the Brothers in attendance took their Craft far more seriously that do many modern Masons. The intent of Symbolic Lodge Freemasonry is not to be a jovial club; there are other organizations that fulfill that need. Symbolic Lodges should be dedicated to the meaning of things philosophical and empirical. They should guard well the gate to the Temple. Potential initiates should meet with well-informed Brothers as well as Lodge officers to discuss their interest in the Fraternity and their reason for *knocking at the door.* The investigation should not be *pro forma,* and the background check should be extensive. Candidates should be asked difficult and pointed questions, and it should be understood that Freemasonry is not something one can inherit—it should not *grandfather* its members.

Too often Freemasonry has penalized a Brother for taking the time necessary to learn our valuable lessons and has enforced too rapid advancement of unprepared individuals resulting in less informed and less Masonically educated Brothers assuming leadership positions in the Lodge. This does not mean that procrastination is acceptable; time is a factor in Freemasonry as it is in real life. Deadlines are deadlines, and meeting them indicates the ability of the initiate as well as his willingness to conform to the Fraternity's rules and regulations; but it is not unreasonable to allow a new Brother to participate in some Lodge activities other than advanced Degree work while he *learns his lessons* and proves himself ready for further advancement. Our ancient operative brothers gave a young man seven years or more to learn the *mysteries* of the craft and many were not successful. Those who did, however, demonstrated more than proficiency in their work when they produced their apprentice piece and met the judgment of the Masters.

Finally, Freemasonry should not be done *on the cheap*. It is not a public service. All of us find the money to do those things that we consider important personally and professionally, be it tickets to a sporting event or concert or the price of a fine meal at a high-quality restaurant. None of our members *NEEDS* to be a Mason; they are here of their own free will and accord. Historically, guild dues were set high with reports in England of dues equaling as much as a month's wages for craftsman and more for a master. Members of the operative guilds dressed in livery or distinctive clothing. Modern Masons should consider the example of their forefathers and dress in accordance with their respect for the Craft and their evaluation of its worth. As in the craft guilds, advancement should be based on merit not seniority. If an officer, elected or appointed, fails to fulfill his obligation and his duties to the Lodge, he should remove himself from the line. It is the nature of Freemasonry that he who would be first should first be last.

Freemasonry gives no man the answers. It provides him with the working tools necessary to the attainment of *further light* (ongoing light). It presents him with a mirror. The author well remembers a full-length mirror in a barracks at an Army Officer Candidates School. On top of the mirror were the words *IS THIS THE BEST YOU CAN BE?* Every Masonic Lodge might consider installing such a mirror in its anteroom.

NOTES

1. W.L. Wilmshurst. *Meaning of Masonry, 1927.* (LaVergne, TN: NuVision Publishing, 2007), p.15.

2. Silas H. Shepherd. "The Spiritual Significance of Freemasonry," in *The Builder Magazine, Vol., No. 11* located at http://www.themasonictrowel.com/masonic_talk/the_builder_magazine/files_month/1926_11.htm.

3. Cathy Grossman. "Survey: 72% of Millennials 'more spiritual than religious." USA Today, April 27, 2010.

4. Pew Research Center. "A Portrait of 'Generation Next." Located at http://www.people-press.org/2007/01/09/a-portrait-of-generation-next, January 9, 2007.

5. Theodore Roosevelt quotes located at http://www.lakeharrietlodge.org/lhl277/MainMenu/Home/MasonicEducation/MasonicLibrary/MasonicQuotes/tabid/356/Default.aspx, retrieved 1 October 2015.

6. Gilbert Weisman. *Grand Oration, Grand Lodge of Florida, May 2015.* Located at http://grandlodgefl.com/archive-2014/grand_oration_2014.html.

7. Cliff Porter. *A Traditional Observance Lodge: One Mason's Journey to Fulfillment.* (Colorado Springs, CO: Starr Publishing, LLC, 2013), p. 9.

8. Andrew Hammer. *Observing the Craft: The Pursuit of Excellence in Masonic Labour and Observance.* (New York: Mindhive Books, 2012), p. ix.

9. John Bizzack. *For the Good of the Order; Examining the Shifting Paradigm within Freemasonry.* (Lexington, KY: Autumn House Publishing, 2013), pp. 99-100.

10. William Preston, *Illustrations of Masonry William Preston.* 1861. Reprint. (London: Forgotten Books, 2013) p. 14.

Chapter Eleven

A Closing Charge

"Forget not the duties you have heard so frequently inculcated and forcibly recommended in this Lodge. Be diligent, prudent, temperate, and discrete . . . These principles are to extend further. Every Human being has a claim upon your kind offices. Do good unto all" reads a closing Charge. My favorite, however, is a Scottish Charge.

Picture, if you will, newly made Masons, appearing for the first time before those grand Collared and Aproned leaders of his Lodge; a bag pipe plays in the background and a giant Scotchman, looking about six foot ten with his bearskin hat adding another two solemnly intones:

When is a man a Mason?
Aye, Laddie, look about, and ask yourself and others.

When is a man a Mason?
Is it when he passes thru that door, into a Lodge room?
Is it when he is conducted, around, and cannot see, but is
Guided to the stations, and the words are passed?

When is a man a Mason?
Is it when he can look over the majestic hills, and mountains,
and looks beyond the vast oceans . . . aye and immense deserts,
the valleys, abundant with flowers, and in the vast scheme
of this creation, of the Supreme Architect, know with a
profound sense of his own littleness?
And yet has faith, hope, and courage, and which he accepts
as the root of all virtue.

When is a man a Mason?
When he knows down in the recesses of his own heart,
that every m an is as noble, as vile, as Devine, and aye as
diabolical . . . and yes . . . as lonely as he is within himself?

When is a man a Mason?
Is it when he seeks to follow, to forgive, and for all cause to
love his fellow man?

When is a man a Mason?
When he knows how to sympathize with men in their sorrows
And aye, Lad, even in their sins, knowing that each man
fights the hard fight against many odds in life's span?

When is a man a Mason?
When he has learned to make friends and to keep them,
and above all, to keep friends with himself.

When is a man a Mason?
When he loves the flowers of the fields, aye, he can hunt
the birds of the forest . . . without a gun . . . and indeed knows
and feels the thrill of the old and forgotten joy when he hears
the laughter of a child.
When he can be happy and high minded amid the meaner
drudgeries of a life time.

When is a man a Mason?
When the star-crowned trees and the glint of sunlight
on flowing waters subdue him as the thoughts of a much
loved one and now long gone.

When is a man a Mason?
When no voice of distress reaches his ear in vain
and no hand seeks his aid without response.
When he finds good in every faith that helps any
man lay hold of Divine thoughts toward the majestic
meaning of life . . . whatever the name of that faith may be.

When is a man a Mason?
When he can look into a wayside puddle, see something
beyond the mud . . . the reflection of a face of a most
forlorn fellow mortal . . . and . . . aye, he sees something
beyond sin.

When he knows how to pray, how to love, and how to
retain hope.
When he keeps faith with himself, his fellow man,
and his God.

When is a man a Mason?
If in his hand, he carries a sword against evil, but bears
in his heart a bit of a song, always glad to live . . .
Aye . . . but nar'e afraid to die for his just cause.

Such a man . . . aye such a man . . . has found the secrets
of Masonry and this is the message we are trying to share
with the world.
Look abo't, ye lad, the man in this Lodge –every one of us—
is a Mason. So mote it be. [1]

The evidence of God speaks in his creation through our senses. All things
are consistent with the Word of God. The whole universe is His creation.
Every inhabitant of this planet enjoys the same opportunities for knowledge.
Our ideas of the Creator, His wisdom, and His benevolence are as limitless as
His creation. The practice of moral truth is not a mystery; it is an imitation of
the goodness of the Deity. It is the moral character of a man that makes him
in the Deity's image. Our reason, our insight, our search, enables us to find
Him, and the creation that we behold is His real Word. Our moral duty is to
imitate this moral goodness and beneficence, and to realize fully that any
persecution and revenge between man and man is a violation of His will for
us. All nations believe in the Deity, so therefore let every man imitate His
divine plan, worship as he prefers, and, above all, do unto others as he would
have them do unto him.

"And until we are called upon the level of time toward that undiscovered
country from whose borne no traveler returns; it is our responsibility to pass
the excellent Tenets of our institution through our Lodges pure and unim-
paired from generation to generation so that our childrens' children will
celebrate with joy and gratitude the Freemasonry that we love." [2]

NOTES

1. Scottish Charge compliments of R. W. Chuck Estano, Grand Historian, Grand Lodge of
New Hampshire.
2. Lecture, "Order of the Rusty Nail," Grand Lodge of Florida.

Appendix I

Old Charges

MANUSCRIPT NAME & DATE (IF KNOWN)

Operative Masons Charges
Edict of Rothari A.D. 643
Constitutions York 926
Charter of Bologna 1248
York 1370 (French Translation)
Preambolo Veneziano relativoalle Mariegole dei Taiapiera, dei tagliatori
    dipietra (1307)
Anglo-Norman Charges 1356 England
King David and the Temple of Jerusalem
Regius 1390 British Museum
Cooke 1450 British Museum
Strassburg, Ratisbona 1459 Germany
Torgau Ordinances 1462 Germany
Watson MS series 1535
Grand Lodge No.1 1583 London
Schaw 1598
The Sinclair MS 1601
Jones 1607 (Possibly 1655)
Wood 1610 Worcester
Thorp 1629 Leicester
Sloane No. 3848 1646 British Museum
Inigo Jones MS 1655
Sloane No.3323, 1659 British Museum

Atcheson Haven 1666, Grand Lodge of Scotland
Aberdeen 1670, Aberdeen Lodge No.1 (copy published "Voice of Masonry" December 1874)
Henery Heade 1675, Inner Temple, London
Melrose No.2 1675, Melrose St. John Lodge No.1
Stanley 1677 West Yorkshire Library
The Thomas Tew MS 1680
Plot 1686 Epitome in Nat. Hist. Staffordshire
Clerke 1686
Antiquity 1686, Lodge of Antiquity No.2
William Watson 1687, West Yorkshire Library
Beaumont 1690, West Yorkshire Library
Waistell 1693, West Yorkshire Library
York No.4 1693, York Lodge No.236
Edinburgh 1696
Edinburgh 1696 (French Translation)
Foxcroft 1699
Buchanan 1600's
Phillips No.1 1600's Cheltenham
Phillips No.2 1600's Cheltenham
Speculative Masons Charges
York No.1 1600's York
York No.5 1600's York
York No.6 1600's York
Kilwinning, 1600's Kilwinning Lodge No.0
Lansdowne 1560—1600's British Museum
Harleian No.1942 1600's British Museum
Harleian No.2054, 1600's British Museum
Grand Lodge No.2 1600's London
Colne No.1 1600's Royal Lancashire Lodge No.116, Colne
Harris No.1 1600's Bedford Lodge No.157, London
Dumfries No.1 1600's Dumfries Kilwinning Lodge No.53
Dumfries No.2 1600's Dumfries Kilwinning Lodge No.53
Dumfries No.3 1600's Dumfries Kilwinning Lodge No.53
Stirling 1600's, Ancient Lodge No.30, Stirling
Hope 1600's Benevolent Lodge No.303, Teignmouth
Bain 1600's London
Dring-Gale 1600's London
Langdale 1600's Rochdale
Clapham 1600's West Yorkshire Library
Dauntesey 1600's Manchester
Taylor 1600's West Yorkshire Library
Lechmere 1600's Worcester

Beswicke-Royde, 1600's East Lancashire
David Ramsay, 1600's Hamburg
Embleton 1600's, West Yorkshire Library
Sloane No.3329, 1700 British Museum (French Translation)
Drinkwater No.1, 1700 Manchester Association
Drinkwater No.2, 1700 Manchester Association
Chetwode Crawley 1700 (French Translation)
Boyden 1700, Washington, DC.
Strachan 1700 QC Lodge No.2076
Alnwick 1701 Newcastle
York No.2, 1704 York Lodge No.236
Heaton 1705 England
Scarborough, York 1705 Grand Lodge of Canada
Dumfries N.4 1710 London (French Translation)
Talents 1700-20 London
Brooks Hill 1700-20 London
Cama Circa 1705 London
Inigo Jones 1705 Worcester
Trinity College 1711 (French Translation)
Kevan 1714
Robert's Constitutions 1722
Roberts 1722 (original)
Macnab 1722
Ancient Charges of a Free Mason 1723
Regulations of a Free Mason 1723
Post Boy Sham Exposure 1723
Haddon 1723 London
Briscoe 1724 Printed
Grand Mystery of Freemasons 1724 Printed
Grand Mystery of Freemasons 1724 (French Translation)
Institution of Free Masons 1725
Institution of Free Masons 1725 (French Translation)
Whole Institution of Free-Masons Opened 1725
Spencer 1726 Massachusetts
Graham 1726 London (French Translation)
Songhurst Circa 1726 London
Fisher 1726 London
Dundee 1727
Wilkinson 1727 (french Translation)
Tho. Carmick 1727 Pennsylvania
Woodford 1728 London
Cole 1728 Engraved in Cole's Constitutions
Free Masonry according to the Scriptures 1737 (spanish translation)

La Reception d'un Frey Maçon 1737
Langley 1738 Printed
Dodd 1739 Printed
Levander-York 1740 Port Sunlight
Free Masons Catechism 1740 Harry Carr (Spanish translation)
Le Parfait Maçon 1744
Le Sceau rompu 1745
Holywell 1748 Lancashire
Fortitude 1750 Fortitude Lodge No. 281, Lancaster
Essex 1750 Harry Carr
Thistle Manuscript 1756, Thistle Lodge No. 62, Dumfries
The Free Mason Examin'd 1758
Three Distinctive Knocks 1760 Printed
Melrose No.3, 1762 Melrose St. John Lodge No.1
Jachin and Boaz 1762
Tew 1700's West Yorkshire Library
Portland 1700's Wilbick Abbey
Hughan 1700's West Yorkshire Library
Papworth's 1700's London
Phillips No.3, 1700's Cheltenham
Newcastle College 1700's Newcastle
Probity 1700's Probity Lodge No.61, Halifax
Colne No.2, 1700's Royal Lancashire Lodge No.116, Colne
Harris No.2, 1700's British Museum
Rawlinson 1700's Bodleian Library
Dumfries No.4, 1700's Dumfries Kilwinning Lodge No.53
Gateshead 1700's Lodge of Industry No.48
Krause 1806 (Printed from an Older MSS)
Dowland MSS (An Older MSS which was Printed in 1815 date unknown)
Hargrove 1818 Printed
Tunnah 1828 London
The Albury MS.1875
MHC No.1 The Act of Regularity 2005
MHC No.2 The Observances of Freemasonry 2005
MHC No.3 The Constitutions of the Craft 2005
MHC No.4 The Foundations of Regular Craft Ritual 2006
List of several manuscripts that are presumed missing
Melrose No.1 1600's
York No.3 1630—Constitutions a parchment Roll of Charges on Masonry
    (last seen in 1779)
Bolt-Coleraine 1728
Crane No.1 1700's
Crane No.2 1700's

Wren 1852
Baker
Morgan
Wilson
Masons Company
Newcastle Lodge
T. Lamb Smith
Anchor & Hope
Drake

Appendix II

British Liberate Rolls

The Anglo-American Legal Tradition (Robert Palmer, University of Houston Law Center) Miscellaneous Chancery Records enrolled at Common Law (WAALT: The Wiki for the Anglo-American Legal Tradition Website)

CHARTER ROLLS

Thomas Duffus Hardy, ed. Rotuli Chartarum in Turri Londinensi Asservati. Volume 1, part 1. [1199-1216] (1837) (Google Books [Hints and tips])
   Latin transcripts in record type. No more published.
   [Other copies at: Bavarian State Library.]

Calendar of the charter rolls preserved in the Public Record Office. Volume 1. Henry III. A.D. 1226-1257. (1903) (Internet Archive–Text Archive)
   [Other copies at: Google Books: 1 ; 2 [Hints and tips].]

Calendar of the charter rolls preserved in the Public Record Office. Volume 2. Henry III- Edward I. A.D. 1257-1300. (1906) (Internet Archive–Text Archive)
   [Other copies at: Google Books [Hints and tips].]

Calendar of the charter rolls preserved in the Public Record Office. Volume 3. Edward I, Edward II. A.D. 1300-1326. (1908) (Google Books [Hints and tips])

[Other copies at: Google Books [Hints and tips]; Internet Archive–Text Archive.]

Calendar of the charter rolls preserved in the Public Record Office. Volume 4. 1-14 Edward III. A.D. 1327-1341. (1912) (HathiTrust)

Calendar of the charter rolls preserved in the Public Record Office. Volume 5. 15 Edward III–5 Henry V, A.D. 1341-1417 (1916) (Internet Archive–Text Archive)

Calendar of the charter rolls preserved in the Public Record Office. Volume 6. 5 Henry VI–8 Henry VIII. A.D. 1427-1516. With an appendix, A.D. 1215-1288. (1927) (HathiTrust)[Other copies at: HathiTrust.]

CLOSE ROLLS

Thomas Duffus Hardy, ed., Rotuli litterarum clausarum in Turri Londinensi asservati. Volume 1. 1204-1224. (1833) (Mecklenburg-Vorpommern Digital Library)
    Transcripts, in record type.

Thomas Duffus Hardy, ed. Rotuli litterarum clausarum in Turri Londinensi asservati. Volume 2. 1224-1227. (1844) (Google Books [Hints and tips])
    Transcripts, in record type.
    [Other copies at: Mecklenburg-Vorpommern Digital Library.]

Close rolls of the reign of Henry III preserved in the Public Record Office . . . A.D. 1227-1231. (1902) (Internet Archive–Text Archive)
    Latin transcripts.
    [Other copies at: Google Books [Hints and tips]; Harold B. Lee Library, Brigham Young University.]

Close rolls of the reign of Henry III preserved in the Public Record Office . . . A.D. 1231-1234. (1905) (Harold B. Lee Library, Brigham Young University)
    Latin transcripts.
    [Other copies at: Internet Archive–Text Archive.]

Close rolls of the reign of Henry III preserved in the Public Record Office . . . A.D. 1234-1237. (1908) (Harold B. Lee Library, Brigham Young University)
    Latin transcripts.

[Other copies at: Google Books: 1 ; 2 [Hints and tips]; Internet Archive–Text Archive: 1 ; 2; Harold B. Lee Library, Brigham Young University.]

Close rolls of the reign of Henry III preserved in the Public Record Office . . . A.D. 1237-1242. (1911) (Harold B. Lee Library, Brigham Young University)
  Latin transcripts.
  [Other copies at: Internet Archive–Text Archive.]

Close rolls of the reign of Henry III preserved in the Public Record Office . . . A.D. 1242-1247. (1916) (Internet Archive–Text Archive)
  Latin transcripts.

Close rolls of the reign of Henry III preserved in the Public Record Office . . . A.D. 1247-1251. (1922) (Harold B. Lee Library, Brigham Young University)
  Latin transcripts.
  [Other copies at: Internet Archive–Text Archive.]

Close rolls of the reign of Henry III preserved in the Public Record Office . . . A.D. 1251-1253. (1927) (Harold B. Lee Library, Brigham Young University)
  Latin transcripts.

Close rolls of the reign of Henry III preserved in the Public Record Office . . . A.D. 1254-1256. (1931) (Harold B. Lee Library, Brigham Young University)
  Latin transcripts.

Close rolls of the reign of Henry III preserved in the Public Record Office . . . A.D. 1256-1259. (1932) (Harold B. Lee Library, Brigham Young University)
  Latin transcripts.

Close rolls of the reign of Henry III preserved in the Public Record Office . . . A.D. 1259-1261. (1934) (Harold B. Lee Library, Brigham Young University)
  Latin transcripts.

Close rolls of the reign of Henry III preserved in the Public Record Office . . . A.D. 1261-1264. (1936) (Harold B. Lee Library, Brigham Young University)
  Latin transcripts.

Close rolls of the reign of Henry III preserved in the Public Record Office . . . A.D. 1264-1268. (1937) (Harold B. Lee Library, Brigham Young University)
  Latin transcripts.

Close rolls of the reign of Henry III preserved in the Public Record Office . . .
A.D. 1268-1272. (1938) (Harold B. Lee Library, Brigham Young University)
Latin transcripts.

Calendar of the close rolls preserved in the Public Record Office . . . Edward
I. A.D. 1272-1279. (1900) (Harold B. Lee Library, Brigham Young Univer-
sity)
[Other copies at: Internet Archive–Text Archive: 1 ; 2; 3 .]

Calendar of the close rolls preserved in the Public Record Office . . . Edward
I. A.D. 1279-1288. (1902) (Harold B. Lee Library, Brigham Young Univer-
sity)
[Other copies at: Internet Archive–Text Archive: 1 ; 2.]

Calendar of the close rolls preserved in the Public Record Office . . . Edward
I. A.D. 1288-1296. (1904) (Harold B. Lee Library, Brigham Young Univer-
sity)
[Other copies at: Internet Archive–Text Archive: 1 ; 2; 3 .]

Calendar of the close rolls preserved in the Public Record Office. Edward I.
Vol. 4. A.D. 1296-1302 (1906) (Google Books [Hints and tips])
English abstracts.
[Other copies at: Harold B. Lee Library, Brigham Young University;
Internet Archive–Text Archive: 1 ; 2; 3 ; 4 .]

Calendar of the close rolls preserved in the Public Record Office. Edward I.
Vol 5. A.D. 1302-1307 (1908) (Google Books [Hints and tips])
English abstracts.
[Other copies at: Harold B. Lee Library, Brigham Young University;
Internet Archive–Text Archive: 1 ; 2.]

Calendar of the close rolls preserved in the Public Record Office. Edward II.
A.D. 1307-1313 (1892) (Google Books [Hints and tips])
English abstracts.

Calendar of the close rolls preserved in the Public Record Office. Edward II.
A.D. 1313-1318 (1893) (Google Books [Hints and tips])
English abstracts.
[Other copies at: Internet Archive–Text Archive: 1 ; 2; 3 .]

Calendar of the close rolls preserved in the Public Record Office. Edward II.
A.D. 1318-1323 (1895) (Internet Archive–Text Archive)
[Other copies at: Internet Archive–Text Archive.]

Calendar of the close rolls preserved in the Public Record Office. Edward II. A.D. 1323-1327 (1898) (Internet Archive–Text Archive)
[Other copies at: Internet Archive–Text Archive.]

Calendar of the close rolls preserved in the Public Record Office . . . Edward III. A.D. 1327-1330. (1896) (Harold B. Lee Library, Brigham Young University)
[Other copies at: Google Books: 1;2[Hints and tips]; Internet Archive–Text Archive: 1, 2, 3, 4.

Calendar of the close rolls preserved in the Public Record Office . . . Edward III. A.D. 1330-1333. (1898) (Harold B. Lee Library, Brigham Young University)
[Other copies at: Google Books [Hints and tips]; Internet Archive–Text Archive: 1 ; 2; 3 .]

Calendar of the Close Rolls preserved in the Public Record Office. Edward III. A.D. 1333-1337 (1898) (Google Books [Hints and tips])
English abstracts.
[Other copies at: Google Books [Hints and tips]; Harold B. Lee Library, Brigham Young University; Internet Archive–Text Archive: 1 ; 2; 3 .]

Calendar of the close rolls preserved in the Public Record Office . . . Edward III. A.D. 1337-1339. (1900) (Harold B. Lee Library, Brigham Young University)
[Other copies at: Google Books [Hints and tips]; Internet Archive–Text Archive: 1 ; 2.]

Calendar of the close rolls preserved in the Public Record Office . . . Edward III. A.D. 1339-1341. (1901) (Harold B. Lee Library, Brigham Young University)
[Other copies at: Google Books [Hints and tips]; Internet Archive–Text Archive: 1 ; 2; 3 .]

Calendar of the close rolls preserved in the Public Record Office. Edward III. Vol 6. A.D. 1341-1343 (1902) (Google Books [Hints and tips])
English abstracts.
[Other copies at: Internet Archive–Text Archive: 1 ; 2; Harold B. Lee Library, Brigham Young University.]

Calendar of the close rolls preserved in the Public Record Office . . . Edward III. A.D. 1343-1346. (1904) (Harold B. Lee Library, Brigham Young University)

[Other copies at: Internet Archive–Text Archive: 1 ; 2.]

Calendar of the close rolls preserved in the Public Record Office . . . Edward III. A.D. 1346-1349. (1905) (Harold B. Lee Library, Brigham Young University)

[Other copies at: Internet Archive–Text Archive: 1 ; 2.]

Calendar of the close rolls preserved in the Public Record Office . . . Edward III. A.D. 1349-1354. (1906) (Harold B. Lee Library, Brigham Young University)

[Other copies at: Internet Archive–Text Archive: 1 ; 2.]

Calendar of the close rolls preserved in the Public Record Office . . . Edward III. A.D. 1354-1360. (1908) (Harold B. Lee Library, Brigham Young University)

[Other copies at: Internet Archive–Text Archive: 1 ; 2.]

Calendar of the close rolls preserved in the Public Record Office . . . Edward III. A.D. 1360-1364. (1909) (Harold B. Lee Library, Brigham Young University)

[Other copies at: Internet Archive–Text Archive.]

Calendar of the close rolls preserved in the Public Record Office . . . Edward III. A.D. 1364-1368. (1910) (Harold B. Lee Library, Brigham Young University)

[Other copies at: Internet Archive–Text Archive.]

Calendar of the close rolls preserved in the Public Record Office . . . Edward III. A.D. 1369-1374. (1911) (Harold B. Lee Library, Brigham Young University)

[Other copies at: Internet Archive–Text Archive.]

Calendar of the close rolls preserved in the Public Record Office . . . Edward III. A.D. 1374-1377, &c. (1913) (Harold B. Lee Library, Brigham Young University)

With supplementary close rolls, 1341-1342 and 1355-1357.
[Other copies at: Internet Archive–Text Archive: 1 ; 2.]

Calendar of the close rolls preserved in the Public Record Office . . . Richard II. A.D. 1377-1381. (1914) (Harold B. Lee Library, Brigham Young University)

[Other copies at: Harold B. Lee Library, Brigham Young University; Internet Archive–Text Archive.]

Calendar of the close rolls preserved in the Public Record Office . . . Richard II. A.D. 1381-1385. (1914) (Harold B. Lee Library, Brigham Young University)

[Other copies at: Internet Archive–Text Archive.]

Calendar of the close rolls preserved in the Public Record Office . . . Richard II. A.D. 1385-1389. (1914) (Harold B. Lee Library, Brigham Young University)

[Other copies at: Internet Archive–Text Archive.]

Calendar of the close rolls preserved in the Public Record Office . . . Richard II. A.D. 1389-1392. (1922) (Harold B. Lee Library, Brigham Young University)

[Other copies at: Harold B. Lee Library, Brigham Young University; Internet Archive–Text Archive.]

Calendar of the close rolls preserved in the Public Record Office . . . Richard II. A.D. 1392-1396. (1925) (Harold B. Lee Library, Brigham Young University)

With supplementary close roll (exchange roll), 1382-1394.

[Other copies at: Harold B. Lee Library, Brigham Young University.]

Calendar of the close rolls preserved in the Public Record Office . . . Richard II. A.D. 1396-1399. (1927) (Harold B. Lee Library, Brigham Young University)

Calendar of the close rolls preserved in the Public Record Office . . . Henry IV. A.D. 1399-1402. (1927) (Harold B. Lee Library, Brigham Young University)

Indexed in separate volume (see below).

Calendar of the close rolls preserved in the Public Record Office . . . Henry IV. A.D. 1402-1405. (1929) (HathiTrust Digital Library)

Indexed in separate volume (see below).

Calendar of the close rolls preserved in the Public Record Office . . . Henry IV. A.D. 1405-1409. (1931) (Harold B. Lee Library, Brigham Young University)
　　Indexed in separate volume (see below).

Calendar of the close rolls preserved in the Public Record Office . . . Henry IV. A.D. 1409-1413. (1932) (Harold B. Lee Library, Brigham Young University)
　　Indexed in separate volume (see below).

Calendar of the close rolls preserved in the Public Record Office . . . Henry IV. Index volume. A.D. 1399-1413. (1938) (HathiTrust Digital Library)

Calendar of the close rolls preserved in the Public Record Office . . . Henry V. A.D. 1413-1419. (1929) (HathiTrust Digital Library)
　　Indexed in following volume.

Calendar of the close rolls preserved in the Public Record Office . . . Henry V. A.D. 1419-1422. (1932) (Harold B. Lee Library, Brigham Young University)
　　Includes an index for 1413-1422.

Calendar of the close rolls preserved in the Public Record Office . . . Henry VI. A.D. 1422-1429. (1933) (Harold B. Lee Library, Brigham Young University)

Calendar of the close rolls preserved in the Public Record Office . . . Henry VI. A.D. 1429-1435. (1933) (Harold B. Lee Library, Brigham Young University)

Calendar of the close rolls preserved in the Public Record Office . . . Henry VI. A.D. 1435-1441. (1937) (Harold B. Lee Library, Brigham Young University)

Calendar of the close rolls preserved in the Public Record Office . . . Henry VI. A.D. 1441-1447. (1937) (Harold B. Lee Library, Brigham Young University)

Calendar of the close rolls preserved in the Public Record Office . . . Henry VI. A.D. 1447-1454. (1941) (Harold B. Lee Library, Brigham Young University)

Calendar of the close rolls preserved in the Public Record Office . . . Henry VI. A.D. 1454-1461. (1947) (HathiTrust Digital Library)

Calendar of the close rolls preserved in the Public Record Office . . . Edward IV. A.D. 1461-1468. (1949) (Harold B. Lee Library, Brigham Young University)

FINE ROLLS

Thomas Duffus Hardy, ed. Rotuli de Oblatis et Finibus in Turri Londinensi asservati, tempore Regis Johannis [1199-1216]. (1835) (Google Books [Hints and tips])Latin transcripts, in record type.
[Other copies at: Internet Archive–Text Archive; Bavarian State Library.]

Charles Roberts, ed., Excerpta e Rotulis Finium in Turri Londinensi Asservatis, Henrico Tertio Rege, A.D. 1216-1272. Volume 1. A.D. 1216-1246. (1835) (Google Books [Hints and tips])
Latin extracts, in record type.
[Other copies at: Google Books: 1;2[Hints and tips].]

Charles Roberts, ed., Excerpta e Rotulis Finium in Turri Londinensi Asservatis, Henrico Tertio Rege, A.D. 1216-1272. Volume 2. A.D. 1246-1272. (1836) (Internet Archive–Text Archive)
Latin extracts, in record type.
[Other copies at: Google Books [Hints and tips].]

Henry III Fine Rolls Project (National Archives/King's College, London/ Canterbury Christ Church University, Kent)
English calendar of the fine rolls of the reign of Henry III (1216-1272), in progress, for publication on the Internet and in print. The website includes both searchable draft text and images of the original documents. As an alternative to the interactive viewer, a directory of image files is available here.
So far three volumes of *Calendar of the Fine Rolls of the Reign of Henry III* have been published, covering 1216–1242 (Woodbridge, 2007-2009).

Calendar of the fine rolls preserved in the Public Record Office . . . Volume 1. Edward I. A.D. 1272-1307. (1911) (Harold B. Lee Library, Brigham Young University)

Calendar of the fine rolls preserved in the Public Record Office. Volume 2. 1307-1319. (1912) (Internet Archive–Text Archive)
[Other copies at: Harold B. Lee Library, Brigham Young University.]

Calendar of the fine rolls preserved in the Public Record Office. Volume 3. 1319-1327. (1912) (Internet Archive–Text Archive)
 [Other copies at: Harold B. Lee Library, Brigham Young University.]

Calendar of the fine rolls preserved in the Public Record Office. Volume 4. 1327-1337. (1913) (Internet Archive–Text Archive)
 [Other copies at: Harold B. Lee Library, Brigham Young University.]

Calendar of the fine rolls preserved in the Public Record Office . . . Volume 5. Edward III. A.D. 1337-1347. (1915) (Harold B. Lee Library, Brigham Young University)

Calendar of the fine rolls preserved in the Public Record Office . . . Volume 6. Edward III. A.D. 1347-1356. (1921) (Harold B. Lee Library, Brigham Young University)

Calendar of the fine rolls preserved in the Public Record Office. Volume 7. 1356-1368. (1913) (Internet Archive–Text Archive)
 [Other copies at: Harold B. Lee Library, Brigham Young University.]

Calendar of the fine rolls preserved in the Public Record Office . . . Volume 8. Edward III. A.D. 1368-1377. (1924) (Harold B. Lee Library, Brigham Young University)

Calendar of the fine rolls preserved in the Public Record Office . . . Volume 9. Richard II. A.D. 1377-1383. (1926) (Harold B. Lee Library, Brigham Young University)

Calendar of the fine rolls preserved in the Public Record Office. Volume 10. 1383-1391. (1929) (Internet Archive–Text Archive)
 [Other copies at: Harold B. Lee Library, Brigham Young University.]

Calendar of the fine rolls preserved in the Public Record Office. Volume 11. 1391-1399. (1929) (Internet Archive–Text Archive)
 [Other copies at: Harold B. Lee Library, Brigham Young University.]

Calendar of the fine rolls preserved in the Public Record Office. Volume 12. 1399-1405. (1931) (Internet Archive–Text Archive)
 [Other copies at: Harold B. Lee Library, Brigham Young University.]

Calendar of the fine rolls preserved in the Public Record Office. Volume 13. 1405-1413. (1933) (Internet Archive–Text Archive)
[Other copies at: Harold B. Lee Library, Brigham Young University.]

Calendar of the fine rolls preserved in the Public Record Office. Volume 14. 1413-1422. (1934) (Internet Archive–Text Archive)

Calendar of the fine rolls preserved in the Public Record Office. Volume 15. 1422-1430. (1935) (Internet Archive–Text Archive)

Calendar of the fine rolls preserved in the Public Record Office. Volume 16. 1430-1437. (1936) (Internet Archive–Text Archive)
[Other copies at: Harold B. Lee Library, Brigham Young University.]

Calendar of the fine rolls preserved in the Public Record Office. Volume 17. 1437-1445. (1937) (Internet Archive–Text Archive)

Calendar of the fine rolls preserved in the Public Record Office. Volume 18. 1445-1452. (1939) (Internet Archive–Text Archive)

Calendar of the fine rolls preserved in the Public Record Office. Volume 19. 1452-1461. (1939) (Internet Archive–Text Archive)

Calendar of the Patent Rolls preserved in the Public Record Office . . . Edward VI. A.D. 1547-1553. (1926) (Harold B. Lee Library, Brigham Young University)
Patent rolls for 1553, with fine rolls for 1547-1553 and various chancery warrants.

The Gascon Rolls Project (1317-1468) (Oxford University/Liverpool University/King's College, London)
Work in progress, to provide an online calendar of the unpublished rolls (C 61/32-144), together with images of the original documents, searchable indexes and a historical introduction.
The Gascon Rolls: 1387-1399 (Tony Jebson)
Partial draft Latin transcripts of C 61/102-105.
Inquisitions Miscellaneous:

Calendar of Inquisitions Miscellaneous (Chancery) . . . volume 1. [Henry III and Edward I] (1916) (HathiTrust Digital Library)

Calendar of Inquisitions Miscellaneous (Chancery) . . . volume 2. [Edward II and 1-22 Edward III] (1916) (Internet Archive–Text Archive)

Calendar of Inquisitions Miscellaneous (Chancery) . . . volume 3. [22-51 Edward III] (1937) (HathiTrust Digital Library)

Calendar of Inquisitions Miscellaneous (Chancery) . . . volume 4. 1377-1388. (1957) (HathiTrust Digital Library)

Calendar of Inquisitions Miscellaneous (Chancery) . . . volume 5. 1387-1393. (1962) (HathiTrust Digital Library)

Calendar of Inquisitions Miscellaneous (Chancery) . . . volume 6. 1392-1399. (1963) (HathiTrust Digital Library)

Calendar of Inquisitions Miscellaneous (Chancery) . . . volume 7. 1399-1422. (1968) (HathiTrust Digital Library)

IRELAND

CIRCLE: A Calendar of Irish Chancery Letters, c. 1244-1509 (Irish Chancery Project, Department of History, Trinity College Dublin)
    Online resource incorporating all known transcripts and calendars of Irish chancery letters, including a digitized version of the calendar published by the Record Commission in 1828. The original records were lost when the Irish Public Record Office was destroyed in 1922.

James Morrin, ed., Calendar of the Patent and Close Rolls of Chancery in Ireland, of the reigns of Henry VIII., Edward VI., Mary, and Elizabeth. Volume 1. (1861) (Internet Archive–Text Archive)
    Covers c. 1514-c. 1576.

James Morrin, ed., Calendar of the Patent and Close Rolls of Chancery in Ireland, from the 18th to the 45th of Queen Elizabeth. Volume 2. (1862) (Internet Archive–Text Archive)Covers c. 1576-1603.

James Morrin, ed., Calendar of the Patent and Close Rolls of Chancery in Ireland, of the reign of Charles I. [1625-1633] (1863) (Internet Archive–Text Archive)
    [Other copies at: Internet Archive–Text Archive: 1 ; 2.]

LIBERATE ROLLS

T. Duffus Hardy, ed., Rotuli de Liberate ac de Misis et Praestitis, regnante Johanne. (1844) (Internet Archive–Text Archive)
Latin transcripts, in record type.
[Other copies at: Google Books: 1 ; 2 [Hints and tips].]

Calendar of the liberate rolls . . . Henry III. Volume 1. A.D. 1226-1240. (1916) (Internet Archive–Text Archive)
English abstracts.

Calendar of the liberate rolls . . . Henry III. Volume 2. A.D. 1240-1245. (1930) (Digital General Collection, University of Michigan)
English abstracts.

Calendar of the liberate rolls . . . Henry III. Volume 3. A.D. 1245-1251. (1937) (Digital General Collection, University of Michigan)
English abstracts.

Calendar of the liberate rolls . . . Volume 4. 1251-1260. (1959) (Digital General Collection, University of Michigan)
English abstracts.

Calendar of the liberate rolls . . . Volume 5. 1260-1267. (1961) (Digital General Collection, University of Michigan)
English abstracts.

Calendar of the liberate rolls . . . Volume 6. 1267-1272 with Appendices 1220-1267. (1964) (Digital General Collection, University of Michigan)
English abstracts.

NORMAN ROLLS

Thomas Duffus Hardy, ed., Rotuli Normanniae in Turri Londinensi Asservati, Johanne et Henrico Quinto Angliae Regibus. Volume 1 [1200-1205, 1417] (1835) (Google Books [Hints and tips])
Latin transcripts in record type.
[Other copies at: Internet Archive–Text Archive: 1 ; 2; Bavarian State Library.]

PARLIAMENT ROLLS

Chris Given-Wilson, general ed., The Parliament Rolls of Medieval England, 1275-1504 (printed edition, 17 volumes, Boydell and Brewer; CD-ROM, Scholarly Digital Editions; 2005)

Transcripts of all the surviving parliamentary rolls from the reign of Edward I to that of Henry VII (Latin, French and English), together with new translations into modern English, appendices of supplementary material, a general introduction and an introduction for each parliament. The digital editions include more than a hundred specimen images of the original documents. Also available to subscribers at British History Online.

Rotuli Parliamentorum; ut et petitiones et placita in parliamento . . . volume 1 [1272-1327] [1783] (Harold B. Lee Library, Brigham Young University)
    Latin and French transcripts.

Rotuli Parliamentorum; ut et petitiones et placita in parliamento . . . volume2[1327-1377] [1783] (Harold B. Lee Library, Brigham Young University)
    Latin and French transcripts.

Rotuli Parliamentorum; ut et petitiones et placita in parliamento . . . volume 3 [1377-1399] [1783] (Harold B. Lee Library, Brigham Young University)
    Latin and French transcripts.

Rotuli Parliamentorum; ut et petitiones et placita in parliamento . . . volume 4 [1413-1439] [1783] (Harold B. Lee Library, Brigham Young University)
    Latin and French transcripts.

Rotuli Parliamentorum; ut et petitiones et placita in parliamento . . . volume 5 [1439-1472] [1783] (Harold B. Lee Library, Brigham Young University)
    Latin and French transcripts.

Rotuli Parliamentorum; ut et petitiones et placita in parliamento . . . volume 6 [1472-1504] and Rolls of Parliament, to Supply the Deficiencies in the Journals of the House of Lords [1513-1553]. [1783 and 1771] (Harold B. Lee Library, Brigham Young University)
    Latin and French transcripts.

PATENT ROLLS

Calendarium Rotulorum Patentium in Turri Londinensi (1802) (Harold B. Lee Library, Brigham Young University)
   Latin extracts, 1201-1483.

Thomas Duffus Hardy, ed., Rotuli Litterarum Patentium in Turri Londinensi Asservati. Volume 1, part 1. [1201-1216] (1835) (Jon Crump, The Itinerary of King John Project)Page images of Latin transcripts in record type. The site also includes an interactive timeline and map based on the itinerary in Hardy's edition.
   [Other copies at: Google Books [Hints and tips]; Bavarian State Library.]

Joseph Hunter, ed., Rotuli selecti ad res Anglicas et Hibernicas spectantes . . . (1834) (Internet Archive–Text Archive)
   Latin transcripts in record type of the patent roll, 7 John, original writ and return of all discharges of debt, etc., granted by the Irish exchequer, Henry V and Henry VI, and six rolls of pleas de terris datis et occupatis, etc., Henry III.
   [Other copies at: Google Books [Hints and tips].]

Patent Rolls of the Reign of Henry III . . . A.D. 1216-1225 (1901) (Harold B. Lee Library, Brigham Young University)
   Latin transcripts.
   [Other copies at: Internet Archive–Text Archive.]

Patent Rolls of the Reign of Henry III . . . A.D. 1225-1232 (1903) (Harold B. Lee Library, Brigham Young University)
   Latin transcripts.
   [Other copies at: Google Books [Hints and tips]; Internet Archive–Text Archive.]

Calendar of the Patent Rolls preserved in the Public Record Office . . . Henry III. A.D. 1232-1247 (1906) (Harold B. Lee Library, Brigham Young University)
   [Other copies at: Internet Archive–Text Archive.]

Calendar of the Patent Rolls preserved in the Public Record Office . . . Henry III. A.D. 1247-1258 (1908) (Harold B. Lee Library, Brigham Young University)
   [Other copies at: Internet Archive–Text Archive; HathiTrust Digital Library.]

Calendar of the Patent Rolls preserved in the Public Record Office . . . Henry III. A.D. 1258-1266 (1910) (Harold B. Lee Library, Brigham Young University)
[Other copies at: HathiTrust Digital Library.]

Calendar of the Patent Rolls preserved in the Public Record Office . . . Henry III. A.D. 1266-1272 (1913) (Harold B. Lee Library, Brigham Young University)

Calendar of the Patent Rolls preserved in the Public Record Office . . . Edward I. A.D. 1272-1281. (1901) (Internet Archive–Text Archive)
[Other copies at: Google Books [Hints and tips]; Internet Archive–Text Archive: 1; 2; Harold B. Lee Library, Brigham Young University; HathiTrust Digital Library.]

Calendar of the Patent Rolls preserved in the Public Record Office . . . Edward I. A.D. 1281-1292 (1893) (Harold B. Lee Library, Brigham Young University)
[Other copies at: Internet Archive–Text Archive; HathiTrust Digital Library.]

Calendar of the Patent Rolls preserved in the Public Record Office . . . Edward I. A.D. 1292-1301. (1895) (Internet Archive–Text Archive)
[Other copies at: Google Books: 1 ; 2 [Hints and tips]; Internet Archive–Text Archive: 1 ; 2; Harold B. Lee Library, Brigham Young University; HathiTrust Digital Library.]

Calendar of the Patent Rolls preserved in the Public Record Office . . . Edward I. A.D. 1301-1307. (1898) (Internet Archive–Text Archive)
[Other copies at: Google Books: 1 ; 2 [Hints and tips]; Internet Archive–Text Archive: 1 ; 2; Harold B. Lee Library, Brigham Young University; HathiTrust Digital Library.]

Calendar of the Patent Rolls preserved in the Public Record Office . . . Edward II. A.D. 1307-1313. (1894) (Internet Archive–Text Archive)
[Other copies at: Google Books: 1 ; 2 [Hints and tips]; Internet Archive–Text Archive: 1 ; 2; Harold B. Lee Library, Brigham Young University; HathiTrust Digital Library.]

Calendar of the Patent Rolls preserved in the Public Record Office . . . Edward II. A.D. 1313-1317. (1898) (Harold B. Lee Library, Brigham Young University)

[Other copies at: Internet Archive–Text Archive; HathiTrust Digital Library.]

Calendar of the Patent Rolls preserved in the Public Record Office . . . Edward II. A.D. 1317-1321. (1903) (Internet Archive–Text Archive)
[Other copies at: Google Books [Hints and tips]; Internet Archive–Text Archive; Harold B. Lee Library, Brigham Young University; HathiTrust Digital Library.]

Calendar of the Patent Rolls preserved in the Public Record Office . . . Edward II. A.D. 1321-1324. (1904) (Internet Archive–Text Archive)
[Other copies at: Google Books [Hints and tips]; Internet Archive–Text Archive; Harold B. Lee Library, Brigham Young University; HathiTrust Digital Library.]

Calendar of the Patent Rolls preserved in the Public Record Office . . . Edward II. A.D. 1324-1327. (1904) (Harold B. Lee Library, Brigham Young University)
[Other copies at: Internet Archive–Text Archive; HathiTrust Digital Library.]

Calendar of the Patent Rolls preserved in the Public Record Office . . . Edward III. A.D. 1327-1330. (1891) (Internet Archive–Text Archive)
[Other copies at: Google Books: 1 ; 2 [Hints and tips]; Internet Archive–Text Archive: 1 ; 2; HathiTrust Digital Library.]

Calendar of the Patent Rolls preserved in the Public Record Office . . . Edward III. A.D. 1330-1334. (1893) (Internet Archive–Text Archive)
[Other copies at: Google Books [Hints and tips]; Internet Archive–Text Archive; HathiTrust Digital Library.]

Calendar of the Patent Rolls preserved in the Public Record Office . . . Edward III. A.D. 1334-1338. (1895) (HathiTrust Digital Library)

Calendar of the Patent Rolls preserved in the Public Record Office . . . Edward III. A.D. 1338-1340. (1898) (HathiTrust Digital Library)

Calendar of the Patent Rolls preserved in the Public Record Office . . . Edward III. A.D. 1340-1343. (1900) (Internet Archive–Text Archive)
[Other copies at: Google Books: 1 ; 2 [Hints and tips]; Internet Archive–Text Archive: 1 ; 2; HathiTrust Digital Library.]

Calendar of the Patent Rolls preserved in the Public Record Office . . .
Edward III. A.D. 1343-1345. (1902) (HathiTrust Digital Library)

Calendar of the Patent Rolls preserved in the Public Record Office . . .
Edward III. A.D. 1345-1348. (1903) (HathiTrust Digital Library)

Calendar of the Patent Rolls preserved in the Public Record Office . . .
Edward III. A.D. 1348-1350. (1905) (Internet Archive–Text Archive)
    [Other copies at: Google Books [Hints and tips]; Internet Archive–Text
Archive; HathiTrust Digital Library.]

Calendar of the Patent Rolls preserved in the Public Record Office . . .
Edward III. A.D. 1350-1354. (1907) (Internet Archive–Text Archive)
    [Other copies at: Google Books: 1 ; 2; 3 [Hints and tips]; HathiTrust
Digital Library.]

Calendar of the Patent Rolls preserved in the Public Record Office . . .
Edward III. A.D. 1354-1358. (1909) (HathiTrust Digital Library)

Calendar of the Patent Rolls preserved in the Public Record Office . . .
Edward III. A.D. 1358-1361. (1911) (HathiTrust Digital Library)

Calendar of the Patent Rolls preserved in the Public Record Office . . .
Edward III. A.D. 1361-1364. (1912) (HathiTrust Digital Library)

Calendar of the Patent Rolls preserved in the Public Record Office . . .
Edward III. A.D. 1364-1367. (1912) (Harold B. Lee Library, Brigham Young
University)
    [Other copies at: HathiTrust Digital Library.]

Calendar of the Patent Rolls preserved in the Public Record Office . . .
Edward III. A.D. 1367-1370. (1913) (Harold B. Lee Library, Brigham Young
University)
    [Other copies at: HathiTrust Digital Library.]

Calendar of the Patent Rolls preserved in the Public Record Office . . .
Edward III. A.D. 1370-1374. (1914) (Harold B. Lee Library, Brigham Young
University)
    [Other copies at: HathiTrust Digital Library.]

Calendar of the Patent Rolls preserved in the Public Record Office . . .
Edward III. A.D. 1374-1377. (1916) (Harold B. Lee Library, Brigham Young
University)

With additions for January-February 1340 and July 1345.
[Other copies at: HathiTrust Digital Library.]

Calendar of the Patent Rolls preserved in the Public Record Office . . .
Richard II. A.D. 1377-1381. (1895) (Internet Archive–Text Archive)

Calendar of the Patent Rolls preserved in the Public Record Office . . .
Richard II. A.D. 1381-1385. (1897) (Harold B. Lee Library, Brigham Young
University)
[Other copies at: HathiTrust Digital Library.]

Calendar of the Patent Rolls preserved in the Public Record Office . . .
Richard II. A.D. 1385-1389. (1900) (Internet Archive–Text Archive)
[Other copies at: Google Books [Hints and tips]; Harold B. Lee Library,
Brigham Young University; HathiTrust Digital Library.]

Calendar of the Patent Rolls preserved in the Public Record Office . . .
Richard II. A.D. 1388-1392. (1902) (Harold B. Lee Library, Brigham Young
University)
[Other copies at: Internet Archive–Text Archive; HathiTrust Digital Library.]

Calendar of the Patent Rolls preserved in the Public Record Office . . .
Richard II. A.D. 1391-1396. (1905) (Harold B. Lee Library, Brigham Young
University)
[Other copies at: Google Books [Hints and tips]; Internet Archive–Text
Archive; HathiTrust Digital Library.]

Calendar of the Patent Rolls preserved in the Public Record Office . . .
Richard II. A.D. 1396-1399. (1909) (Harold B. Lee Library, Brigham Young
University)
[Other copies at: HathiTrust Digital Library.]

Calendar of the Patent Rolls preserved in the Public Record Office . . . Henry
IV. A.D. 1399-1401. (1903) (Internet Archive–Text Archive)
[Other copies at: Google Books [Hints and tips]; Harold B. Lee Library,
Brigham Young University; HathiTrust Digital Library.]

Calendar of the Patent Rolls preserved in the Public Record Office . . . Henry
IV. A.D. 1401-1405. (1905) (Harold B. Lee Library, Brigham Young University)
[Other copies at: Internet Archive–Text Archive; HathiTrust Digital Library.]

Calendar of the Patent Rolls preserved in the Public Record Office . . . Henry IV. A.D. 1405-1408. (1907) (Harold B. Lee Library, Brigham Young University)
[Other copies at: HathiTrust Digital Library.]

Calendar of the Patent Rolls preserved in the Public Record Office . . . Henry IV. A.D. 1408-1413. (1909) (Harold B. Lee Library, Brigham Young University)
[Other copies at: HathiTrust Digital Library.]

Calendar of the Patent Rolls preserved in the Public Record Office . . . Henry V. A.D. 1413-1416. (1910) (Harold B. Lee Library, Brigham Young University)
[Other copies at: HathiTrust Digital Library.]

Calendar of the Patent Rolls preserved in the Public Record Office . . . Henry V. A.D. 1416-1422. (1911) (Harold B. Lee Library, Brigham Young University)
[Other copies at: HathiTrust Digital Library.]

Calendar of the Patent Rolls preserved in the Public Record Office . . . Henry VI. A.D. 1422-1429. (1901) (Harold B. Lee Library, Brigham Young University)
[Other copies at: HathiTrust Digital Library.]

Calendar of the Patent Rolls preserved in the Public Record Office . . . Henry VI. A.D. 1429-1436. (1907) (Harold B. Lee Library, Brigham Young University)
[Other copies at: Google Books [Hints and tips]; Internet Archive–Text Archive; HathiTrust Digital Library.]

Calendar of the Patent Rolls preserved in the Public Record Office . . . Henry VI. A.D. 1436-1441. (1907) (Internet Archive–Text Archive)
[Other copies at: Harold B. Lee Library, Brigham Young University; HathiTrust Digital Library.]

Calendar of the Patent Rolls preserved in the Public Record Office . . . Henry VI. A.D. 1441-1446. (1908) (Google Books [Hints and tips])
[Other copies at: Harold B. Lee Library, Brigham Young University; Internet Archive–Text Archive; HathiTrust Digital Library.]

Calendar of the Patent Rolls preserved in the Public Record Office . . . Henry VI. A.D. 1446-1452. (1909) (Harold B. Lee Library, Brigham Young University)
[Other copies at: HathiTrust Digital Library.]

Calendar of the Patent Rolls preserved in the Public Record Office . . . Henry VI. A.D. 1452-1461. (1910) (Harold B. Lee Library, Brigham Young University)
[Other copies at: HathiTrust Digital Library.]

Calendar of the Patent Rolls preserved in the Public Record Office . . . Edward IV. A.D. 1461-1467. (1897) (Internet Archive–Text Archive)
[Other copies at: Google Books [Hints and tips]; Harold B. Lee Library, Brigham Young University.]

Calendar of the Patent Rolls preserved in the Public Record Office . . . Edward IV. Henry VI. A.D. 1467-1477. (1900) (Harold B. Lee Library, Brigham Young University)
[Other copies at: Google Books [Hints and tips]; Internet Archive–Text Archive.]

Calendar of the Patent Rolls preserved in the Public Record Office . . . A.D. 1476-1485. (1901) (Internet Archive–Text Archive)
[Other copies at: Google Books [Hints and tips]; Harold B. Lee Library, Brigham Young University.]

Calendar of the Patent Rolls preserved in the Public Record Office . . . Henry VII. A.D. 1485-1494. (1914) (Harold B. Lee Library, Brigham Young University)

Calendar of the Patent Rolls preserved in the Public Record Office . . . Henry VII. A.D. 1494-1509. (1916) (Harold B. Lee Library, Brigham Young University)

Calendar of the Patent Rolls preserved in the Public Record Office . . . Edward VI. A.D. 1547-1548. (1924) (Harold B. Lee Library, Brigham Young University)

Calendar of the Patent Rolls preserved in the Public Record Office . . . Edward VI. A.D. 1548-1549. (1924) (Harold B. Lee Library, Brigham Young University)

Calendar of the Patent Rolls preserved in the Public Record Office . . . Edward VI. A.D. 1549-1551. (1925) (Harold B. Lee Library, Brigham Young University)

Calendar of the Patent Rolls preserved in the Public Record Office . . . Edward VI. A.D. 1550-1553. (1926) (Harold B. Lee Library, Brigham Young University)

Calendar of the Patent Rolls preserved in the Public Record Office . . . Edward VI. A.D. 1547-1553. (1926) (Harold B. Lee Library, Brigham Young University)
    Patent rolls for 1553, with fine rolls for 1547-1553 and various chancery warrants.

Calendar of the Patent Rolls preserved in the Public Record Office . . . Edward VI. Index. (1929) (Harold B. Lee Library, Brigham Young University)

Calendar of the Patent Rolls preserved in the Public Record Office . . . Philip and Mary. A.D. 1553-1554. (1937) (Harold B. Lee Library, Brigham Young University)

Calendar of the Patent Rolls preserved in the Public Record Office . . . Philip and Mary. A.D. 1554-1555. (1936) (Harold B. Lee Library, Brigham Young University)

Calendar of the Patent Rolls preserved in the Public Record Office . . . Philip and Mary. A.D. 1555-1557. (1938) (Harold B. Lee Library, Brigham Young University)

Calendar of the Patent Rolls preserved in the Public Record Office . . . Philip and Mary. A.D. 1557-1558. (1939) (Harold B. Lee Library, Brigham Young University)

OTHER

Calendar of various chancery rolls: supplementary close rolls, Welsh rolls, scutage rolls. A.D. 1277-1326. (1912) (Harold B. Lee Library, Brigham Young University)

Appendix III

Account Books

City of London Records, Books of Weekly Payments at London Bridge, 1652-1694
Propositions and Proposals, Greenwich Hospital, 1696
Office of Works Accounts, 1662-1658
Rebuilding Accounts
St. James Palace Accounts, 1644
St. Paul's Cathedral Accounts 1632-1697
White Hall Banqueting Account, 1619-1622
Winchester Palace Account, 1682-1686
Calendars of State Papers, Domestic
Calendars of Treasury Books

Bibliography

Act of Common Council, City of London, Journals of the Court of Common Council, 11 September 1694.

Allen, Reginald E. (ed.). *Greek Philosophy: Thales to Aristotle, 3rd Edition, Revised and Expanded.* New York: The Free Press, 1991.

Allison, Henry. *Lessing and the Enlightenment: His Philosophy of Religion and its Relationship to Eighteenth Century Thought.* Mindhivebooks.com, 2010.

Allmand, Christopher. *Henry V.* New Haven, Conn.: Yale University Press, 1997. Anderson, James. *The Constitutions of Free-Masons: Containing the History, Charges, Regulations, of That Ancient and Right Worshipful Fraternity, for the Use of the Lodges, London, printed by W. Hunter, for J. Senex and J. Hooke in that Year Of Masonry 7523, Anno Domioni 1723.* New York: Masonic Publishers, 1855.

Anonymous. *Jachin and Boaz or an Authentic Key to the Door of Free-Masonry.* London: Nichol at the Paper Mill, 1763. Reprint, White Fish, Montana, Kessinger Publishing, 2014.

————. The *Three Distinct Knocks or the Door of the Most Antient Free-Masonry.* London: H. Sergeant without the Temple. Reprint, Whitefish, Montana: Kessinger Publishing, 2014.

Aristotle. *Nicomachean Ethics* at http://classics.mit.edu/Aristotle/nicomachaen.html, retrieved September 1, 2015.

Ashmole, Elias. *Memories of the Life of the Life of the Learned Antiquary Elias Ashmole, Esq: Drawn up by Himself by Way of Diary: With an Appendix of Original Letters. Publish's by Charles Burman, Esq.* New York: ECCO Press, 2012.

Austin, Justin. *How to Do Things with Words.* Cambridge: Harvard University Press, 1962.

Bacon, Francis. *The Advancement of Learning.* Edited by G.W. Kitchin. Cambridge: Harvard University Press, 1962.

Barber, Malcolm. *The New Knighthood: A History of the Order of the Temple, 12th Edition.* Cambridge, UK: Cambridge University Press, 2015.

————. *The Trial of the Templars.* Cambridge, UK: Cambridge University Press, 2012.

Barber, Malcolm, and Bate, Keith. *The Templars: Selected Resources.* Manchester, UK: Manchester University Press, 2002.

Barlow, Frank. *The Feudal Kingdom of England 1042-1216, Fifth Edition.* Essex, England: Pearson Education Limited, 1999.

Beadle, Richard and Fletcher, Alan (eds.). *The Cambridge Companion to Medieval English Theatre, 2nd Ed.* London: Cambridge University Press, 2008.

Bede. *Ecclesiastical History of the English People.* New York: Penguin Books, 1990.

————. *The Ecclesiastical History of the English Nation and Lives of Saints and Bishops.* London: Veritatis Splendor Publications, 2014.

Bell, Catherine. *Ritual: Perspectives and Dimensions.* New York: Oxford University Press, 1997.

———. *Ritual Theory: Ritual Practice.* New York: Oxford University Press, 1992.

———. *Teaching Ritual.* New York: Oxford University Press, 2007.

Begg, D.J. Ian. "An Archeology of Palatial Mason's Marks on Crete." In *XAPIE: Essays in Honor of Sara A. Immerwahr.* Edited by Anne P. Chapin, pp.1-15. Athens: The American School of Classical Studies, 2004.

Bevington, David. *Medieval Drama.* Boston: Houghton Company, 1975.

Bizzack, John. *For the Good of the Order: Examining the Shifting Paradigm within Freemasonry.* Pittsburg, PA: Autumn House Publishing, 2013.

Bloom, Paul. *Just Babies: The Origins of Good and Evil.* New York: Crown Publishers, 2013.

Bogdan, Henrik. *Western Esotericism and Rituals of Initiation.* Albany: University of New York Press, 2007.

Bogdan, Henrik, and Snoek, Jan (eds.). *Handbook of Freemasonry.* Boston: Brill, 2014.

Bonhoeffer, Dietrich. *Ethics.* New York: McMillian Publishing Co., 1955.

Borst, William A. *The Scorpion and the Frog: A Natural Conspiracy.* Bloomington, IN: Xlibris Corporation, 2004.

Brockett, Oscar, and Hildy, Franklin. *History of the Theatre, Tenth Edition.* New York: Pearson, 2007.

Brooke, Christopher. *From Alfred to Henry III 871-1272.* New York: The Norton Library, 1966.

Burke, James. *Connections: From Ptolemy's Astrolabe to the Discovery of Electricity: How Inventions are Linked—and How They Cause Change Throughout History.* New York: Simon and Schuster, 1978.

Burkert, Walter. *Ancient Mystery Cults.* Cambridge, Mass.: Oxford University Press, 1987.

Campbell, Joseph with Moyers, Bill. *The Power of Myth.* New York: Doubleday, 1988.

Carr, Harry (ed.). *The Early Masonic Catechisms.* Kila, MT: Kessinger Publishing Company, undated.

Carr, Harry. *The Early Masonic Catechisms Transcribed and Edited by Douglas Knoop, M.A., G.P. Jones, M.A. and Douglas Hamer, M.A.* London: Manchester University Press, 1963.

Cassirer, Ernst. *The Philosophy of Symbolic Forms.* Chicago: Open Court Publishing, 1923.

Castor, Helen. *She-Wolves: The Women Who Ruled England before Elizabeth.* New York: Harper-Perennial, 2011.

Chabris, Christopher and Simons, Daniel. *The Invisible Gorilla and Other Ways Our Intuitions Deceive Us.* New York: Crown Publishers, 2010.

Chapin, Anne (ed.). *XAPIS: Essays in Honor of Sara A. Immerwahr.* Athens: American University of Classical Studies, 2004.

"Character of a Freemason" in *A Farmer's Almanac,* Andover, Mass., 1823.

Churton, Tobias. *The Magus of Freemasonry: The Mysterious Life of Elias Ashmole—Scientist, Alchemist, and Founder of the Royal Society.* Rochester Vermont: Inner Traditions, 2006.

Condor, Edward. *Records of the Hole Crafte and Fellowship of Masons: With a Chronicle of the History of the Worshipful Company of Masons of the City of London; Collected from Official Records in the Possession of the Company, the Manuscripts in the British Museum, the Public Record Office, the Guildhall Library, Etc. Et.* London: Swan, Sonnenschein & Company, 1894.

Cua, Antonia. *Human Nature, Ritual and History: Studies in Xanzi and Chinese Philosophy.* New York: The Catholic University Press, 2005.

Davis, Robert. *The Mason's Word: The History and Evolution of the American Masonic Ritual.* Guthrie, OK: Building Stone Publishing, 2013.

———. *Understanding Manhood in America: Freemasonry's Enduring Path to the Mature Masculine.* Lancaster, VA: Anchor Communication LLC, 2005.

DeLuna, D. *The Political Imagination in History: Essays Concerning J.G.A. Pocock.* Baltimore, Maryland: Archangul, Inc., 2006.

Duncan, Hugh. *Symbols in Society.* New York: Oxford University Press, 1968.

Duncan, Malcolm. *Duncan's Masonic Ritual and Monitor or Guide to the Three Symbolic Degrees of the Ancient York Rite and to the Degrees of Mark Master, Past Master, Most Excellent Master, and the Royal Arch.* 1866. Reprint. New York: Crown Publishers, 2008.

Dyson, R.W. (ed.). *Augustine: The City of God against the Pagans.* Cambridge UK: Cambridge University Press, 1998.

"Early Masonic Manuscripts." Located at http://www.rgle.org.uk/RGLE_Old_Charges-htm.

Eaton, Tim. "Old Ruins, New World" in *British Archelogy, Issue 60,* August 2001 at http://www.archaeologyuk.org/ba/ba60/feat2.shtml.

Ehrman, Bart D. *Lost Christianities: The Battles for Scripture and the Faiths We Never Knew.* New York: Oxford University Press, 2003.

———. *Truth and Fiction in The Da Vinci Code.* New York: Oxford University Press, 2004.

"English Royal Freemasons" located at www.freemasonry.london.museum.

"Famous American Freemasons" located at http://phoenixmasonry.org/famous_masons.htm.

Fischer, Barbara and Fox, Thomas (eds.). *A Companion to the Works of Gotthold Ephraim Lessing.* New York: Woodbridge Press, 2005.

Flew, Anthony. *An Introduction to Western Philosophy: Ideas and argument from Plato to Popper.* New York: Thames and Hudson, 1989.

Fort, George. *A Critical Inquiry into the Condition of the Conventional Builders and Their Relations to Secular Guilds in the Middle Ages.* New York: J.W. Bouton, 1894.

"Four Crown Martyrs", *The Catholic Encyclopedia, Vol. 6.* New York: Robert Appleton Company, 1909, p. 163.

Fried, Albert and Elman, Richard (eds.) *Charles Booth's.* –London: Hutchinson, 1969.

Garforth, F.W. *Bede's historia ecclesiastica: Introduction, Text, Notes, and Vocabulary.* Wauconda, Illinois: Bolchazy-Carcucci Publishers, Inc., 2003.

Gertz, Clifford. *The Interpretations of Cultures: Selected Essays by Clifford Gertz.* New York: Basic Books, 1973.

———, (ed). *Myth, Symbol and Culture.* New York: W.W. Norton & Company, Inc., 1971.

Gilbert, Elizabeth. *Eat, Pray, Love: One Woman's Search for Everything across Italy, India and Indonesia.* New York: Riverhead Books, 2007.

Goodrick-Clarke, Nicholas. *The Western Exoteric Traditions.* New York: Oxford University Press, 2008.

Gould, Robert. *A Concise History of Freemasonry.* New York: Macoy Publishing, Co., 1904.

Gould, Robert and Freke, Robert. *A Concise History of Freemasonry.* New York: CreateSpace Independent Publishing Platform, 2013.

———. *The History of Freemasonry: Its Antiquities, Symbols, Constitution, Customs, Etc.* London: Thomas C. Jack, 1885.

Green, Alice. *Town Life in the 15ᵗʰ Century.* London: General Books LLC, 2012.

Gristwood, Sarah. *Blood Sisters: The Women behind the Wars of the Roses.* New York: Basic Books, 2014.

Grossman, Cathy. "Survey 72% of Millennials 'more spiritual than religious'." USA Today, August 27, 2010.

Hamill, John. *The Craft.* London: Crucible, 1986.

Hamill, John and Gilbert, Robert (eds.). *Freemasonry: A Celebration of the Craft.* North Dighton, MA: J.G. Press, 1993.

Hammer, Andrew. *Observing the Craft: The Pursuit of Excellence in Masonic Labor and Observance.* Mindhive Books.com, 2010.

Haskins, Charles. *The Ancient Trade Guilds and Companies of Salisbury.* 1923. Reprint. Lexington, Kentucky: ULAN Press, 2014.

Hayakawa, S.I. *Language as Thought and Action.* New York: Harcourt Brace, 1952.

Heatley, H.R. *A Selection of Pliny's Letters with Notes, Maps, and plates.* London: Rivingtone, 1889.

Hextall, W.B. *The Hiramic Legend and The Ashmolean Theory.* Derbyshire, UK: Self-Published, not dated.

Higgins, Frank. *The Beginning of Masonry.* New York; Self-published, 1916.

Hilton, Rodney. *Bond Men Made Free: Medieval Peasant Movements and the English Rising of 1381* 2nd Edition. London: Routledge, 2003.

Hobbes, Thomas. *Leviathan* located at https://ebooks.adelaide.edu.au/h/hobbes/thomas/h681/chapter13.html, retrieved, July 9, 2015.

Hodapp, Christopher. *Freemasons for Dummies.* New York: John Wiley & Sons Inc., 2013.

Hourihane, Colum (ed.). *The Grove Encyclopedia of Medieval Art and Architecture, 6 Vols.* New York: Oxford University Press, 2012.

Hubert, Henri, and Mauss, Marcel. *Sacrifice: Its Nature and Function.* Chicago: University of Chicago Press, 1964.

Hume, David. *The History of England Vols. I – VI.* Indianapolis, IN: The Liberty Fund, 1985.

Hursthouse, Rosalind. *On Virtue Ethics.* Oxford, UK: Oxford University Press, 1999.

Huxley, Julian (ed.). "A Discussion on Ritualization Behavior in Animals and Man" in *Philogophical Transactions of the Royal Society,* series B, 251, 1966.

Ingulf, Peter and Riley, Henry. *Ingulph's Chronicle of the Abbey of Croyland.* London: George Bell and Sons, 1908.

Johnson, Melvin. *Freemasonry in American Prior to 1750: Being an Address by Most Worshipful Melvin Maynard Johnson Grand Master to the Grand Lodge of Massachusetts.* Cambridge, Mass.: Caustic-Claflin Company, 1917.

Kahn, David. *The Code Breakers: The Comprehensive History of Secret Communication from Ancient Times to the Internet.* New York: Scribner, 1996.

Kant, Immanuel (1785); translated by James W. Ellington. *Grounding for the Metaphysics of Morals, 3ʳᵈ Ed.* New York: Hackett, 1993.

———. (1797). "The Good Will and the Categorical Imperative," in Mary Gregor *Groundwork Of the Metaphysics of Morals.* London: Cambridge University Press, 1998.

Karg, Barb, and Young, John. *100 Secrets of the Freemasons: The Truth Behind the World's Most Mysterious Society.* Avon, Massachusetts: Adams Media, 2009.

Knoop, Douglas and Jones, G.P. *A Short History of Freemasonry to 1730.* London: Manchester University Press, 1940.

———. *An Introduction to Freemasonry.* London: Manchester University Press, 1937.

———. *The Evolution of Masonic Organizations.* Manchester, UK: Manchester University, 1932.

———. *The Genesis of Freemasonry: An Account of the Rise and Development of Freemasonry in Its Operative, Accepted, and Early Speculative Phases.* Manchester, UK; Manchester University Press, 1949.

———. *The London Mason in the Seventeenth Century.* Manchester, UK: Manchester University Press, 1935.

———. *The London Freemasons in the Seventeenth Century.* Manchester, UK: Manchester University Press, 1935.

———. *The Mediaeval Mason.* Manchester, UK: Manchester University Press, 1933.

Kolko-Rivera, Mark. *Freemasonry: An Introduction.* New York: Penguin Group, 2007.

Kossellec, Reinhart, *Critique and Crisis: Enlightenment and the Pathogenesis of Modern Society* (Oxford, UK: Berg, 1988).

Langer, Susanne. *Philosophy in a New Key.* Cambridge: Harvard University Press, 1942.

———. *Mind: An Essay on Human Feelings.* 3 Vols. Baltimore: Johns Hopkins University Press, 1982.

Leeson, R.A. *Traveling Brothers: The Six Centuries Road from Craft Fellowship to Trade Unionism.* London: George Allen & Unwin Ltd., 1979.

Little Masonic Library, 5 Vols. Richmond, Virginia: Macoy Publishing, 1977.

Littlejohn, Stephen. *Theories of Human Communication.* Columbus, Ohio: Charles E. Merrill Publishing Company, 1978.

Littlejohn, Stephen, and Foss, Karen. *Theories of Human Communication, Ninth Edition.* New York: Wadsworth, 2008.

Ludolph of Suchem. *Liber de Itinere Terre Sancte,* F. Deycks, ed. Stuttgart, Germany, 1851.

Lukes, Steven. *Emile Durkheim: His Life and Work: A Historical and Critical Study.* New York: Penguin Books, 1977.

Mackey, Albert. *The History of Freemasonry V Volumes.* New York: The Masonic History Company, 1898.

Mackey, Albert and Singleton, William. *The French Masonic Guilds in the Middle Ages.* New York: Kessinger Publishing and Legacy Press, 2012.

Marino, Gordon (ed.). *Ethics: The Essential Writings.* New York: Modern Library, 2010.

Martin, Sean. *The Knights Templar: The History and Myth of the Legendary Order.* New York: Basic Books, 2009.

Masons' Company Account Books, 1619-1706.

Masons' Court Book, 1677-94, An Account of What Companies Were Served with the Copies Of the Act of Common Council.

Masons' Court Book, General Search of April, 1678.

Masons' Court Book, General Search of September, 1694.

Masons' Court Book, General Search of May, 1696.

Masons' Court Book, List of Foreigners, 1686.

Masons' Court Book, List of Members Made Free by Redemption, 1670-1694.

Masons' Court Book, Stone Imported into London Since 1`3th Day of April 1678.

McClendon, Charles. *The Origins of Medieval Architecture: Building Europe, A.D. 600-900.* New Haven, Conn.: Yale University Press, 2005.

Meade, George. *Mind, Self and Society.* Chicago: The University of Chicago Press, 1934.

Melzer, Arthur. *Philosophy between the Lines.* Chicago: The University of Chicago Press, 2014.

Millar, Angel. *Freemasonry: A History.* San Diego, CA: Thunder Bay Press, 2005.

Mommsen, Theodor and Gustav, Friedrich Haenel. *De collegiis et sodaliciis Romanorum.* In libraria Schwersiana, 1843.

Moore, Charles. *The New Masonic Trestle-Board: Adapted to the Work and Lectures as Practiced in Lodges, Chapters, Councils, and Encampments of Knights Templars, in the United States of America.* 1868. Reprint. London: Forgotten Books, 2012.

Morris, Errol. *Believing is seeing: Observations on the Mysteries of Photography.* New York: The Penguin Press, 2011.

Newman, Sharan. *The Real History Behind the Templars.* Berkley, CA: Berkley Trade Publishing, 2007.

Newton, Joseph. *The Builders: A Story and Study of Masonry.* New York: George H. Doran, Co., 1914.

Nicholson, Helen. *The Knights Templar: A New History.* Gloucestershire, UK: The History Press, 2010.

Nisbet, H.B. *Gotthold Ephraim Lessing: Philosophical and Theological Writings.* New York: Cambridge University Press, 2005.

Nuland, Sherwin B. *Doctors: The Biography of Medicine.* New York: Vintage Books, 1988.

Odiorne, James. *Opinions on Speculative Masonry, Relative to Its Origin, Nature, and Tendency.* Boston: Perkins & Marvin, 1830.

Ogilvie, Sheilagh. *Institutions of European Trade: Merchant Guilds, 1000-1800.* London: Cambridge University Press, 2011.

Paine, Thomas. *Age of Reason: The Definitive Edition.* Grand Rapids, Michigan: Michigan Legal Publishing Ltd., 2014.

Paine, Thomas. *Common Sense.* 1776.

Paine, Thomas. *On the Origin of Freemasonry.* New York: Elliott and Crissy, 1810.

Partner, Peter. *Murdered Magicians: The Templars and their Myth.* Oxford, UK: Oxford University Press, 1982.

Patterson, Oscar III. *Interpreting Masonic Ritual.* Lanham, Maryland: Hamilton Books/Rowman & Littlefield, 2016.

Pew Research Center. "A Portrait of 'Generation Next: How Young People View Their Lives, Futures and Politics." Located at http://www.people-press.org/2007/01/09/a-portrait-of-generation-next.htm, January 9, 2007.

Plato. *The Laws of Plato,* Thomas Pangle (trans.). Chicago: The University of Chicago Press, 1980.

Plot, Robert. *A Natural History of Strafford-Shire by Robert Plot, 1686.* London: Printed at the Theatre, 1686.

Pocock, J.G.A. *The Ancient Constitutions and the Feudal Law: English Historical Thought in the Seventeenth Century.* London: Cambridge at the University Press, 1957.

Pogge, Richard. "An Introduction to Solar System Astronomy", the Ohio State University, www.astronomy.ohio-state.edu/~pogge/Ast161/unit3/response.html, retrieved July 3, 2015.

Poll, Michael (ed.) *Ancient Manuscripts of Freemason: The Transformation from Operative to Speculative Freemasonry.* New Orleans: Cornerstone Books, 2013.

———. *Masonic Enlightenment: The Philosophy, History and Wisdom of Freemasonry.* Lafayette, LA: Cornerstone Book Publishers, 2006.

Pope John Paul II, *L'Osservatore Romano N. 44 (1264)* – November 4, 1992.

Prescott, Andrew. *A History of British Freemasonry 1425-2000.* Sheffield, UK: Centre for Research into Freemasonry and Fraternalism (CRFF) at the University of Sheffield, 2001.

Preston, William. *Preston's Masonry.* 1779. Reprint, Whitefish, Montana: Kerssinger Publishing, 2014.

———. *Illustrations of Masonry William Preston.* 1861. Reprint. London: Forgotten Books, 2013.

———. *Masonry Dissected.* New York: Poemandres Press, 1996.

Proceedings of the National Masonic Convention: Held at Baltimore, Maryland, May, A.L. 5853—A.D. 1843. Baltimore: Joseph Robinson, 1843.

Quill, Elizabeth. "Did This Map Guide Columbus" in *Smithsonian*, June 2015, p. 12.

Ralls, Karen. *Knights Templar Encyclopedia.* Wayne, NJ: New Page Books, 2007.

Rebold, Emmanuel and Brennan, J. Fletcher. *Primitive Masonic Laws and Charters (Extracted From General History of Freemasonry in Europe Based Upon the Ancient Documents Relating to and the Monuments Erected by This Fraternity from its Foundation in the Year 715 BC and the Present Time.* 1867. Reprint, New York: Kessinger Publishing, 2014.

Renard, George. *Guilds in the Middle Ages.* London: G Bell and Sons, LTD, 1918.

Reports and Papers of the Architectural and Archaeological Societies of the Counties of Lincoln and Northampton, 1887. London: Forgotten Books 2012. (Original work published 1887).

Reports and Papers of the Architectural and Archaeological Societies. Associated Architectural Societies, 1850-1931. Lincoln, UK.

Robinson, John. *Born in Blood: The Lost Secrets of Freemasonry.* New York: M. Evans, 1989.

Rogers, James. *Six Centuries of Work and Wages: The History of English Labour.* New York: Forgotten Books, 2015.

Roosevelt, Theodore. Quotes located at http://www.lakeharrietlodge.org/lhl277/MainMenu/Home/MasonicEducation/MasonicLibrary/MasonicQuotes/tabid/356/Default.aspx, retrieved 1 October 2015.

Ross, W.D. (1930). "What Makes Right Acts Right?" in Russ Shafer-Landau *The Ethical Life: Fundamental Readings in Ethics and Moral Problems.* (New York: Oxford University Press, 2015), p. 121.

Ruggeri, Amanda. "The Lost History of the Freemasons" located at http://www.bbc.com/travel/story/20161209-secret-history-of-the-freemasons-in-scotland retrieved December 20, 2016.

Russell, Bertrand. *The History of Western Philosophy.* New York: Simon & Schuster, 1945.

Salzman, L.F. *Building in England down to 1540: A Documentary History.* London: Clarendon Press (1st ed. reprinted with corrections and additions edition), 1967.

Santayana, George, and William G. Holzberger (ed.). *The Letters of George Santayana, Book Five, 1933-1936: The Works of George Santayana, Volume V.* Boston: MIT Press, 2003.

Scott, Leader. *The Cathedral Builders: The Story of a Great Masonic Guild.* New Orleans: Cornerstone Book Publishers, 2013.

Segal, Robert. "The Myth-Ritualist Theory of Religion," in *Journal for the Scientific Study of Religion, 19, No. 2,* 1980.

Shafer-Landau, Russ. *The Ethical Life: Fundamental Readings in Ethics and Moral Reasoning.* New York: Oxford University Press, 2015.

———. *The Fundamentals of Ethics.* New York: Oxford University Press, 2015.

Sharpland, Michael. "Buildings of Secular and Religious Leadership: Anglo-Saxon Tower-nave Churches," PhD thesis. University College of London, 2012.

Smith, Philip. *The History of the Christian Church during the First Ten Centuries, from its Foundation to the Full Establishment of the Holy Roman Empire and the Papal Power.* New York: Ulan Press, 2012 reprint of 1923 original.

Sommers, Susan M. *The Revical of a Patriotic Order: Knights Templars in England and New York.* Located at http://www.knightstemplar.org/KnightTemplar/articles/patroits.html.

Stanford Encyclopedia of Philosophy (Spring 2015 edition) at http://plato.stanford.edu/contents.html.

Steinmetz, George. *The Lost Word, Its Hidden Meaning: A Correlation of the Allegory and Symbolism of the Bible with that of Freemasonry and the Exposition of the Secret Doctrine.* New York: Macoy Publishing, 1953.

Stokes, Philp. *Philosophy 100 Essential Thinkers: The Ideas That Have Shaped Our World.* London: Arcturus, 2014.

The Freemasons' Quarterly Magazine and Review, Vol. 22, January-June 1888.

The Historical Thinking Project. Located at http://historicalthinking.ca/.

Thiroux, Jacques and Krasemann, Keith. *Ethics: Theory and Practice.* New York: Pearson, 2009.

Turner, R.V. *Eleanor of Aquitaine: Queen of France, Queen of England.* New Haven, Conn,: Yale University Press, 2009.

Twersky, Isadore, (ed.). "Mishneh Torah Book 1" in *A Maimonides Reader.* New York: Behrman House, 1972.

Unwin, George. *The Gilds & Companies of London.* George Allen & Unwin Ltd., 1908.

Van Duzer, Chet. http://www.academia.edu/2357451/_The_Yale_Martellus_Map_c._1491_as_a_Source_for_Waldseem%C3%BCller_s_1507_World_Map.

Vibert, Lionel. *Freemasonry before the Existence of Grand Lodges.* London: Spencer & Co., Not dated.

"Voltaire" at http://deism.com/voltaire.htm, retrieved, June 5, 2015.

von Mises, Ludwig. *Theory and History: An Interpretation of Social and Economic Evolution.* Auburn, AL: Ludwig von Mises Institute, 1957.

Webb, Thomas. *The Freemason's Monitor or Illustrations of Freemasonry.* 1802. Reprint. New York: Kessinger Publishing, 2015.

Weisman, S. Gilbert. *Grand Oration, Grand Lodge of Florida, May 2015.* Located at http://grandlodgefl.com/archive_2014/grand_oration_2014.html.

Weir, Allison. *Elizabeth of York: A Tudor Queen and Her World.* New York: Ballantine Books, 2014.

Wilmhurst, Walter L. *Meaning of Masonry.* Sioux Falls, SD: NuVision Publications, 2007, originally published in 1927.

———. *The Relation of Masonry to the Ancient Mysteries Extracted from The Meaning of Masonry.* New York: Kessinger Publishing and Legacy Press, 2012.

Wokeck, Marianne, and Coleman, Martin (eds.). *The Life of Reason: Introduction and Reason In Common Sense; Critical Edition, Vol. 11.* Boston: MIT Press, 2011.

Index

About the author

Dr. Oscar Patterson III is Worshipful Master of Ashlar Lodge No. 98 Free and Accepted Masons in St. Augustine, Florida, for 2017. He holds the Gold Proficiency Card and is State Chairman for Public Education and Citizenship. He is also a member of the York and Scottish Rites, York Rite College, Allied Masonic Degrees, and Red Cross of Constantine as well as The Masonic Society, The Philalethes Society, Quatuor Coronati Lodge No. 2076's Correspondence Circle, and several research Lodges in the United States. His research has appeared in Masonic journals and magazines in the United States and the United Kingdom. His book, *Interpreting Masonic Ritual,* is published by Hamilton Books.

Patterson holds the B.A. in religion and philosophy, the M.F.A. in design, and the Ph.D. in Communication Theory and Research. He is retired after having served as a professor and administrator at several universities in the U.S. during his thirty-five-year teaching career. He lectured at universities in Africa, Europe, and South America as well as the United States, and was appointed as a Fulbright Fellow. His scholarly articles appeared in major academic journals and he presented papers at numerous conferences.

Prior to beginning his academic career, Patterson was a juvenile officer, a Methodist minister, and an infantry officer with command and staff assignments in Vietnam. He also spent time as an actor and theatrical designer. He is a native of North Carolina who worked his way through college surveying land and in a textile mill. He and his wife, Julie, live in Ponte Vedra Beach, Florida, where he does administrative work as a volunteer for the St. Johns County Sheriff's Office.